Spring 2001   Vol. XXI, no. 1
ISSN: 0276-0045   ISBN: 1-56478-274-3

THE REVIEW OF CONTEMPORARY FICTION

The Review of Contemporary Fiction is published three times a year (January, June, September) by The Review of Contemporary Fiction, Inc., a nonprofit organization located at ISU Campus Box 4241, Normal, IL 61790-4241. ISSN 0276-0045. Subscription prices are as follows:

  Single volume (three issues):
      Individuals: $17.00; foreign, add $3.50;
      Institutions: $26.00; foreign, add $3.50.

DISTRIBUTION. Bookstores should send orders to:

Dalkey Archive Press, ISU Campus Box 4241, Normal, IL 61790-4241. Phone 309-874-2274; fax 309-874-2284.

This issue is partially supported by a grant from the Illinois Arts Council, a state agency.

Indexed in *American Humanities Index, International Bibliography of Periodical Literature, International Bibliography of Book Reviews, MLA Bibliography,* and *Book Review Index.* Abstracted in *Abstracts of English Studies.*

The Review of Contemporary Fiction is also available in 16mm microfilm, 35mm microfilm, and 105mm microfiche from University Microfilms International, 300 North Zeeb Road, Ann Arbor, MI 48106-1346.

www.centerforbookculture.org
www.dalkeyarchive.com

THE REVIEW OF CONTEMPORARY FICTION

Call for Casebook Editors and Contributors

www.dalkeyarchive.com

Dalkey Archive Press/The Review of Contemporary Fiction is seeking editors and contributors for its new web-based casebook series: Studies in Modern and Contemporary Fiction. Each casebook will focus on one novel. It will include an overview essay on the book (its place in the author's oeuvre; its critical reception; the scholarly conversations about it) and four other essays looking at specific dimensions of the book. (Recommended length of essays: 20-25 double-spaced pages.) Also included will be a selected bibliography of critical works on the book. The anticipated audience includes professors teaching the book and graduate and undergraduate students studying it.

All casebooks will be refereed. Successful casebooks will be published on the Dalkey Archive Press website.

The duties of the casebook editor will be to write the overview essay and develop the critical bibliography, to coordinate the other essays, especially avoiding overlapping among them, and to coordinate with the series editor.

The following are the books for which we are seeking casebook editors and contributors:

Yuz Aleshkovsky
  Kangaroo
Felipe Alfau
  Locos
  Chromos
Andrei Bitov
  Pushkin House
Louis-Ferdinand Céline
  Trilogy (*North, Castle to Castle, Rigadoon*)
Peter Dimock
  A Short Rhetoric for Leaving the Family
Coleman Dowell
  Island People
Rikki Ducornet
  The Jade Cabinet
William Eastlake
  Lyric of the Circle Heart
Stanley Elkin
  The Dick Gibson Show
William H. Gass
  Willie Masters' Lonesome Wife
Aldous Huxley
  Point Counter Point
Tadeusz Konwicki
  A Minor Apocalypse
José Lezama Lima
  Paradiso
Osman Lins
  The Queen of the Prisons of Greece

D. Keith Mano
  Take Five
Wallace Markfield
  Teitlebaum's Window
Harry Mathews
  Cigarettes
Steven Millhauser
  The Barnum Museum
Nicholas Mosley
  Impossible Object
  Accident
Flann O'Brien
  The Poor Mouth
Fernando del Paso
  Palinuro of Mexico
Raymond Queneau
  Pierrot Mon Ami
Jacques Roubaud
  The Great Fire of London
Gilbert Sorrentino
  Imaginative Qualities of Actual Things
  Mulligan Stew
  Aberration of Starlight
Piotr Szewc
  Annihilation
Curtis White
  Memories of My Father Watching TV

Applicants should send a CV and a brief writing sample.

Send applications to:

Robert L. McLaughlin
Dalkey Archive Press, Illinois State University, Campus Box 4241, Normal, IL 61790-4241

Inquiries: rmclaugh@ilstu.edu

Contents

www.centerforbookculture.org/review

The Review of Contemporary Fiction is seeking contributors to write overview essays on the following writers:

Georges Bataille, Michel Butor, Italo Calvino, Julieta Campos, Jerome Charyn, Emily Coleman, Stanley Crawford, Carol De Chellis Hill, Jennifer Johnston, Gert Jonke, Violette Le Duc, Wallace Markfield, David Markson, Rick Moody, Olive Moore, Nicholas Mosley, Julián Ríos, Severo Sarduy, Joanna Scott, Gilbert Sorrentino, Gertrude Stein, Esther Tusquets, Luisa Valenzuela, Louis Zukofsky.

The essays must:

- be 50 double-spaced pages;
- cover the subject's biography;
- summarize the critical reception of the subject's works;
- discuss the course of the subject's career, including each major work;
- provide interpretive strategies for new readers to apply to the subject's work;
- provide a bibliographic checklist of each of the subject's works (initial and latest printings) and the most
- important (no more than five) critical pieces about the subject;
- be written for a general, intelligent reader, who does not know the subject's work;
- avoid jargon, theoretical digressions, and excessive endnotes;
- be intelligent, interesting, and readable;
- be documented in MLA style.

Authors will be paid $250.00 when the essay is published. All essays will be subject to editorial review, and the editors reserve the right to request revisions and to reject unacceptable essays.

Applicants should send a CV and a brief writing sample. In your cover letter, be sure to address your qualifications

Send applications to:

Robert L. McLaughlin
Dalkey Archive Press, Illinois State University, Campus Box 4241, Normal, IL 61790-4241

Inquiries: rmclaugh@ilstu.edu

Introducing David Antin

Stephen Cope

The work of David Antin—storyteller and narrativist, as well as talker, artist, performer, critic, poet, thinker, philosopher, and one-time novelist—attends a singular position within American art and literature. It does so not solely because of its diverse generic range (although this is remarkable enough) but because, more importantly, this diversity is often evident in a single, given work. His talk pieces, for instance—commonly thought of as poems and curiously gathered under that rubric—are far from the wrought and uniform objects often associated with that term. Instead they encompass, while rarely eschewing, elements of narrative and performance, of story, plot, and gesture, of lecture and comedic irreverence, of philosophical speculation and exact, demonstrative content. Similarly, in his early "poems," found language from sources as diverse as novels, insurance manuals, and philosophical texts collides with and critiques generic expectations. (In one early piece, aptly entitled "Novel Poem," Antin typed no more than a line or a phrase from a page of a novel—works by Ayn Rand, Gore Vidal, Doris Lessing, Iris Murdoch, Han Su Yin, Alberto Moravia, among others—to compose what appear in the book as songs.)

So why the *Review of Contemporary Fiction*, a forum whose generic allegiances seem so clearly spelled out in advance? It is not solely that Antin's work involves at its very core a concern with narrativity (and/or its manifestation as story, novel, talk, song, essay, lecture). Nor is it simply because Antin himself has tried his hand at fiction—a story entitled "Balanced Aquarium" (published in the *Kenyon Review*) and, later, *The Stigmata,* a novel that was never published. Nor is it only that Antin does in fact tell stories, and tells stories about stories, and talks about himself doing so. It is also because Antin—a formally trained linguist, among other things—sees the very work that language, and the various ways in which it does this work, as being a finally more primary issue than that of literary taxonomy. One of the most famous of Antin's pronouncements, for instance (one that will be repeated in the pages that follow):

if robert lowell is a

poet I don't want to be a poet   if robert frost was a

> poet I don't want to be a poet   if socrates was a poet
> ill consider it

If this is a declaration of allegiances—and, indeed, it is—its aim is not so much to define what a poet is or should be (nor simply to call any such definition into question) as to bring the very act of thinking—as active Socratic discipline, and thus distinguished from static *thought*—directly to the fore, irrespective of the mannered formalities in which that thinking takes place or by which it is mediated, mitigated, or altogether dissolved. (At a recent talk in Minneapolis, Antin added John Coltrane to the list of those whose thinking he considered close to his own, suggesting a leap beyond not only genres but media as well.) The point is that poetry—or any stipulation not rooted in the specificity of a given utterance—becomes a facile designation when it serves merely presentational ends. Antin *is* a poet because in many ways Socrates is (and if Lowell's and Frost's poetries were themselves any kinds of examples of serious thinking, they too might be included). The same goes for fiction, and Antin, while talking, constructs fictions that are real (which is to say, they are true), yet he does so without deference (although most certainly *not* without reference) to established modes of exposition.

Born in New York City on 5 February 1932, Antin grew up with a working competence in several European languages. He attended Brooklyn Technical High School, and, later, City College of New York, where he befriended a number of artists and writers—Jerome Rothenberg, Robert Kelly, the late Armand Schwerner, and Eleanor Fineman (who later became his wife, the artist Eleanor Antin)—all of whom have remained lifelong companions. He graduated in 1955, having earned numerous degrees in both the arts and the sciences, and in 1966 he received a master's degree in linguistics from New York University. In the interim he worked as a freelance editor and translator of technical books, wrote both fiction and poetry, and, due to the publication of a number of important and influential pieces of art criticism, emerged as an important figure in both the art and literary worlds. He spent 1967 as a curator at the Institute of Contemporary Art in Boston, and, the following year, he was appointed an assistant professorship in the Visual Arts Department at the University of California—San Diego, where he served as curator of the UCSD Art Gallery from 1968 to 1971, and where, despite his recent retirement, he remains an active and vital member of the literary and art communities.

Early on, however, Antin fashioned himself an engineer (he attended Brooklyn Tech with this at least partly in mind). He never entirely abandoned this pursuit. I recall a recent conversation in which Antin offered the story of a creative writing workshop—the only one he ever taught—which included among its participants the late Kathy Acker and the fiction writer Melvyn Freilicher. "I told my students," I paraphrase Antin, "that writing is like engineering. The technology is language. In order to invent something useful, you have to know what is needed now, but also you have to know the present state of the technology." Or something to that effect. He sent his students to the library to study the state of the technology. He wanted them, as he said to another group of students, to construct an art machine ("an art machine," Antin explains in a recent talk piece that tells the story of this second class, is "a system whose parts when put in motion act upon each other in such a manner as to cause you to see things differently"). "Otherwise," he concluded, "all you end up doing is re-inventing the wheel."

Antin's career to date might be rightly summarized as an ongoing attempt to "see things differently"— or to develop a practice carried out thereby: a commitment to surpass prior technological advances and to invent workable art machines, which are also language machines, culture machines, thought and thinking machines. Yet to be an engineer in this fashion is to be committed as well to experimentation, in the most literal sense of that term: a testing of the given and a questioning of what is assumed for the purposes of further discovery. Antin is unique in letting us witness his early experiments, often as he carries them out (as in the talk pieces) rather than expecting us to be satisfied with the published results (those recorded in his books). Indeed, like John Coltrane—of whom some critics complained that he merely "practiced in public"—Antin realizes that the pursuit itself is a good part of the results. He does not offer simple proofs, but the terms and techniques of questioning. And although he may lead us to arrive at numerous revelations, like a good engineer, he also shows his work.

The essays gathered here show decisively, I think, that we are all the better for his having insistently done so.

An Interview with David Antin

Charles Bernstein

The following is taken from a conversation between Charles Bernstein and David Antin that took place by way of E-mail over a period of several months in late 1999 and early 2000. This excerpt comprises roughly half of the conversation, the entirety of which will be published as a special edition by Granary Books.

Charles Bernstein: Last year, I had the opportunity to tour Brooklyn Technical High School with my daughter Emma, who was just going into ninth grade. I was enormously impressed with the place: it reminded me of Bronx Science, where I went to high school, but was far more imposing and I would say more severe, or anyway focussed, directed. It seemed a place that would really turn out engineers, technicians, and scientists, more than the lawyers and doctors that Science seemed to produce in my day. Yet Brooklyn Tech graduated two of my favorite wandering poets, you and Nick Piombino. I wonder if you could say how you came to go to Brooklyn Tech?

David Antin: Growing up in Brooklyn in the forties and following the war in the papers and on the radio every day, tracing the paths of my cousins, one a bomber pilot whose military career took him through bases in North Africa and Italy, the other an engineer who wound up at the Remagen Bridge, and my next door neighbor, who survived Okinawa, the world looked very different to us then. Because there was always the war until suddenly it wasn't. And I had to pick a high school. There were only three—Bronx Science—that was too far away—Stuyvesant and Tech. Tech was closer, even though it was a train ride away, and somehow more tangible. I wanted to be an inventor, whatever I thought that meant then. I guess I was thinking of Edison or maybe James Watt. Or maybe even Newton. I had read all about his optical discoveries and I had managed to figure out how the steam engine worked from the *Encyclopaedia Britannica*. I had played around with radios and dynamos and I figured I'd have to study engineering to invent anything electrical or mechanical. The great thing was they had all those shops—a foundry, sheet metal shops, machine shops. I loved making tool bits in the machine shop and working on the bench lathe. They also had a year-long course called Industrial Processes that taught us how everything that was manufactured up to then was made. And we had to make drawings of open-hearth furnaces and Bessemer converters. And everything in the world around me became more tangible and solid. So there I was, taking the F-train every morning, that started underground and came out into the light at 7th Avenue, where it turned into an elevated and stayed above ground till Smith-9th Street, where I always changed for the GG, even in bad weather, although I could have changed at Carroll Street or Bergen, where it was back underground. Because from the Smith-9th station that was poised high over the Gowanus Canal, I could look out to the Statue of Liberty. In spite of everything that's happened in America since the end of that war, I've always had a strong feeling for the Statue of Liberty, because it became the statue of my personal liberty. The great green statue appearing at the center of the train trip out of my childhood neighborhood, that started in the dark and came out into the light, taking me to the first school I had ever chosen, became the mark of my personal liberation—from life with my mother, from the mythology of childhood and family and even the war—liberation from everything but a future I was going to be free to discover or invent.

CB: I want to get back to invention in a minute, but before that I want to know about what you received. What was the family mythology? What were your parents' designs for you? And what were their designs for themselves—their backgrounds and aspirations, their realities and their destinies. In other words: some family history.

DA: Most of that material is scattered throughout my earlier talk pieces. But to simplify— You have to understand, the world I entered into was the 1930s. My family were European émigrés. They came to this country at the beginning of the century and they had just gotten themselves situated, when there was a Great War. Then came a short period of flush times that went bust, and I arrived just at the beginning of the Great Depression. After which there was an even Bigger War. Nobody had any designs or expectations—only hopes for survival.

My father died when I was two. He got a strep throat before there was penicillin or sulfa. That was his second mistake. His first was marrying my mother, who was apparently quite beautiful, but so what. My mother was a social climber heading downward. She started with a high-school education, a high degree of literacy and a Pennsylvania accent acquired by arriving in Scranton at age seven. In those days the family had expectations. In the twenties they were successful business people and figured she would go to college. They figured wrong. She took a job as a bookkeeper in the family business, spent her money on looking pretty and married my father as soon as she could. When he died a couple of years later, she turned into a professional widow. By the forties she was already a marginally competent examiner in the dress business. She couldn't understand why I wanted to be an engineer; she thought I should be a chicken farmer in Lakewood.

None of my other relatives had any expectations—either for me or for themselves. All their expectations seemed to turn out wrong. My mother's older brother Sam was a great chess player. At the age of fourteen he held Lasker to a draw in a game he could have won. Lasker was then the national champion. Sam was fourteen. It was one of those matches where the champion takes on twenty or thirty players at one time, usually finishing off the weaker ones as quickly as possible so he has more time for the tougher ones. My uncle had the advantage, but he was only fourteen. The champion, seeing he might lose, offered him a draw. My uncle thought about it hard but accepted, and I don't think he ever recovered from it.

He was sixteen when the U.S. entered the First World War. He was so big, people thought he was much older. Instead of going to college, he took a job in the coal mines and spent his leisure time beating up miners who called him a slacker. Her younger brother was a charming bohemian drifter—a labor organizer, a steward on cruise ships, a mountain climber. He fell off a cliff in Yosemite. Nobody paid that much attention to the girls. Three of my mother's older sisters married. One of them, my Aunt Sarah, married my father's older half-brother. An interesting man, he'd been a revolutionary in Russia in 1905, but became a successful dress manufacturer in the United States. A man who loved materials, wore dark tweed suits in winter and seersuckers in summer, and always wore hats to work. A judicious and generous man, he was the family arbiter. When my mother left her second husband, she wrote her autobiography and presented it to him for his approval. I got my first job working for him after school, and I used to practice my German with my Aunt Sarah when I lived with them. Nobody noticed when the youngest sister, a gorgeous and independent redhead, without saying a word to anyone, got herself accepted into nursing school and became a registered nurse. Nobody expected that either.

My earliest family memories were living with my grandmother and my aunts—all beautiful women—living in a great old house in Boro Park. It was the depression and everybody was poor but you'd never have known it. People kept coming from all over the world to visit, to play cards or chess and to tell stories and argue in a handful of European languages about people and facts and politics. My Aunt Bessie always took the upside. A noble white-haired widow with

CHARLES BERNSTEIN | 13

two grown daughers she almost never saw, she used to say she was an optimist because something good could always happen, and if it turned out bad, you didn't have to waste your time worrying about it till it did. When her beloved husband suddenly died, she gave up her beautiful brownstone near the Navy Yard and took up a career as a dietitian. When she wasn't working, she'd take the Culver Line down to Coney Island, find a seat on one of the benches on the boardwalk and take pleasure in simply breathing in the clear salty air. My Aunt Bette usually took the dark view and on principle refused to suffer stupidity. Of one comfortable relative she said once as she was leaving, "We have a perfect relationship. She thinks I'm a horse and I think she's a cow." And my grandmother presided over the entire household in a droll, mischievous manner. This is the household I most remember. It was noisy, cheerful, and gay, and a world away from the austere prison of living with my mother, which happened only once in a while. And I was on my own from the age of sixteen anyway.

CB: Of course, I know well that you have told some stories about this before—but a story is always a little bit different every time you tell it, no? Speaking of stories, what was the oral culture—the telling culture—like in your immediate environment when you grew up? You speak of being surrounded by stories at your grandmother's house. Was it books or talk that made the most impact on you? Or the arguing in different languages? I'm interested in the difference among argument and conversation and stories, but also the fact that you were surrounded by languages other than English and how this affected your approaches to English, to "the American," as the French say, in your writing. And indeed how writing, how books, came into play for you.

DA: Yeah, stories are different every time you tell them—because they allow so many possible narratives. For years I've been thinking of stories and narratives as two related but different things—the inside and the outside of the human engagement with transformation. For me, story's the shell, a kind of logical structure, a sequence of events and parts of events that shape a significant transformation, while a narrative is the core, the representation of a desiring subject, somebody's confrontation with a significant transformation that he or she works to bring about or avoid. So any time you tell a story from a different point of view, you get a different narrative. The same events look different because their parts look different and combine differently. So the events are also different, and they become a new story that may have the same beginning and ending or different ones, or no ending and no real beginning. But you want to know about my experience, not my theory.

The people I grew up with told stories almost all the time, and the stories always seemed to go together with arguments, in which they functioned as examples, evidence and counterevidence, testimony, mostly from experience—direct or overheard—though they could have been read about in a newspaper or a book or maybe only imagined, or dreamed—but always internalized in the language and experience of the speaker. They also functioned as models, metaphors, parables, or as paradoxes, as jokes that exploded other arguments—or their own. But they always functioned. Barbara Kirschenblatt-Gimlet has an essay somewhere on Jewish storytelling, where she talks about the way stories usually seem to be woven into discourse to such an extent that in Yiddish speaking circles, when the story's function becomes unclear, the speaker is usually confronted with the question, "Nu, voss i de sof?" (So, what's the point?) And while the stories I heard were told in lots of other languages and many of them may have been told for the sheer hell of it, the artistry of the telling always left you with a strong sense of their consequentiality and meaning.

Which raises the question of language. When you grow up in a family of languages, you develop a kind of casual fluency, so that languages, though differently colored, all seem transparent to experience. Reading Elias Canetti's "History of a Youth," which I happened to read in French because it was lent to me by my friend, the filmmaker Jean-Pierre Gorin, though it was written in German, I remember Canetti wondering over the fact that he remembered every frightening detail of the stories of vampires and werewolves that his little Bulgarian girl playmates terrified themselves with. But he remembered them in German not Bulgarian, which he had forgotten completely. So I hardly ever remember what language I first heard a story in. But I started reading pretty early. And that introduced the kind of opacity of language you experience when you see a word and don't know how to pronounce it or what it means. Looking at newspapers, when I was about four, the Sunday editions were illustrated with brown photographs and I would try to figure out the captions, trying to sound out words like *negotiations* or *typhoon*. My mother taught me some spelling. Then she bought a candy store in Astoria with my Uncle Irving, and I really learned to read from comic books. "Ach, you kicked me in the stomach!" When I was seven, I was once again living with my mother—this time in the attic apartment of an old wood-frame house in Kensington on the block where my Uncle Dave and my Aunt Sarah shared a solid, two-family, brick house with his business partner. We rented the attic apartment from two Kentuckians, Jeanie and Lucille, who were married to a pair of truck drivers. When the guys were home and weren't fighting with their wives, they'd be listening to country music. So there was radio again. The guys weren't much for storytelling, but they talked lots of baseball over beer, and sometime I would sit with them and listen to Red Barber broadcast Dodger games. My mother always had a few books around, remnants of some earlier reading. *Point Counter Point, The Sound and the Fury*, and *Immortal Marriage*—Aldous Huxley, William Faulkner, and Gertrude Atherton. I was seven or eight and I read them all, but the one that got to me was *Immortal Marriage*. I don't know how I read it, because I never paid any attention to the central romance of Pericles and Aspasia. But the Greeks, the Agora, Pericles' philosophical court, Anaxagoras, Socrates and Alcibiades and the image of the Parthenon and Phidias' gold and ivory statue of Athena, that's what got me. On the strength of the book I snuck into the adult section of the local library to read the poems of Pindar. But they were disappointing.

CB: I often get a sense of poetry being disappointing to you, that the failure of poetry to do something it could be doing or doing better was a kind of inspiration for writing poetry (well you know that's my current theory, speaking of theories, and I do see you as a particularly good model for it). What do you or did you think poetry should be doing? Were you looking to make improvements? Then I also want to ask whether you consider your early work as a kind of invention or innovation (it certainly looks that way to me). But I know you wrote poetry before the work that you collected in *definitions* in 1967, and I suppose there is a big narrative bridge that you may want to make from Brooklyn Tech in the forties to CCNY in the fifties to the earliest work I know of yours from the late sixties.

DA: I hardly remember how I started to write poetry. It was somewhere in the middle of high school. The English classes we took at Tech were in some ways very good, but the poems they showed us, especially in early high school, were things like Alfred Noyes's "The Highwayman" with lines like "the road was a ribbon of moonlight over the purple moor" or "the moon was a ghostly galleon tossed upon cloudy seas." It's the only English poem I know with an Aztec horse. The hooves go "Tlot, Tlot!" There was Kipling's supremely silly "Gunga Din," there were poems by the two Benets, by Elinor Wylie, Edna St. Vincent Millay, bowdlerized Emily Dickinson, and Nathalia Crane's "I'm in love with the janitor's boy / and the janitor's boy loves me." Confronted by this trivia, it's hard to imagine what I thought poetry could do.

But I also had a memory of driving one summer day with my Uncle Julius, my father's twin brother, up toward his family's bungalow on Sackett Lake; and as we were cruising through the green summer landscape, he suddenly burst into this poem by Pushkin, producing a cascade of cadenced Russian I barely understood that brought tears to his eyes. For just a moment. Then he corrected himself, laughed and said "What nonsense!" Maybe I remembered this. Maybe I heard of it somewhere else, but I thought somewhere there must be something called modern poetry that meant something to us living now at the end of the Second World War. So I started to look.

I found an anthology by Conrad Aiken. It had a lot of imagist stuff—John Gould Fletcher's "Symphonies," some early Pound. There was one very short poem by Pound with a Greek title Δώρια— the one that begins with a bleak wind and gray waters. Somehow it got to me—the Greek title, maybe because of Gertrude Atherton, or maybe its severity. It felt like New York in winter. It felt modern. Its cadences were nothing like the tiresome metrics of Noyes or Millay, but it also felt old, and I thought I could try to bring it up to date. So I did. With the confidence of a sixteen-year-old, I composed a "poem in a minor key," an image piece that got in the bleak wind, the gray sky. I replaced Pound's cliffs with a deserted el, left out the gods and the underworld, and I thought it was okay but a little too descriptive for my taste. So thinking of Fletcher, I did some poems that were more abstract or maybe more concrete—verbal toccatas or fantasias without any apparent subject matter. But they didn't seem to go anywhere.

The Tech library was helpful. I discovered *Three Lives* and was blown away by the flattened blues music of "Melanctha." These were stories, but it never occurred that these were not poetry. So from there on, it got easier. I found the *Dubliners* in the same library, but I had to buy *Ulysses*. I found Eliot's *Collected Poems 1909-1935* in a used bookstore in Greenwich Village. I had an Irish drinking buddy and we spent late night hours in Fourth Avenue bars fantasizing making a movie out of *Finnegans Wake*.

By the time I got to City College, I learned that the literary world was in a conservative mode. Poets were supposed to be picking up the meters again. Novelists were writing novels of manners. I wasn't interested. I met Jerry Rothenberg and we were both struggling to find a way out, but it was 1950 or so and it was not a good time as we saw it. We listened to jazz. It was the age of McCarthy. The Korean War was on. Jerry got drafted and went off to Germany to write for *Stars and Stripes*. I met a kid painter, Gene Kates; he introduced me to Heidegger, to abstract expressionism, took me downtown to people's studios. I was into physiological psychology, reading Norbert Weiner on negative feedback systems, Cannon on the *Wisdom of the Body*. Hebb on neural functioning. Kurt

Goldstein. Heidegger's *Sein und Zeit*. Wittgenstein's *Tractatus* and Hölderlin. Anything but Richard Wilbur or Delmore Schwartz. Still, I edited the school's literary magazine and wrote mostly stories, looking back to Stein, and through her, further back—to Flaubert. Hearing the sound of the great French sentences in my head, I started working under the spell of the *Trois Contes*. Each word worked into place as in a kind of mosaic. It was a disaster. I shifted gears, wrote a faux folktale, drawing on an imagined Yiddish tradition.

Suddenly I was graduated, after over five years and three majors at City College. I got a job with a scientific translation outfit, where I edited the translation of the Soviet *Journal of Automation*. My faux folktale got published in a Jewish magazine. I wrote a Flaubertian parable set in Brooklyn. I got a rejection slip with an apology from the editor of *Esquire,* who said the publisher wouldn't let them print it because it was too dark. A couple of years and ten rejections later, it got published by John Crowe Ransom in the *Kenyon Review* after he cut out the word *Sex,* describing the behavior of a pair of tropical fish. Jerry had come back from the army and was translating Eric Kaestner. We helped found the *Chelsea Review* with Ursule Molinaro and Venable Herndon and Robert Kelly, a poet and friend I had known from City College. Jerry started putting out *Poems from the Floating World* and was translating postwar German poetry and I was looking back at Breton, Apollinaire, and Cendrars. I was also translating books on physics and mathematics for Dover Press. Jerry started Hawk's Well Press and the two of us translated Martin Buber's *Tales of Angels Spirits and Demons*. We met Paul Blackburn, who dragged us around to every poetry reading in sight. Bob and Joby Kelly started *Trobar* with the poet and translator George Economou.

It was within this space that Jerry came up with the notion of a "deep image" poetry, out of a certain sense, I think, that an image core had to be at the center of a truly exploratory expressive poetry. About as soon as he came up with the term—around 1960—almost everybody we knew had some disagreement with it, or parts of it. I had a Wittgensteinian distrust of the word *deep,* though I could imagine a system of communicative or expressive gestures relying on the metonymic function of images to take a poem around the systematized clichés of the language. Bob Kelly, following what seemed a kind of Olson-like argument, thought the emphasis on image understated the issues of musicality and the line. Rochelle Owens hated it. Jackson Mac Low claimed not to understand it. Armand Schwerner had his doubts about it. Only Diane Wakoski seemed more or less content with it. But the one thing that should have told us to kill the term was that Robert Bly was enthused by it. His promotion of it in his magazines, the *Sixties* and the *Seventies*, eventually eviscerated any intellectual significance it had. But I didn't pay so much attention to all this, because I was working on a novel. Ever since the *Kenyon Review* published my much-rejected story, I'd been getting letters from publishers wanting to get a first crack at my novel. What novel? Everybody supposed then that if you wrote a short story, you were working on a novel. Elly and I moved out of the city to North Branch, a small town in the western corner of Sullivan County, so that I could write my novel and she could work at her paintings—she was making paintings then—in quiet. But I was a little too Steinian—or too Flaubertian—to write a novel, and she didn't need quiet, she needed the art scene.

So back we came to the city. I'd ditched the novel and was writing poems again. With a difference. When we first came back to the city around September of 1963, we were staying in a house in a corner of the Bronx not far from the Whitestone Bridge that we were subletting from a dentist who was traveling in Asia collecting Buddhist art, and the local library was specially rich in philosophical Catholic works and books on business. So in the afternoons, when I wasn't translating, I'd go down to the library past the teenagers who were busy "beatling" every adult who walked by—the Beatles were about to come to America then—to get in several hours of reading before Elly finished painting. Reading through Simone Weil's journals and an insurance manual, there were lots of sentences whose meaning I didn't really understand. They weren't unusually difficult sentences. They often contained words that were cultural commonplaces or clichés, ordinary abstract terms that everybody seems to understand. "Loss." "Value." "Power." But as I looked at them I found out I didn't understand them at all. So I started to write them down, thinking that by writing them down, I could concentrate on them, ask them questions and find out what meanings they might conceal. And I saw that my not-understanding could be a way to go on. And as I went on with this writing down I didn't think about whether I was writing poems. I was thinking. And the more I was thinking, the more there was I didn't understand. The first part of "definitions for mendy" with its questions about "loss" and "value" and "power" and "brightness" were written this way and temporarily stopped on the day Jack Kennedy was killed in the fall of 1963. My two first books—*definitions* and *Code of Flag Behavior*—were written this way, bringing not-understanding as a set of questions to puzzling commonplaces and clichés—linguistic and cultural acceptances of every kind. So I was trying to find out what it was that everybody else understood without giving up my stubborn and hard-won lack of understanding. Of course my lack of understanding kept expanding. To the image of personal knowledge represented by *autobiography,* to the nature of the represention of human experiential knowledge in the novels of "novel poem," to the meaning of meditation in an environment of power and violence provided by the war in Vietnam in "the separation meditations." Finally this extended to my attack on the idea of "understanding" altogether in "tuning." Though the "talk pieces" are obviously very different in certain ways from the earlier poems through "The November Exercises."

CB: I read in the paper just a few days ago that Lita Hornick died last weekend. And of course Kulchur published your 1972 book *Talking*, which marked your second break with previous work. Certainly, the poems from 1963-1973 gave you less opportunity for the kind of discursive and philosophical writing in your essays; the poems and the essays remained quite distinct genres. But with the talks, your poems and essays came into close proximity, if not identity. *Talking*—the practice and the book—was a more expansive way to work allowing you to go wherever you wanted to go and say whatever you wanted to say, which was perhaps not the case with the earlier poems. But *Talking* also suggests a more decisive break from most ideas about the form of poetry. Why did you give up the way you had been working around 1971?

DA: There were two reasons that I remember. One was my experience of poetry readings. I remember giving a reading at SUNY— Binghamton around that time, and I was there to read these "process poems." And I was very committed to the process of composing, working at poems, putting things together and taking them apart like some kind of experimental filmmaker. But when I got to the reading all the work was done, and I was reduced to being an actor in an experimental play that I'd already written. And I didn't want to be an actor. I didn't want to illustrate the way I had worked. I wanted to work. At being a poet. In the present. So at this reading I started revising poems while I was reading them. Changing poems that were already written. It was a disaster. I tried to invent a poem, my kind of poem—an interrogation of a sort. I started thinking out loud and that was somewhat better. I was committed to a poetry of thinking—not of thought but of thinking. And now it seemed possible. But my way of thinking is very particular and concrete. It doesn't follow a continuous path. When I come up against an obstacle, some kind of resistance, I often find myself looking for some concrete example—a story that could throw light on it or interfere with it, kick it into a different space. So I found myself telling stories or, to use my term, constructing narratives, as part of my thinking. I had resorted to narrative before, my kind of fragmented narrative—in my comically titled "autobiography" back in 1967, which was probably closer to the "Aztec Definitions" that Jerome and I published in *some/thing* back in 1965 than to conventional stories. So the two notions—of improvisation, of doing it there, thinking while talking, and thinking by any means I could, which meant thinking by telling—stories—came to me at pretty much the same time.

CB: You didn't want to be an actor, you wanted to act. And yet in grounding your work in performance you are brought inevitably into some relation to the performing arts, to theater. But I take the essential part of this move is related to the unscripted or improvised nature of the performance. There is certainly some connection here with the happenings and related performance art: art coming off the walls into an unplanned action. And yet saying that, I am struck more by dissimilarities than by the similarities. The apparently chaotic or dadaistic quality to happenings is not reflected in your talks. The visual dimension is kept to a minimum: if you were not an actor you wouldn't wear makeup or costumes or have sets. In some ways the talks most suggest the stand-up comic; Lenny Bruce's late talk pieces (as I've noted elsewhere) in terms of their extended improvisations. In other ways, I think especially of the poet's talk and the interest there in thinking out loud. And in still other ways, I think of the Socratic tradition of philosophy as a form of thinking out loud rather than written composition—and there are still some philosophers who continue to work that way, who don't write essays or articles but who do their philosophy out loud, either in monologue or dialogue (Wittgenstein's Cambridge talks would be a good example but there are many others). Of course, I am not even mentioning in any detail the unscripted "speech" — whether political or—let's say—civic? And finally, there is the sermon, and many kinds of those. How do you see your talks in relation to these related types of performance?

DA: Back around the spring or summer of 1971, I got a call from Dore Ashton inviting me to be part of a series of talks she was organizing for a group of philosophers, historians, and critics at Cooper Union. It sounded interesting so I agreed. "What's the title of your piece?" she asked. Without having a minute to think, I said, "The Metaphysics of Expectation," and hearing the silence on the other end of line, I added, ". . . or the Real Meaning of Genre." "Great," she said and gave me a date in December. I had given myself a title that left me a lot of working space. But how to prepare for this talk. I figured I would prepare a variety of related issues, and I began researching and taking notes . . . on the diagnosis of disease, on the history of molecular theory, on a particular turn in nineteenth-century French painting—from Manet to Monet—on contemporary sculpture in relation to performance. And I took all these notes on little index cards that I planned to bring with me to use for the talk. When December came around and I got to Cooper Union, they put me in one of those theater-like lecture halls in back of a stone-topped table. I felt like I was back at Brooklyn Tech. All I needed was a glass retort and Bunsen burner. I put my tape recorder on the table, I looked up at the audience and started to speak. I forgot about my index cards and talked for about ninety minutes and took questions for about another thirty. The talk seemed to work, but the transcription of the tape took forever, and the whole thing was so long I never sent Dore a text, and she had to publish the volume without me. This piece was a turning point. I wasn't thinking of poetry, I was thinking of giving myself more room, freeing my mind to work in a wider space than the critical essays at whose boundaries I was already pushing. But it took a second piece at Pomona College to let me see what I was doing. Guy Williams had read the rather violent critical essay I had written about the LA County's "Art and Technology" show and invited me to talk at Pomona, where I think he was running the art department. I agreed. But at Cooper Union I knew I'd be talking to the art world and maybe some of the poetry world, and I had no idea where these kids at a small private college in the San Fernando Valley were coming from, why they were coming to hear me, or what they needed to know. So I arranged to go up there early, do some studio visits, and generally hang out with them during the afternoon. That evening I did the talk and the next morning Elly, who had come up with me, suggested I play the tape on the drive home. So on the long drive from Pomona to Solana Beach on old 395 we listened to the tape. "That's a poem," Elly said. And she was right.

I hadn't been consciously aware of it myself, but what I'd apparently been doing was working to bring together my critical thinking and my poetry into a kind of blend that took place on the ground of improvisation. "talking at pomona" got published in 1972 in my Kulchur book *Talking*, along with the written improvisation "November Exercises," and the two collaborative but controlled and taped improvisations, "three musics for two voices" and "the london march," that I completed in 1968. I played both tape pieces at St. Mark's that year, but I still hadn't put my way of working into action "live" in front of a "poetry" audience. But in the spring of 1973 Kathy Fraser invited me to give a joint poetry reading with Jerome at the San Francisco Poetry Center. This time I told Elly I wasn't going to bring any of my books with me to read from. The place was filled with poets and Jerry led off with a great reading. Then I went up there without any poems to read and asked the question "what am i doing here" and proposed to answer my own question by talking. The talk was successful enough in my terms. But it seemed to make everybody nervous, because parts of the talk engaged directly with George Oppen and Robert Duncan, who were in the audience; and, because there was no telling what I might say, everybody else seemed worried about what I might say about them. It's hard being a hostage in somebody else's mouth—or a character in somebody else's novel.

So this is roughly how the talks started—but it's not the whole story. "The November Exercises" was a kind of improvisatory composition with found material somewhat like "the separation meditations"—but the mode of composition and quickness of the choices of both emphasized improvisation in private for me. "three musics for two voices" started as a commissioned work. I was a curator at the I.C.A. in Boston in 1967, and when I went to California in 1968, Sue Thurman, the director, asked me to do some new kind of recording for gallery visitors to listen to when they came into the exhibition hall. I started working on it, but it very quickly radicalized far away from its original intention. Sue Thurman left the I.C.A. And Dan Graham asked me to do a piece for the "Information Theory" issue of *Aspen Magazine* he was editing. The piece I finally did was the controlled improvisation with Eleanor as the second actor— "three musics for two voices" —and it was originally published in that issue of *Aspen* in a little pamphlet designed by George Maciunas to look like a Fluxus score on pages about 1.5 inches high and 6 inches long. "the london march" was a second "theatrical" dialogue between Elly and me that we did in one unedited shot with a news radio background. So those two were audio performances accomplished through improvisation. And these were not my first entries into some form of theater. During the period of antiwar protests in 1967, Bob Nichols organized a long reading in a Methodist church not far from Judson and asked me to read from one of the pieces in *definitions*. I designed a special performance in which I was to read the "pain" section of "the black plague" —the Wittgenstein section—but in a peculiar setting. I recorded two AM radio collages putting one on each channel of my old reel-to-reel stereo recorder and enlisted Elly to play randomly with the volume controls and the switching while I was reading, alternately overriding my meditation on pain and letting fragments of it through. While I was reading and Elly was cutting into my reading, I had intended to tear apart a wooden chair with my bare hands, breaking it down to the smallest parts. Bob vetoed the chair breaking, but got me to perform the piece twice to punctuate the other readings. Elly did a great job with the tape recorder, and the piece in some way was a performance transformation of some of the issues of my procedural poems, in that my speech—already distanced through the screen of Wittgenstein screened through Anscombe—was situated in rising and falling tides of noise—talk shows, news fragments, d.j. chatter, commercials, Spanish-language baseball broadcasts. That piece should throw some light on my acceptance of agency in the procedural poems of *Code, Meditations,* and *Talking.* In a way I suppose I was dramatizing our human situation by situating "myself as poet" in a textual sea filled with the sea wrack of language and the flotsam and jetsam of wrecked human intentions.

But in going this long narrative way around your questions about situating my talk pieces, I think the mix of backgrounds can give you some idea of the variety of impulses leading to the work and the way in which it came about. Still, I would like to add a cautionary note on your comment about the chaos of Happenings. I didn't see Happenings as chaotic. Almost every Happening I saw or took part in was carefully scripted. There is certainly in the sixties work a kind of baroque painterly quality to the surfaces. But Robert Whitman's work, Ken Dewey's, Allan Kaprow's work in particular, were tightly scripted. Allan's performers usually received very precise instructions and had specific jobs to carry out. The chaotic appearance resulted from the collision of many precise tasks. Allan's later work is absolutely pristine. And in the clarity of his work, he's somewhat typical of Fluxus, and has a lot in common, in this sense, with George Brecht. And while I don't script and I don't use other performers, I think my taste for underlying precision—precision of mind—gives me something in common with Allan and George Brecht. And this taste for precision, not of surface, but of underlying procedure, is what brings me closer to the philosophical tradition—from Wittgenstein to Socrates. And in some way to Emerson, who belongs in that tradition as well. My connections to performers like Lenny Bruce are a little more oblique. First I never accepted for myself the genre of "entertainment." And Bruce's beginnings are situated at a particular moment within that arena. He gradually pushes its envelope to the breaking point, but there is always at least the ghost of that genre haunting him in the memory of the audience that came to hear him. I always had the feeling I should put up a sign over the entrance to any of my performances "Abandon hope, all ye who enter here" because I don't feel obligated to "entertain" —though I reserve the right to tell shaggy dog stories or even common jokes as part of what I'm doing. But I also don't give a damn if half the audience walks out. This separates me not only from Bruce, but from other entertainers like Spaulding Gray or Garrison Keillor, all of whom I enjoy. I'm standing up on my feet thinking. Anybody who wants to listen is welcome. If not, I'm happy to see them go.

CB: By "chaotic" I really meant busy or multiplicitous, not unstructured: lots of stuff going on, lots of, as you say, scripted action and its attendant distraction, all of which made these events so particular and memorable. In the case of the talk pieces, as they evolved, though, we have a much more minimal direction (to use another loaded term), a person standing up alone in street clothes talking with modulated performance gestures (thinking in terms of vocal dynamics and rhythms and physical movements). Yet the work is hardly minimal in terms of content, quite the opposite. That is, contrasted with much performance art of the sixties and early seventies, including the ones of your own that you describe in such a tantalizing way (I am sorry not to have been able to see them), you are foregrounding one thing—the verbal production—with few distractions or disruptions. In this context, I'd like to pursue your remark about "entertainment"—in an age of cultural studies I think the meaning of the distinction you are making is being eroded, so I'd welcome further thoughts on this. But I would also note that, in contrast to some of my favorite poetry of the time, your "talks" might well be experienced as entertaining, and I suspect that your move to storytelling is not completely divorced from the dynamics of sustaining an audience's attention over a period of time, avoiding distraction (I won't mention "absorption"). But it's apparent that you are not working in the same genre as monologists such as Gray and Keillor, which is why I think of your work—but not theirs—as poetry (which is not an evaluative comment but a comment on genre). Yet I don't know the criteria I would use to make the distinction, though I agree that it would have to do with improvisation as a way of "doing" thinking, thinking as act, as activity, in contrast to a more narrative-driven storytelling. But storytelling threads through both. So that brings me round to another comparison (I know: comparisons are the hobgoblin of the ardent conversationalist): the many "telling" traditions in analphabetic cultures. Certainly your close proximity to "ethnopoetics" would suggest that this was another frame of reference for your all-talking poetry performances.

DA: Look, the Sophists' paradoxical talk pieces and their public debates were "entertainment" in fifth-century Greece. And in that world Socrates was an "entertainer." The rhetorical performances, the show speeches of Lysias or Gorgias, were also entertainments. So were the performances of the troubadours and their jongleurs in twelfth-century Europe. And the performances of the Commedia dell Arte, and Shakespeare's plays and Donne's sermons or Emerson's sermons and his lectures; and Buster Keaton and Charlie Chaplin and Laurel and Hardy films are also entertainments I feel close to. Still, something has happened to the idea of entertainment that brings it into the corporate embrace of Disneyland and Time-Warner. From this entertainment industry, may the gods of language protect us. I have nothing against seeing my work having affinities with Lenny Bruce, and Maria Damon wrote a whole essay on our relationship. But the nightclub audiences he started from were expecting diversions from the tedium of their lives as they experienced it. They went to the nightclub to get a little drunk, hear some aggressive dirty talk, have fun, and forget the business of the day. Disney made a fortune out of inventing the businessman's idea of the imaginary as the contradictory of the businessman's idea of the real. So Bruce had to insult and slug his audience back into some connection with the real. The ones who didn't stay insulted, shook off the slugging and enjoyed hearing everybody else get insulted and slugged. In the course of this kind of performance he was able to introduce serious and broad-ranging social criticism that was only incidentally funny. He's a special case because he pushed the aggressive stand-up comic genre beyond its "entertainment" envelope. But all you have to do is go to your local comedy club to see the generic stand-up form in all its numbed emptiness. It's not that these are simply poor or mediocre comics. They may be funnier than Bruce, because they're doing their job, and he wasn't. He was inventing a new job. Now, I don't have his audience and I don't want it. My rejection of the idea of "entertainment" in its current form is essentially based on the audience that comes with it. I don't want Keillor's audience either. And when I say audience, I mean the specific group membership created by the performance form they're involved with. I'm sure there are people who come to hear my talks who've listened with pleasure to Garrison Keillor. So have I. But I have no intention of engaging with the sentimental, mock-nostalgia expectations of that audience, and if they come to hear me they'll have to reorient themselves or let me reorient them. So yes, I'm aware of my audience in a way and I do try to engage with them while I'm trying to go about my business of thinking, and I believe they help me with it by providing a focus and a sense of urgency for a process that could otherwise go on forever. But in its present form, I absolutely reject the idea of entertainment.

As for the "ethnopoetics discourse," I could hardly deny a connection to it. I was a contributing editor to *Alcheringa,* and I was probably what you might call "a member of the Central Committee" along with Jerome and Diane Rothenberg and Dennis and Barbara Tedlock, since I was there from the beginning. Like my close friends, I was interested in the widest range of poetries in the broadest sense of the term poetry. So I was one of the readers in the reading of "primitive poetries" Jerome organized for Jerry Bloedow's "Hardware Poets Theater" in the early sixties and part of the Folkways recording. When we started *some/thing* in 1964, Jerome was quick to see affinities between my "definitions for mendy" and the "Aztec Definitions" collected by Sahagun, and we deliberately juxtaposed them alongside Jerry's "Sightings" in the first issue. *Alcheringa* published a part of "talking at pomona" in 1972, "the sociology of art" in 1976 and "talking to discover" in 1976, and "tuning" in 1977. So we were all involved in the question of the relations between poetry and art of so-called "primitive cultures" or "oral cultures" and the work of contemporary experimental poets and artists in the "technically advanced" cultures. Coming from linguistics, I was probably the one among the group most committed to the secular, the colloquial and the vernacular. I was studying Black Vernacular English and the marginal grammar of Gertrude Stein, so it was only reasonable for me to attack the ancient anthropological idea of primitivity with its cloud of secondary associations of the originary, the natural and the simple, and the romantic emphasis on myth and ritual. "the sociology of art" began as a talk I gave to a seminar in "primitive art," in which I tried to lay out what I thought was a more reasoned and less romanticized idea of the difference between what I preferred to call oral and literal societies. It might have seemed a little shocking for a journal dedicated to ethnopoetics to publish a talk that argued that "a myth is the name of a terrible lie told by a smelly little brown person to a man in a white suit with a pair of binoculars." But once we could get past the noble savage and quasi-religious ideas of surrounding myth, we could get back to the idea of myth as just one kind of storytelling and discuss more concrete issues of how people went about the business of living, making things and using and enjoying and talking about them. In the course of that piece I tried to replace the theory of the primitive by offering a theory of the difference between "oral societies" and "literal societies" based on a more general notion than the simple and obvious question of "writing" versus "no-writing"—a distinction between a society that was committed to processes and a society committed to objects. It went on to make the case that innovation probably proceeded more fluidly, casually and regularly in oral societies, where you learned how to make a pot or a canoe or a spear thrower by learning the right way to make it rather than by copying an idealized standardized object. So in a traditional "oral culture," a potter might make several pots that looked to an outsider very different from each other, all of which counted for the potter as the same. While in what I called "literal societies," the artist was always consulting a standard model from which the least deviation looked like a revolution. In the ethnopoetics discourse I tended to emphasize the secular, the casual, the colloquial, the vernacular against the sacred, a view I shared probably mainly with Diane Rothenberg, whose doctoral thesis on the history of Seneca relations with the Quakers I still regard as one of the most important ethnopoetic works because of the way it documented the pragmatic reasonableness of both groups in a history of dreadful misunderstandings. But I was strongly affected by Dennis Tedlock's versions of Zuni storytelling, most particularly by the way his translations placed the tale in the mouth of a speaker and situated the telling in an occasion in a way similar to Labov's transcriptions of the stories told by young black teenagers in the New York ghetto. And by Jerry's translations of the songs of contemporary Seneca songmen. So yes, I also saw my talking within the wider framework that Jerome's great collage anthologies *Technicians of the Sacred* and *Shaking the Pumpkin* suggest.

CB: Your talk poems raise a number of issues about the relation of orality to textuality and I wanted to get your thoughts on a few of these. For one thing, is the term *orality* useful for you to describe the compositional practice involved in your talk poems? My own sense would be to call this work postalphabetic just as I think we are now entering an age of postliterary: one that assumes alphabetic literacy but in which that is only one form of textuality. That is, I would take your work as textual practice even though it is composed in improvised speaking, since it exists in the context, and is "read" against, alphabetically composed poetry (your own and others) and relies on a range of writing technologies (if not to say modalities) for its realization. I realize the fundamental ambiguity of all these terms. But there are some significant distinctions here, amid the terminological morass. One stream of thinking from Walter Ong's *Presence of the Word* to David Abraham's *Spell of the Sensuous* has suggested that alphabetic literacy, compared to what preceded it, puts its users in a fundamentally more alienated relationship to language and the body. Such thinking suggests the value of a return to "orality," which often strikes me as nostalgic, in the sentimental sense of the word, although I find the idea of "return" *(nostos)* that allows a reimagining of where we are quite resonant. That may be close to Olson's sense of such things, and again his idea of composition by "breath" in "Projective Verse" is another possible frame for your talk poems. Do you find that terms of "Projective Verse" valorize speech over writing? An alternative is, I think, provided by Olson's articulation of a poetics of embodiment in "Proprioception": a person speaking their mind through their body (can you say "speaking their body"?). OK—then there is the relation between your performances and the writing that comes out of them. These are not, it seems to me, "documentation" in the conceptual art sense of that term, but literary works on their own terms. They are not "transcriptions" in the sense that Dennis Tedlock talks about in *The Spoken Word and the Work of Interpretation*. Nor are they, in my interpretation, "secondary" (and I say this as an extension of the argument I make in the introduction of *Close Listening: Poetry and the Performed Word* that the performance of a poem at a reading is also not "secondary" but a distinct realization or version of the work—this is where I propose the idea of "anoriginality"). Finally, there is the insistence on the vernacular in your work—vernacular essays, vernacular poems—*vernacular thinking,* which is not just a matter of vocabulary or syntax but of composition. This insistence on the vernacular is, as you suggest, in Stein, and also Williams, and is, in that sense, fundamental to radical modernist writing. Here again the relation of "speech" to "writing" is complex and productive.

DA: I don't really think the distinction between "alphabetic" and "analphabetic" is a good one. There are many forms of writing down that are not "alphabetic," that are not based on graphemic analyses of phonological distinctions. Chinese writing is only the most obvious example. But my main objection to the term is that the distinction is not fundamental enough. I am also quite unsatisfied by the distinctions between the "oral" and "literate" laid out by Ong and Havelock, brilliant as their pioneering work in this area has been. The two fundamentally different ways of proceeding still seem to me the ones I laid out twenty-five years ago in "the sociology of art": the differences between an "oral" and a "literal" culture—the "oral" conceived as embracing all the ways of organizing behavior relying upon the wide range of mental and physical procedures (including body learning) we can call remembering; and the "literal," which includes the whole range of procedures laying access to some form of "recording" or spatialization of memory, including drawing and mark-making of any sort, and perhaps also nonspatialized but ritualized repetitional, recitational memorizing. You can see the most extreme form of this spatialization in the ancient "art of memory," whose invention is usually attributed to the sixth-century Greek poet Simonides but was apparently handed down in the classic rhetorical tradition to the Greek and Roman rhetoricians and from them to their successors in the European Middle Ages and Renaissance. This tradition is described in great detail by Frances Yates in her marvelous book *The Art of Memory*. The idea was to call to mind a familiar and complicated building and stage a mental walking tour of all of its rooms, imagining precisely and in their places all of its decorative details, and then to place each of the images of a projected speech in a particular detail of the building in the sequential order that it would have to be recalled in the speech. It's a kind of mental road map with illustrated "view points" or "rest areas." This isn't writing, but it is a way of spatializing memory, especially if you bear in mind that the "images" that the rhetoricians intended to place were visual images either of "arguments" or of "words." So what they placed were like emblems or rebuses that could evoke a chain of logical connections or particular phrases that they wanted to make use of. Now the Greeks already had writing in the sixth century. Simonides' lyrics were written down and were memorized. So they could place texts on columns or niches, physically as well as mentally. But memorization of texts, the mode of the rhapsode who recited a poem that had a completely accomplished verbal form, is very different from remembering. Memorizing isn't remembering, and recording isn't remembering. But I don't want to be pious about the oral. The literal recording has distinct advantages. The tape recorder that recovers my talk pieces distinctly belongs to "literal" culture. I couldn't be having this E-mail dialogue with you and I certainly couldn't go back and reread Frances Yates or "the sociology of art" without it. The ancient Greek "oral poets" all had this anxiety about the deficiencies of their memories and always began poems by praying to the Muse to help them remember. The invocation of the Muses may have been a purely formal element by the time we encounter it, but it very likely reflected a real sense of the anxiety that the memory of forgetting could induce in a sensitive artist of an "oral society." But the situation, as I tried to describe it in "the sociology of art," is more complicated. There probably never were any purely "oral" societies, as there are no purely "literal" ones. Because the self is an oral society in which the present is constantly running a dialogue with the past and the future inside of one skin. So we're really dealing with two different cognitive modalities. The oral in my sense is present in the most literal societies, though it may be underground. There is good reason to consider how readers in "literal" societies actually read. Any reader will find that the act of reading evokes uncontrolled and uncontrollable memories, and these haven't been stored in building niches, and they may or may not be similar to the memories out of which the author created the text. On the other hand there is probably no oral society that fails to mark the spatial distinction of left and right, peculiar as this distinction may be for bilaterally symmetrical animals, and all societies I know of make the easier distinction between front and back, that is supported so clearly by the difference between our own front and back. And once they have this settled, they all seem to be able to orient themselves by facing in the fairly constant direction of the rising sun and distinguishing the four directions of frontal east and dorsal west, sinistral north and dextral south in the real world. This is the beginning of a literal mapping strategy. I suppose the whole "sociology of art" piece is an elaborate enactment of this argument, which it makes at great length. But that's not the whole story. The epistemological argument I make against the notion of "understanding" in the twin pieces "tuning" and "gambling" is a direct consequence of my argument about the "oral." Understanding is a literal idea based on a geometrical notion of congruence, and tuning is a notion of a negotiated concord or agreement based on vernacular physical actions with visible outcomes like walking together or making love. So here we are back at the vernacular again. That being said, I am not pious about the idea of the "oral" and my written pieces draw on all the aspects of "literal" culture I find useful for my purposes. In a way, I suppose my works—the "talk performances" and the written "talks"—run a kind of dialogue with each other. I wasn't always aware of this, and it may have been pointed out to me by others—Fred Garber and Henry Sayre. But I've come to believe it's true, because there's no other way I can account for my persistent attachment to both ways of working.

CB: I agree with you that the alphabet is one among a number of modalities or technologies for inscribing, recording, mapping, and remembering and should not be taken to stand for all forms of textuality, as it sometimes does. When we awaken to the specific potentialities of different media, we can use each according to its possibility without feeling that the one obliterates the other, as in some progressivist and binary models. When you refer to *The Art of Memory*, it sounds as if you are speaking from a practical engagement with the spatialization of memory, but also that you see your talk pieces as "literal" as much as "oral." Can you apply what you have just been saying (I mean writing) to your talk pieces: What forms of memory and what structural principles do you employ and how do these kinds of choices change the results? This also relates to improvisation in your work. Improvisation is never starting from scratch but rather moving around in material brought to an occasion (or at least I recall your saying something like that to me not long ago). The most common model for improvisation is jazz: How does this relate to your own use of improvisation—but also are there other forms of improvisation that seem relevant to you for contextualizing your talks? (You see I can't ask even this question without saying *text*.) I'm also thinking of improvisation as a writing practice—your own earlier work, for one thing, but also someone like Clark Coolidge, thinking of his frequent invocation of "spontaneous bop prosody" in Jack Kerouac. To what degree are your improvisations spontaneous and, if to some degree (it's a leading question), what is the equivalent of editing? (Isn't repetition with slight variation a form of temporal editing?) It seems to me that one could map out one of your pieces in terms of its structure, perhaps as one might a musical composition—development, digression, theme, repetition; anecdote, commentary, allusion; variation in length of segments. I'm interested to know about the compositional or architectonic decisions for the piece, what are ground plans, what's made in the process, or is it impossible to say because they are so intertwined? And as you say, here we are, engaged in a conversation by E-mail, that is fundamentally different from taping it (as we had considered). But then, with all your experience (I'm not suggesting it could be done if you didn't have extensive experience doing talks), couldn't you write one of your talks? Who would know the difference besides you? What would be the telltale signs?

DA: Taking your last question first, I used to think it was the speed at which it had to be done. In a talk piece I usually have between half an hour and an hour and a half to do whatever I have to do. I can't walk away to check sources for quotations. If I am trying to analyze something, I have to live with whatever abilities and resources I bring to the occasion. I have to have complete confidence in my abilities for the occasion. If they turn out to be not completely adequate, I have to find a way to turn my momentary inadequacy to dramatic advantage. I once gave a talk that hinged on an elaborate story about the difference in character between two salesmen in my uncle's dress business and while building up the characterization of one of them, I realized I couldn't remember his name. So I turned my inability to name him into the dramatic conclusion of the piece. Readiness is all. If I make a slip of the tongue, I can't erase it, though I can correct it publicly if I catch it. But then the audience may not catch it either. I can also edit it out in the talk by the way I move past it. You're absolutely right that there are editing procedures for talks just as there are editing procedures in jazz improvisation. And you're right about not starting from ground zero. Think of Charlie Parker or Thelonius Monk: you know they didn't walk in without things on their mind, habits in their way of proceeding, musical sounds in their head. Usually somebody gives me a title for a piece or I give them a title that serves as a kind of seed for the talk. I may think about this a lot or a little before I get to the occasion. I often let my mind play loosely over images and ideas evoked by the title. Sometimes something wildly digressive enters my thinking. I try not to lock myself in. But sometimes I haven't been thinking about a talk at all until I'm nearly there. In France last December, at Blerancourt, I thought I was going to read—up to the point at which Jacques asked me to do a talk piece. So I had no time to prepare beforehand. Of course I had my nearly thirty years of experience working this way. So the act of going up there to start set me off. We were in a museum, with all those unimpressive paintings by American painters of no great distinction. The cold weather and the topiaried bushes made me think of *Last Year at Marienbad*. Which reminded me of the photograph of Jack Youngerman and the beautiful star of *Marienbad,* his wife, sitting on a rooftop in Soho. The photograph was used as the cover for *Das Kunstwerk*, a German magazine I was the American correspondent for. The raw weather and the photograph and Serge Fauchereau, who was involved with the American art world, brought me to the frozen winter day that was the opening for the Brit sculptor from the American University at Beirut. My image of him at the Fischbach gallery that winter was a little like my image of myself coming out of California to perform a month later at the Beaubourg in what must surely be a bit of a poetic vacuum for a talk piece. So that's how the piece went. The twenty-minute length left the piece less worked out than it might have been. Your insight into that was on the money. I'm not used to working that short. So I had to leave it slightly fragmented and take advantage of the difference of potential among the image fragments, letting the piece take a somewhat more lyrical character I didn't foresee but also didn't mind.

Now is this really different from improvisatory writing—say by Clark Coolidge? Certainly not insofar as the improvisation is concerned. We probably have a great deal in common, though I'm not sure Clark would see it, because we start from different kinds of material. But the main difference for me between "writing" a talk piece and "talking" one by now is the presence or absence of an audience that gives the work its sense of address. Which is why this E-mail dialogue has some of the feel of the talk pieces, because we can address each other directly. More directly than a talk piece, because it's a dialogue between people who know each other and are specifically setting out to engage with each other. This isn't really the case with the talk piece, where the sense of address is inferred and felt, but an explicit address rarely takes place. Still, at Blerancourt I was working in the presence of quite a few people I knew—you and Jerry and Jackson and Diane and Jacques . . . And some I had recently gotten to know. So there were distinct identities in my mind as I spoke. Sure, I could probably write something very much like a talk piece—now that I've been doing them for so long and now that the computer has made it possible for me to write almost as fast as I think. But the focus that an audience provides—would be missing. For me, writing a letter would probably feel closer to my talk pieces. And of course I've always felt that Diderot's great *Salons* and his *Letter on the Deaf and the Mute*, his *Letter on the Blind*, and his whole correspondence with Sophie Volland, were very close to my talk poems. Diderot is probably a prime example of a writer whose writing is very close to "talking." Among contemporaries there is also Kerouac. And Parker and Coltrane and Monk.

As for architectonics, that's harder to talk about. I know that I start from the tension between an engagement with an audience that's in front of me and an engagement with some discourse. The audience is contingent, the discourse is less so. The greater the distance between the two engagements, the greater the tension of working a kind of tuning between the audience and the material and me. Or at least what I imagine is this kind of tuning. That's where the vernacular comes in. It's the language space I'm working in, regardless of how recondite the discourse seems to be. Though it's my idea of the vernacular. I say that I'm thinking out loud, and I am, but I'm testing my thinking against my image of an intelligent and not necessarily expert audience—I have spoken to expert audiences occasionally, but then no audience is expert over the whole range of things I want to explore. And I'm not expert either—not over the the whole range. So my image of audience is that it's a kind of equivalent of me. Equal but different—equally curious, equally intelligent and equally open to the widest range of experience. Which means I can use any method that comes into my head for making my way forward. So the architectonics occur within the image of a trip, of some kind of traversal of a terrain. But I don't know what the terrain will look like till I've traversed it. I know I've traversed it when I've gone as far as I can at that time in that place. So the architectonics are determined by several factors—the nature of the audience, the nature of the discourse or discourses, the distances between them and me, and my insistence on a kind of tuning over the ground of the vernacular. I don't know if that answers your question.

CB: It does, though perhaps part of what I am asking is something that you are in the wrong position to answer: I think it would be possible to do a structural analysis of some of your talk pieces and come out with some interesting patterns. But to say that doesn't mean you are thinking along those lines. My related question would be to ask if you have any sense of the connection between the talks, the relation of one talk to another? Is there a sense of a series or some way of seeing them as a constellation or constellations?

But let me continue by responding to some of your other comments. The idea that speaking before an audience without a script launches one more directly into vernacular is something well, that works for you, but I suppose someone else could deny that impulse and give a lecture instead of a talk. In your comment on the epistolary nature of the talks, in your insistence on the dialogic space of work that is, after all, monologue, you seem to be intent on address as being the critical element. Do you think modernist and contemporary poetry has lost its sense of address, in the wake of the collapse of the traditional lyric poem, which had a very specific, if not necessarily vernacular, address? Does the vernacular address of the talks create an intimate space? That is, I'm struck by your description of the space of your talk poems as being, fundamentally, an interpersonal space, a space between people. This seems to me a sharp critique of the whole idea of theory as a form of deanimated prose. And yet, aren't you theoretical? Can theory be vernacular? How would the content change? That, in turn, brings up the difference between private reading of a poem (or essay) and public performance. Yet it is crucial to note that the talk poems are not conversations, except in the sense of conversations with yourself. Your work does not draw on the form of the town meeting. They are extended solos. Indeed, your comments on the short talk in France underline your commitment to sustained duration of your pieces. Too many short and discrete segments, as in a discussion format, would elide the shape of the whole. That puts you squarely in the tradition of the long poem, especially in its aversion to the short lyric utterance. But are your talks "long poems"?

I want to follow up on one more thing. You note, quite significantly I think, the difference between memorizing and remembering—and it seems to me that remembering—the act and the theme—riddles these exchanges we are having. The oral poetry of cultures without alphabetic writing systems was necessarily involved with memorization, since this poetry was a technology for the storage and retrieval of cultural memory. It seems to me your talk poems, released from the burden of memorization, are free to explore memory. Maybe this accounts for the autobiographical turn in your work, although again here I would ask you to reflect on the difference between what you do in a talk and the genre of autobiography and memoir that are now so popular. Well, that gives you a baker's half-dozen strands to pick up.

DA: Let me tackle the vernacular first. I never intended to give the impression that simply facing an audience without a paper in my hands would launch me into the vernacular. The vernacular is a social and linguistic space, and the decision to employ it is a social choice. It looks for an engagement with a certain kind of audience. The use of a technical jargon is also a social choice. It looks to engage with a group of experts, who recognize each other's expertise in the facility with which they handle the special language. A few years ago Alan Golding invited me to talk at a conference on postmodernism at the University of Louisville. I was scheduled to speak later in the day, but I wanted to hear some of the other speakers to get a feel for the way they engaged the topic. My plane was delayed in Atlanta because of snow, but I got there in time to hear the first speaker. He had a nice attentive crowd of what I took to be mainly young literature professors, and what he seemed to be doing was comparing Franz Fanon's image of the racial outsider in the white European empire with Homi Bhabha's vision of the racial and cultural migrant in its ruins. But he never bothered to describe or compare anything. Almost all the energy of the talk was spent invoking the spiritual presence of absent but terribly potent critical beings through a gracefully elliptical incantation of their magic words—"hegemony," "subaltern," "archive," "panopticon," "rhizome. . . . " Whenever the speaker uttered one of these words, a shiver of pleasure went through the room, and those who shivered knew they were true members of the expert audience to whom this talk was directed. But it seemed that the talk's only purpose was to celebrate the existence of the group it was designed to animate. In the afternoon I gave a talk about the difficulty of buying a mattress.

Over the years I've come to a thorough distrust of the uses of expert language. It's true that you can't discuss competing phonological theories without mentioning distinctive features or allophones or formants, or gene theory without talking about alleles and phenotypes. But the vernacular is pretty permeable and admits new technical vocabulary when you really need it. Chomsky was able to present his linguistic theory to a nonexpert audience in what I would call an educated vernacular. You ask if theory can be vernacular, and whether my works are theoretical. I'm not sure what theory is, unless it's the pursuit of fundamental questions. And I do the best I can at this in the vernacular. But the philosophical tradition I most admire, the one that runs from Socrates through Kierkegaard and Dewey and Wittgenstein, was conducted in the vernacular. With considerable success. In this time of professional specialization, I probably cost myself a certain of amount of attention in professional philosophical circles because of my choice of language register. But you pay your money, you take your choice. I get the audience my language attracts and I lose the ones it repels. Sometimes it seduces members of the other audience into my space.

I suppose my choice of the vernacular for my talks, some of which are in your sense theoretical and in my sense philosophical, makes them an implicit critique of the professional way in theory or philosophy—or poetry. And there is a sense in which I think of them as conversational, not in the literal dialogical sense of actual conversation, but in the kind of space within which conversation exists. I realized how much I felt this at a huge public reading many years ago at the Fillmore East, when I had the opportunity of hearing Voznesensky, who went on before me. To me he sounded like a Russian general addressing his troops in a stadium—when he didn't sound like the general showing his troops how he breathed his words into his girlfriend's ear. For most of my work I'm aiming at a space that's more humanly intimate than a stadium and less cloistered than a bedroom. Of course I might reserve the right to play in either of these two spaces, but at the moment I don't have either of them in mind. And I like the idea of theory poems or philosophy poems. At least for some of my pieces . . . like "the sociology of art" or the twin pieces "tuning" and "gambling" or in a different way "the structuralist." I think the pieces do form constellations, and I try to use placement in my books to suggest ways in which these constellations can be seen—the way "the sociology of art" sits at the center of *talking at the boundaries,* where I hope it reverberates back through and is energized by the other pieces grouped around it. The way "tuning" and "gambling" sit at the center of *tuning,* or slightly differently, the way "the structuralist" sits at the end of *what it means to be avant-garde.* Nobody has paid much attention to the structure of my books as books—at least so far—probably because the individual works all begin in performance. But since I use the book as one of my modes, I pay a great deal of attention to it. The books are pretty certainly not long poems, but they are long and complexly structured single works. And the structuring may start loosely in the sequence of performances, but it really takes shape only when I put the talk pieces together to form a book.

On the question of remembering versus memorizing. I think you may be relying a little too much on the arguments of Eric Havelock and maybe on Hugh Kenner. It seems to me that any society that has a powerful anxiety about the ability to remember may be tempted toward "literal" memorization and recitation the way medieval Scandinavian society felt the need to "memorize" their body of law and recite it ceremonially in public once a year. Though it's not certain that this recitation was as verbally literal as the performance of the Greek rhapsodes. If it was, it was part of a move along the path of "literalization." But there was no evidence of "memorization" by the Balkan improvisers Parry recorded. What he found was that they employed metrical verbal phrase patterns that could be deployed and *varied* over a wide range of similar but different narrative circumstances. Lord took this further in his examination of the manipulation and redeployment of certain thematic elements in their epic narratives. Still, the Milman Parry, Albert Lord, and Eric Havelock tradition projects a kind of mechanical cobbling together, that Martin Nagler coming later shows is almost certainly not characteristic of the Homeric poems, which exhibit a much more fluid relation to the traditional materials. With the kind of fluid transformations that are more characteristic of remembering than memorization. And much more characteristic of the ordinary operation of mind that the new cognitive science seems to be confirming.

CB: Although, given the nature of your work, even such analysis becomes an extension of the talking more than an explication of it. The elasticity of the work is quite amazing. So that even my prodding of you about the metastructures of the books can be transformed into more "mything" (rimes with riffing) as you say in "sociology of art." Complete with a bit of self-cautioning: not to reify something that is a process (or, in other words, not to become too self-absorbed in the way poets sometimes do).

I think one reason why your comments on the structures of the books is useful is that the visual format of the books may foster a kind of overall or run-on reading. Despite your care in breaking up each piece and giving a short preface about the particular occasion from which each one emerges, there is also a sense in which the one talk flows into the next. It has something to do with the porousness of talk and something to do with the visual format you have created for the talks, with its absence of periods, capitalization, and apostrophes. I was very interested in Marjorie Perloff's talk at Amiens, in which she suggested that concrete poetry brought the visual organization of all poetry into sharper view and that this has had particular importance for prose-format poetry. Which reminds me of your remark that prose is "concrete poetry with justified margins." What I especially appreciated about Marjorie's essay is how she turns that fact around on itself and shows how important is the visual arrangement of proselike works such as Rosmarie Waldrop's and your own. I agree with you when you say, in the note that precedes *talking at the boundaries*, that your pages are not prose, even if your talks are appropriately considered as part of Stephen Fredman's study of poets' prose. Anyone would know the visual format is not prose if they tried to copy a passage accurately: preserving the spacing between word clusters with different right-margin breaks is not only difficult but suggests that what you have created is actually an internalized form of lineation. The format brings to mind transcription, but there is no necessary way to score transcription, as Dennis Tedlock notes so cogently in *The Spoken Word and the Work of Interpretation*. You address this explicitly when you say that the texts of your work are notations or scores of oral poems. But are they?

You have designed a format that has practically become a signature, even though this format could be widely used as an alternative to prose format. (If and as someone else uses this format, the first thing a reader will notice is that it "looks like Antin.") But do you think of the word clusters delineated by white space before and after as something relating to verse lines? I am at some pains here to avoid the word *phrases* for these clusters, but that's probably what they are. That is—and correct me if I'm wrong—you always break at the syntactic or phrasal end; these units are never broken up or enjambed. There is some connection to the practice of lineation suggested by Olson in "Projective Verse," but I wouldn't think you would conceptualize it along those lines. It is also notable, and audible, that you vary the length of the phrases from a few words to a few lines and that the longer units include phrases that in other parts of the talk would be broken into smaller units. So what, then, is the prosody here? What is "talk" rhythm and how do you create it within this format?

I am asking this partly because your citing of "the sociology of art" reminded me that in my second book, *Parsing* (soon to reprinted in *Republics of Reality: 1975-1995),* I end with a poem called "Roseland" (written, I think, in 1975) that incorporates a series of short phrases from that talk (for the most part, shorter than the phrases in the original), scored in "field" style and connected by an associative rather than linear or discursive movement. So this is something I have been thinking about for a while.

What precedents were there for this particular format? Looking back on your "concrete poetry with justification," can you give some account of what the format has allowed and perhaps some notion of the limitations? Can you imagine using a different format in the future?

DA: Back in 1976, in the preface to *talking at the boundaries,* I explained the texts of my talk poems as "the notations or scores of oral performances" and I thought I drew a clear line in the sand, separating them from prose, which I'd characterized earlier as "concrete poetry with justified margins." That made sense to me then, but while I'll still stand by my characterization of prose, I'm no longer satisfied by the earlier description of my texts. In music a score has two primary purposes—to serve as a kind of transducer, allowing "the music" to be stored, transmitted and distributed by other means than live performance, and to enable reperformance by oneself or by other performers. The talk pieces weren't designed for other performers or for reperformance in general. And while I did read one once at a reading celebrating the publication of Jerry's and Pierre's *Poems for the Millennium* and it seemed to satisfy the conditions of a poetry reading, to me it felt a bit weird. A little like Homer reading part of the *Odyssey*. What's more, its sound became different. And I couldn't help it. It became a reading sound instead of a speaking sound—a reading sound that recalled the sound of its speaking but somehow put it in the past tense. It might be interesting to do but it wasn't what I designed my notation for. I didn't start my transcriptions for that purpose, and the transcriptions were made from tape recordings of the performances, which I suppose could have been distributed directly. So the texts weren't strictly necessary for the purposes of recording and distribution, though they may have been a more effective and elegant means of recording and distribution.

When I started doing the performances with the sense that I was doing "talk poems," I had no textification in mind. Contrary to Dennis Tedlock's supposition that they were composed orally with the typewriter in mind, I didn't think at all about textual realizations. Unless what Dennis meant was that as citizens of a textual culture anything we say is conditioned by the instrument used for rendering speech into text—which at that time was the typewriter. That's an Ong-like supposition and has some truth in it—though not as much as one might think. But I did tape-record them—to find out what I'd said. So why did I decide to transcribe and publish them? I think this is where your notion of the surrounding context comes in. I'm sure I believed that the serious discourses of our culture took place in texts. I still believe it. And what I was doing was trying to confront the textual discourses, which were generated at a desk in the language of textification, with a text that was generated by talking, that derived its life and its mode of thinking from talking and carried the traces of its origins into the world of text. How to do it?

Oddly enough I was thinking of *Beowulf*. When I studied the Klaeber edition of the great Anglo-Saxon poem, I was struck by how bizarre the punctuation seemed. Klaeber had made a mad attempt to fit this essentially oral poem to nineteenth-century punctuation complete with commas and semicolons. These marks felt insane. When I examined a facsimile of the manuscript it bore none of these marks. It didn't even respect what careful reading would show were the lines of the poem. It had scribal marks that had nothing to do with the original poem but probably indicated where a scribe stopped for the moment or the day. But once you got used to it, the poem was easier to read this way than it was in the scholarly edition. So I realized I needed to remove marks—commas and periods. And I also realized that regularized margins on the left and on the right were originally only conveniences for printing. Later they became associated with the idea of "prose," which derives from a Latin phrase meaning "straightforward talk," whatever that might be. Verse was something different. But a poetry that wasn't verse and wasn't prose had to declare itself as different. Word spaces still seemed reasonable, and phrase music was apparent. So I took for granted that I would separate words from each other and represent phrasal groupings. In figuring out what these were I tended to follow the pulse of the talking. Mostly these were units that made a kind of grammatical and semantic sense together but this could change if there were hesitation markers or other junctural markers that seemed meaningful. This allowed occasionally different breaks. Then there was the additional fact that I felt free to add to the original material and expand it—with phrases or whole passages that were not in the original but belonged in the talk. These had to be adapted to the pulse of speech. That wasn't hard for me as long as I was sitting at a typewriter or later a computer, composing the material directly as I am now. The sense of address had already been created. So they were merely freely composed interpolations. But if I had to introduce long passages of previously composed materials—as in "the sociology of art"—I tried to set them off in ways that would indicate their separateness. Your question about the formation of the phrase groupings is interesting. I think I mostly tried to follow the pulse of the speaking, whatever way I seemed to understand that. But I also seemed to react to the way this pulse could be most clearly represented on a page, which is a different thing from literal copying of the breaks of my voice. And you're quite right, I wasn't really thinking of this from a "Projective Verse" point of view. Now in talking about "Roseland" you're not really clear about what the origin of your phrases was. You suggest the text originated in some kind of talk and that the phrases were cut out of this talk. If that was the case you may have been doing something very close to what I was doing in representing the phrasal groups. It's quite a different thing to create word clusters that can be imagined as possibly but not certainly going together in some kind of speech. A reader might try to find a possible speaking pulse for such clusters but would probably remain uncertain about their intonation and pacing. The result would be a tendency for such clusters—if they were identified as that—to acquire conceptually a kind of list structured intonation. I'm really interested, but I don't have a copy of *Parsing*. I'd like to see it.

CB: One of the things that interests me is how the talking pulse in your poetry is audible even if you rearrange the order of the phrases—that is part of what I was exploring in the pieces of mine I mentioned. So I want to focus more on this talking pulse, because it raises some fundamental issues for poetry, issues that I think are related to, but distinct from, the questions of the vernacular we have been discussing.

Traditional prosody works by differentiating a poem's sound patterns from those of speech, heightening the sound, which means accenting one form of sound patterning over another. This despite the connection between the iambic line to the "natural patterns" of English speech that is often cited by prosodists. Non-naturalistic in the sense that nonspeech-oriented verbal patterning is also present in cultures without writing systems, through devices such as parallel structure and vocables, among others. Thinking again of the Serbian singers discussed by Lord and Parry, and leaving aside the issue of the technical imperatives for the structure of verse they used, there is again a highly marked verbal patterning that is different from speech.

Then again, there's Wordsworth's famous remark in the preface to his *Lyrical Ballads* that his poems are a "metrical arrangement" of the "language really used by men." His elaboration of this is relevant: "The language, too, of these men is adopted (purified indeed from what appears to be its real defects, from all lasting and rational causes of dislike or disgust) because such men hourly communicate with the best objects from which the best part of language is originally derived; and because, from their rank in society and the sameness and narrow circle of their intercourse, being less under the influence of social vanity they convey their feelings and notions in simple and unelaborated expressions." As with much "real" speech in poetry, Wordsworth is presenting the speech of other people, not himself. In a similar way, speech enters in *The Waste Land* in the form of the barmaid's monologue in "A Game of Chess" ("When Lil's husband got demobbed, I said / I didn't mince my words, I said to her myself"). I mention these two examples as exemplary moments for romanticism and modernism, respectively.

And then there's Williams, and I think here we are closer to what I want to get at. Williams's practice, misleadingly called "free verse," also claimed authority from the spoken language he heard around him, the American idiom. The structures of his lines and stanzas worked to bring this out, often using very short word clusters and isolating individual words for emphasis but also not sticking with any consistent line length, which I think does convey something of a "speech pulse." The crucial intervention in this history is the tape recorder. Transcribing tape-recorded speech doesn't solve the problem of the representation of speech in writing, but it does change it. Access to this technology in a way that could be used to create poems becomes possible, from a practical point of view, only in the 1950s, and even then it would have been cumbersome. As you may know, the first audio tape recorders were manufactured for retail sale in 1935 (in Germany); cassettes were first made available in the mid-1960s. There is of course a substantial body of transcribed speech (and "oral history"), much of it I think of great importance for poetry. But what I think is less common, and particularly significant in terms of this prosodic history I am tracing, is self-transcription, especially given the freedom, within the space of the poem, to edit and alter: to make speech not just to represent it. And this of course is what you are doing in the texts of your talk poems.

There is a question lurking behind all this. In "the sociology of art" you say that poetry in cultures without writing is "a kind of talking." But what about song? In that piece you mention song in passing, and with typical wit, as a kind of constraint ("a special form of talking . . . like telling a story on a tightrope or while swimming"). What is the difference between talk and song? What is the possibility for song in the poetry of the present moment?

DA: While I've had a great distaste for what's usually called "song" in modern poetry or, for that matter, for what's usually called "music," I really don't think of "speech" as so far from song and I don't think of "talk" as "unmusical." Prose may be most of the time unmusical—because it wants to be. It wants to be responsible. And music is playful and irresponsible. Phonologically overdetermined, as Jakobson might say. Jingling or tuning. Think of the blues refrain in Stein's "Melanctha." It sneaks into the novella right after one of the narrator's stiffest "prose" paragraphs.

Why did the subtle, intelligent, attractive, half white girl Melanctha Herbert love and do for and demean herself in service to this coarse, decent, sullen, ordinary, black childish Rose, and why was this unmoral, promiscuous, shiftless Rose married, and that's not so common either, to a good man of the negroes, while Melanctha with her white blood and attraction and her desire for a right position had not yet been really married.

Stein holds this tone for a sentence and then modulates slowly away.

Sometimes the thought of how all her world was made, filled the complex, desiring Melanctha with despair. She wondered, often, how she could go on living when she was so blue.

Finally she lets in the full refrain, slightly flattened by the prose environment

Melanctha told Rose one day how a woman whom she knew had killed herself because she was so blue. Melanctha said, sometimes, she thought this was the best thing for herself to do.

From there on, the refrain haunts the novella in a great number of variations, and it's possible to argue that the whole of "Melanctha" is a struggle between "poetry" and "prose"—prose represented by the narrator's stiff and "unmusical" literary style and "poetry" by the characters' "musical" black speech. What I learned from *Three Lives* when I was sixteen or seventeen was that speech was musical and that the line between talking and singing is very hard to draw. But looking back at "Melanctha" now, it seems to me that even the stiffest prose sections threaten to become musical if the notation would only let them be. What if I took the commas away and printed?

> Why did the subtle
>   intelligent
>   attractive
>   half white
>   girl
>   Melanctha Herbert
>   love and
>   do for and
>   demean her self
>   in service to this
>   coarse decent
>   sullen
>   ordinary
>   black
>   childish Rose

We say that infants are learning to speak when they play with the sounds of our language. They are, but they're also singing. When my son Blaise was about nine months old I used to sing to him an otherwise senseless phrase:

```
Hel-          ca-
    lo   Chi-     go
```

That is, "Hello, Chicago," to the tune starting from the A above middle C and dropping a minor tenth to F# F# then back to A and ending on F# in an accent pattern ´ ^ ^ ´ `, which he would sing back to me over and over again with great pleasure, with the pitches and accents and vowels perfectly imitated and some approximation of the consonants. Children frequently sing meaningful phrases to themselves over and over again before they learn to make a distinction between singing and saying or between talking and playing. And they play with the whole range of the phonology, especially the intonation patterns.

The notion of song itself is not so simple. For several centuries what has passed for song in literary circles was any text that looked like the lyrics for a commonplace melodic setting. In *Code of Flag Behavior,* the first two sections of "Novel Poem"—"10 songs" and "7 songs"—began as parody. But it soon became an idea of liberation. I took lines from popular novels and arranged them as songs. Since the source texts were novels, the language was originally notated as prose. The idea was to find some features of song hidden in the prose and release them in a new notation. "Have you got Prince Albert in the can? Let him out, he's a friend of mine." So we're back to notation and the question you asked me earlier about my own notation.

The notation I developed for the "talk poems" works well enough to represent the pulse and logic of thinking while talking. Which is fairly rapid. And it's hard to slow up. If I wanted to give a novella-like character to a narrative developed in one of them, I can only slow up so much. The conventions of prose fiction permit more detail and different types of representation of subjectivities than I can ordinarily make use of. A piece like "the structuralist," which in some ways approaches the genres of the novella, took a lot of maneuvering to maintain its original relation to the improvised talk piece I did in Toronto while I incorporated richer detail on the origins of Volapuek and its place in Paris in 1889 and greater elaboration of the sound poem that concludes the piece. Like any notation, the one I use has its preferences and maybe it precludes certain possibilities, but I'm not really sure of that. Whenever I've tried to adapt the notation to some uncustomary use, I seem to be able to bring it around. I've also found that I had to turn some "talk pieces" into what looked like essays. A piece in *Critical Inquiry* called "Fine Furs" and another in *Representations* called "Biography" began as talk pieces, that I found I could adapt to the essay genre without terrible difficulty. And some of my earlier art critical essays could very easily have been presented as "talk pieces." Especially the *Art News* essay called "Tingueley's New Machine." I suppose I can manage a prose format as long as I keep closer to Laurence Sterne than to Henry James.

Would I employ another kind of notation? I have recently—over the last year or so—been doing a group of what I call "Micro Films," short poems ten to twelve lines long, that I designed to be seen projected as slide sequences, text over image, one line per slide. So far I've completed three of them and they're really designed for projection in a movie theater as "short films" that take advantage of familiarity with popular film genres to relate text and image. The image is not exactly a "background" except in the case of "Film Noir," where there is nothing but white text on a black ground. But the black ground tends to suggest an image of a night in which the texts work like radio voices and provide cues to imagined images. "Poincaré's Theorem" is a sci-fi film and has its white texts "embedded" in the image of a starry sky. So the sequence appears like a dialogue in outer space. And "Loose Ends" uses texts set under a number of different landscape images in a way that suggests off-camera dialogue. Clearly I could equip my computer with slide capabilities, but I don't think I'd like my little slide films on a computer screen. I really designed them for movie theaters or film festivals. The idea of a seventy- or eighty-second film in which the black leader is longer than the film appeals to me. So what I have when they're printed is a series of ordinary looking short poems, which I could probably print directly on the picture reproduced from the slides. I guess this would be a new version of an old format in which the notation is simply that of the short poem for lines of dialogue that evoke a popular movie genre. The first two were projected as slide sequences at the Laemmle Figueroa, a downtown Los Angeles movie theater, as part of a series of artists' projections sponsored by Side Street Projects. Billed as "Intermission Images," they ran instead of the usual commercials between films in that theater for something over a month—to the apparent bewilderment of the general audience.

Since none of these "films" uses more than fourteen slides, what I would have if I wanted to publish them in book form would be a series of short poems printed one line to a page over a reproduction of the image taken from the corresponding slide. As I see it, this would seem to borrow a conventional children's book format for the presentation of a series of short poems. I've also been doing a sequence of "short stories" that I began as an installation for MOCA Los Angeles. These are very short stories running from a few lines to no more than a page, each one built around a single obligatory word drawn from the dictionary. I intend to work my way from A to Z three times. Right now I have forty stories and they're all presented in a "prose" notation.

CB: I look forward to seeing the "Micro Films." That type of format, where you are actively using the "background" as part of the work, in contrast to the old style white page, reminds me of a range of moving text pieces now being created for the web (I guess "programmable media" is the current word for this). Though in the case of the "Micro Film," you are situating the poem as projection in a performance rather than for private viewing on a computer screen. So: back to the another version of the issue of page versus stage.

But let me postpone that discussion for the moment and go back to what you say about song. I wonder if the more important distinction isn't the one between speech and song but is the one between singing and song? Your comments on this seem to me something of an extension of remarks you made on Stein and prose in your *Occident* essay about the time you were moving into the talk performances—and also talk texts. Stein invents her version of modernist composition, as articulated in the last sections of *The Making of Americans* and then *Tender Buttons,* through a close listening to, and notation of, nonstandard American speech. In the terms I used in "Poetics of the Americas," the origins of Stein's ideolectical poetry is in the dialectic passages of *Three Lives*. Speech "as it is spoken" (WE SPEEK SPEECH HERE) is, for Stein, the source of modernist textuality. This proposes a kind of quantum poetics: the deeper one listens to the spoken the more textual it seems.

It may be a bit of leap to go from Stein to her immediate contemporary, Arnold Schoenberg (both born in 1874 and both living in Vienna when they were the age that Blaise was when he was singing a tune that had not yet become Song), but indulge me with this for just a second. Schoenberg's opera *Moses and Aaron,* begun in 1930, figures the conflict between speech and song in a way that has some bearing on your comments. Schoenberg's libretto is a revisionist's *Exodus*. Moses speaks *(Sprachstimme),* Aaron sings. Aaron's singing enables him to be persuasive but it is also problematic because it involves pandering with images. In other words, for Schoenberg in this work, song is associated with the prohibition against graven images. In contrast, Moses's speaking is associated with thought and ideas. While his speaking lacks the eloquence of Aaron's song, its refusal of image marks its ethical character. The ethical character of speech is that it is dialogic, reciprocal, face to face. Speech refuses spectacle. Song, in contrast, flirts with spectacle ("I worked marvels for eyes and ears to witness" as Aaron says), climaxing in the "operatic" extravaganza of the Golden Calf. At the heart of the agonistic struggle between the two brothers is a conflict between ethical and moral discourse, where moral discourse implies exhortation and ethical discourse implies an encounter, through thought, with the unnamable and unrepresentable. Yet Moses's ethical bearing is also, for Schoenberg, the key to his inaccessibility, his difficulty communicating, and ultimately his isolation from the people. In contrast, Aaron offers something "ordinary, visible, easy to understand, gold forever."

I go on at this length because *Moses and Aaron* seems to me a paradigmatic modernist allegory, where modernist composition is thematized as the difficult and unrepresentable thought for which Moses speaks. The fact that the music for the opera could not be finished in the wake of an unrepresentable Extermination Process that pushed Schoenberg to LA is even more to the point: the opera is complete only in its "text," which is, in the final act, forever uncoupled with music. As Adorno suggests, the opera provides a full-scale critique of reification as a form of idolatry (or vice versa). Schoenberg's Moses, confronted by the Calf (the ur of reification), makes the point succinctly: you cannot "enclose the boundless in an image."

The problem for modernist composition is that its critique of reification may only displace the problem, leaving the reification intact. In this sense, reification returns in the aesthetic distance created by the objectification of the work of art, so that one reads the work or is bowled over by it, rather than participating in it. Stein's dialogism, including her oscillation between speech, song, and "prose" composition, suggests a viable alternative to this form of modernist objectification. I think also of Wittgenstein's reluctance to write down his talking philosophy, about which you've already spoken in this conversation (thinking also of the connection to a Socratic as opposed to Platonic orientation, if such a distinction can be maintained).

Could your move from an image-based poetry to a poetry that shattered images be seen as necessarily iconoclastic: the breaking up of images, idols? And your subsequent move into talk and direct address, with its emphasis on reciprocal presence of the speaker and the spoken—could that be viewed as an ethical turn? That would suggest an interpretation of your disinclination to perform work you had previously written as a refusal to locate value in the poem understood as a fixed, as icon, but rather . . . in what? The thought process? Isn't there, then, a rethinking of modernism here, as prefigured in your *Occident* essay?

DA: I agree. *Moses and Aaron* is the paradigmatic modernist allegory and it's symptomatic of both the virtues and problems of modernism. Specifically in its identification of representation and reification. The weakness of representation is by now pretty clear—whether from Rimbaud's "Je est un autre" or from Wittgenstein's *Tractatus*. But representation and reification are not the same thing. Aaron represents the power that brought the Israelites out of Egypt as a Golden Calf. As an image it's not even so-so. For gold it's pretty impoverished. The gold stands for value, okay. But a calf? An animal notable for weakness, clumsiness, and immaturity. This for the Power that made the deal with Abraham, drove out Hagar and Ishmael, let ancient Sarah conceive a child, demanded the sacrifice of Isaac, brought the plagues on Egypt, divided the Red Sea—the image is a bit laughable, and we can suppose that the writer of Exodus wanted us to laugh at it. It might not have seemed quite so laughable if he'd said a Golden Bull—an image of value married to an image of male power—or a Golden Cow, an image of expansive fruitfulness. The Power provided manna in the desert. Would a Whirlwind have been better? A Fire? All representations are imperfect and some are more imperfect than others. But once one gets engraved in the culture, that's when it becomes the Golden Calf. Yet the weakness of representation is also its strength. That's what the modernists didn't understand. Jerome Bruner in a review of *The Scientist in the Crib,* a recent book on childhood learning, points out that children's need "to construct a world of space, time and causality" requires certain "trade-offs in which some things are represented at the expense of others and that there are forms of blindness to the world that are part of the process of learning." But all representations are at the expense of other representations, and the only way to deal with this is to preserve some sense of their provisionality. Which is to say they're context dependent. So a representation may open the door to the most profound chain of insights in a certain situation and then block the way to further insights once the situation has changed. That's what happened to classical modernism. Schoenberg's absolute distinction between Moses's "ethical" speech and Aaron's "moral" singing is a perfect example of the reification of a profound observation. It is quite true that there is no way of imaging the unknowable Force that Moses bears witness to. Because It's unimaginable. But It is also Indescribable—in prose or speech or song. So what good is Moses's "speech." Its entire value gets used up in its powerful ethical rejection of conventional imaging. This is the difficulty with hieratic high modernism, that includes the painting tradition running from Kandinsky and Malevich and Mondrian to the Rothko Chapel—though it doesn't extend to Duchamp or Cendrars or Satie. And as you say, if we get caught up in overvaluing this eloquent Rejection Speech, we're back to reification. So while I share your feeling for the ethical in Schoenberg's Moses, for me Gertrude Stein's code switching in *Three Lives* from a textified "prose" sound to a "speech" sound that is undifferentiated from singing, to the fully imaged sound of "song," as I was discovering it in my *Occident* essay, prefigured a possible way out of the high modernist impasse. And while there is a strong component of the ethical in my move to the talk pieces, based on my sense of the human value of direct address, it was also based on the promise of the kind of provisionality offered by jazz. Improvisation is the enemy of reification, if you don't count on it too much. The talk pieces are filled with representations—images and stories. There are also places that are very close to the symphonic if not to song, but they emerge somewhat impromptu from the talking and disappear back into it. Which is the way I want it. I tend to think that I learned more from Duchamp, Stein, Cage and Cendrars than I did from Schoenberg and Rothko, much as I admire them both.

And this leads to a question I wanted to ask you. What do you mean by *text?* I'm not sure I really understand it when you say "the deeper we listen to the spoken, the more textual it seems?"

CB: Well, for me, that echoes a quote by Karl Kraus (I seem unable to leave Vienna): "The closer you look at a word, the greater the distance from which it stares back." I am just thinking that as one gets into hyperclose listening to speech, as with detailed tape transcription, all of a sudden the textures and the grains of speech start to loom large: the pauses and interruptions and garbling of words and the rhythms. And it begins to look like something very textual, woven verbal texture. I think Stein, in trying to represent vernacular but also the "broken" English of the second-language speaker (in *Three Lives),* actually discovered "wordness" in speech. That is, she came up with the particular syntactic density of her radical modernist composition. You see this emerging in the end of *Making of Americans* and full blown in *Tender Buttons*. By textual, I mean features especially associated with writing, punctuation for example, or orthography, so it's the transcriptive aspects of speech reproduction that immediately plunge one into the center of the textual imaginary. This is something I was trying to explore, for example, in "A Defense of Poetry" in *My Way,* which is pervaded by typographical errors. What I am interested in is especially evident when the piece is sounded out in performance. And that poem ends with that quote from Kraus (by the way, also born in 1874).

You know there's that often quoted sentence by Robert Grenier, "I HATE SPEECH," which has this paradox because, as is almost never acknowledged, the remark is a speech act above all else, above its purported content. And Grenier's work of the time is all about speech, about the transcribing or realizing "utterance." So that's the quantum part: it's no shock to find the imagined opposition of writing and speech collapses at stress points. You might say that writing and speech are aspects of verbal language and that textuality is a palimpsest: when you scratch it you find speech underneath, but when you sniff the speech, you find language under that. And of course what I have been suggesting in our discussions is that your "talk" poems are quantum entities in just this way.

Well, as I mention Kraus, it brings up something that is "under" maybe or "around" or "next to" key parts of our conversation. I want to ask you if you see a particular turn in Jewish modernism, if the Jewishness is significant for your reading of modernism? But I also want to ask about the significance of Jewishness for you. And, carrying this to the present, in an age of identity poetics, how do you read Jewishness in terms of your work and your life?

DA: Yesterday I had to call our New York accountant and he greeted me as always with a burst of gleeful Yiddish that made me laugh and answer him as well as I could in his mother tongue. "Oy," he said, "you sound like a German. Your Yiddish is verdeitcht." What can I do, Mel, I learned German first. I suppose that's my typical situation in relation to Jewishness. My family was no longer religious. My grandfather, whom I was named for, had turned from a Talmudic scholar into a Spinozan pantheist. As long as I remember I not only had no personal interest in religion, but growing up during the Nazi takeover of most of Europe, I thought the idea of god was not only obscene but at best totally meaningless. Yet I got bar mitzvahed—because my grandmother wanted me to. On her husband's side of the family we claim descent from one of the great Hasidic masters, Wolf Kitzes, a close associate of the Baal Shem Tov. So I learned enough Hebrew to stagger through a meaningless ceremony that I scarcely remember, except that my cousin Betsy, who was principal of a high school, gave me the collected novels of Victor Hugo, which I dutifully read all the way through in spite of the endless descriptions, the small print, and the thickness of the volume. But I recognized something of my family in what Martin Buber wrote about our somewhat absentminded ancestor. It amused me and made me wonder what made him one of the Hasidic Masters. So when Jerome Rothenberg and I had translated a very early work of Buber's and we had occasion to meet him, I asked him what made Wolf Kitzes a Hasidic master, and Buber simply said "He had fire." Jerry and I were in our twenties then and Buber was about seventy. So I left it at that. But early in 1990 Marjorie Perloff and Jerome

CHARLES BERNSTEIN | 51

and I were asked to talk at a *Tikkun* conference in Los Angeles about Writing and Jewishness. I took the occasion to do a talk piece called "writing and exile" that got published in *Tikkun* in September or October. And toward the end of the talk I decided to revisit the Wolf Kitzes story and tell it my way. It goes like this:

The Baal Shem for some reason sent Wolf off on an expedition that required him to travel from Bialostock or wherever they were in Poland or Russia to the shore of some sea across which he had to travel for some time on board a ship that was caught in a storm and wrecked, and clinging to a spar he drifted ashore on what looked like a deserted island. Exhausted and dripping wet, he crawled up the beach, creeping along in his soggy clothing perhaps having lost his stremmel and looking for some sign of human habitation, which appeared on a distant peak or crag to be a lone castle or manor. He made his way painfully up the mountain to the manor and rang at the gate, hoping to be admitted with the servants. But nobody came. The gate simply swung open as did the great door of the principal building, that opened into a grand central hallway where Wolf found himself at the end of a huge table that seemed to stretch an immense distance into the interior of the castle, which appeared so dark and far away that he couldn't make out the head of the table, and this table was set with a heavy tablecloth shot through with gold and silver silken threads on which were set wax candles in golden candlesticks and goblets of Venetian glass among dishes of Chinese porcelain and knives and spoons of beaten gold. And there was food on the table in such measure it seemed as if spilled from some great horn of plenty—nuts and fruits, grapes and peaches and persimmons and melons he had never seen, and great trenchers loaded down with roasted birds and decanters of ruby wine. But there was no one at the table. All the places were empty and he was afraid to begin to eat. So he looked around the room and up toward the other end of the table. But the head of the table that was dark before now seemed to be enveloped in a sort of luminous fog out of which a powerful voice spoke. "Wolf, how is it with my people?" And Wolf, who was at first terrified to hear the voice, reflected and then answered as any true Jew would, "So how should it be?" "So be it," answered the voice and the light dissipated from the end of the table. Wolf lost his fear, took up the decanter of wine nearest him, poured out a goblet full and pronounced the blessing over it and proceeded to eat and drink till he fell asleep at the table. When he woke up he was out at sea again clinging to a spar in the water, from which he was picked up by a fishing boat that carried him to the port from which he eventually made his way back to Bialostock or wherever he had started from on the Polish Lithuanian Russian border, and he went to his beloved master the Baal Shem and reported what had happened. When he got to the part about the voice, the Baal Shem couldn't contain himself and demanded, "So Wolf, what did you say?" And Wolf told him and the Baal Shem got very depressed. "So what should I have said?" my ancestor asked. "If you had told him the truth, he would have made it better."

Thinking about this story and thinking about my ancestor, who might have been distinguished only in being responsible for the troubled fate of the Jews if you took this story straight, I realized this was impossible. What had really happened was this. My ancestor, Wolf, in the spirit I know well from my family, heard a voice coming to him from a distance and asking what he would have had to consider, if he considered it critically, an obscene question—because an omnipotent omniscient boss knows how his people are and it is a stupid offensive question asked by an obscene power—if that's what you think you're confronting. But Wolf knew he was confronting his own delusionary system. His terrible fear and hunger and thirst had got the better of him and produced the delusion that he could ask for his situation to change and that there was some addressable being with the will and the power to change it, who somehow never had the will or the power to change any of all the other terrible situations of the Jews throughout history. So my ancestor realized the ludicrousness of his situation and turned on himself the mockery that's become the true mark of the Jewish tradition by answering in response to the question "How is it with my people?" "So how should it be?" And when he got back home and went to visit his beloved Master of the Holy Name and the Baal Shem Tov asked him "What did you say?," he realized with a feeling of pity as deep as his love that his master had so profound and excessive love of the numinous he could momentarily believe in the absolute status of this event. So taking pity on his great teacher he answered once again in the Jewish tradition, "So what should I have said?" and left it at that. Because there was nothing he should have said. There's nothing an exiled human should say when addressed in this way. You have to refuse this question because it is the imbecilic product of a degrading delusion. That's what I realized at the *Tikkun* talk. I realized the tale was a devastating example of Jewish black humor that Buber just didn't get, because it leaves you with a choice I understood, between a demonic god and no god at all. And that talk piece taught me that what I got from the Jewish tradition was not Yiddish or the religion, but the sense of exile. Now the sense of exile seems to play a very large role in modernist writing. When you asked me about Jewish modernists, I thought first of Kafka—the middle-class, German-speaking Jew caught between Catholic German nationalists and Hussite, Czech Prague. Or Proust, the gay, rich Jew in Catholic France. But why not go back to Marx and Freud, the one baptized and anti-Semitic and the other a resolutely secular atheist Jew. This was modernist exile, confronting blunt European racism. Kafka worked for an anti-Semitic insurance company and could watch a pogrom unfold outside his office window. But he was also exiled from the various forms of Jewishness as well, from Zionism, from Yiddish folk culture, from the language itself, which he thought of the way all cultivated German speakers did, as a low jargon, in spite of the linguistic fact that Yiddish is an older language than Hochdeutsch. It's essentially a socially distinct version of medieval Rhenish, carrying traces of the Andalusian origins of its first speakers and enriched by an elaborate word hoard from Hebrew, Polish, Ukrainian, and Russian, as its largely literate speakers moved eastward. But the Jewish exilic aspect of modernism goes beyond the Jewish modernists themselves, among whom we would have to include Stein and Wittgenstein as well. It's no accident that Joyce chooses Bloom, the Hungarian Jew to play the Odysseus of his novel to Stephen's Telemachus. Marcel Duchamp, a permanent if cheerful exile wherever he went, remarked in an interview that he'd originally intended to give his female persona a Jewish name. The fact is, he did. Rrose Selavy is easily pronounced as the typically European, Jewish Rosa Levy. Everyone from a Jewish family had an aunt Rose. I not only had an aunt Rose, I had three cousins named Rose, one of whom changed her name to Barbara because she thought Rose sounded too Jewish. But this is now, not then. If I draw on the sense of exile, it's more in the cheerful exilic mode of Marcel Duchamp than in the anguished mode of Kafka. Probably because by now it seems clear nobody has a permanent home on the face of the earth. Though Kafka's narrator in the *Gespräch mit dem Beter* appears to have foreseen this in his vision of the city square, around which the buildings were collapsing and across which people were used to being lifted and blown by a weirdly gusting wind.

california—the nervous camel

david antin

the reason i was asked to talk here is obviously that im not a
  native californian   so i must have a clearer view of california
  coming from three thousand miles a way   and theres a certain
  justice in supposing this   because its very hard for fish to get a
  clear view of water   while if youre a land dweller and come into
    the water   you experience it somewhat more sharply than if
  youd always lived there   but ive been living here for a long time
    i came to california back in 1968 after staying away from
  california for a long time   how long?   im not that old   but
  id stayed away from california almost as if id been resisting it   i
  had traveled around the united states as a kid a young man   id
  been to the northwest the middle west   i knew someof the south
    i knew new england   but somehow id always stopped at
  california and i dont know why   though it may have come from
    my earliest experiences of california   which were of course
  representations of california

                                  everybodys heard of california   but what
  id heard was probably not very much like what everyone else had
  heard   the first memory i have of california made me a bit
    nervous   i guess i was about three or four and my next door
  neighbor was a little kid who was called gedaliah inside his house
    and jerry outside   in that part of boro park we lived in two
    different countries in those days   inside my grandmothers
  house where i lived then   we lived in eastern europe and my
  family spoke a variety of eastern european languages that were
  all very pleasant to eavesdrop on   but outside we spoke what
  they used to speak in brooklyn   which was the true american
    english   and so you can tell from my accent that im a truly
  native american   so if i heard this outside sitting on the stoop
    i heard it from jerry   but if i heard it inside sitting in the
  covered porch   i heard it from gedaliah   and i think i heard it
  from gedaliah   that he had a brother an older brother   and i
    wondered where he was

                                i didnt wonder all the time   you know as
  a kid youre busy all the time   youre playing marbles
  youre walking around the corner to watch the police change shifts
    at the police station across the street so you could admire their

crisp blue uniforms and bright brass buttons as they marched out
of the station two by two the way you admired the department of
sanitation workers for their fancy gloves   so you had a lot to do
but somewhere in the midst of all this i remember asking gedaliah
where was his brother   i lived right next door to him in a nice
little house with a covered porch and a glider inside where we
could sit in the evenings eating salmon sandwiches on silvercup
bread and listen to the lone ranger on the radio but id never seen
his brother and i wondered why   so i asked him where is your
brother   and gedaliah said he was killed by an airplane on the
beach in los angeles   now i was a smart little kid and i knew
that los angeles was in california   and the image has never left
me   this image of a plane diving on the beach in los angeles
as i saw it this tall handsome athletic looking guy in a bathing
suit was standing on the beach talking with two girls who were
admiring how handsome and athletic he was when at some point
he suddenly left them to go rushing into the water   because
thats what you do at the santa monica beach
                                                    i didnt know about
santa monica then
                            but i imagined him racing madly down the
beach to dive into the surf   and just as he rushed into the water
a plane fell out of the sky and killed him   that was something
to bear in mind when i thought about california   and then i had
another experience that probably stood in the way of my coming to
california   i had a very interesting uncle   who i didnt know
too well because he was a colorful guy who was always going off
somewhere doing interesting things   being a ships steward or a
labor organizer   that was back in the thirties   and he looked
like douglas fairbanks jr   a stocky little guy with a dandyish
moustache   i remember him mainly from a snapshot that
looked like it was taken in old encinitas   he was standing next
to a model A ford with another guy and a couple of women under
the kind of dusty evergreens that lined highway 101   and
theyre all standing there in the late afternoon sunlight lined up
with their arms around each other smiling into the camera
waiting for their photograph to be taken   a photograph that in
my memory was already brown
              and then i remember a time when i was a very little kid
between three and four   and i was sitting on the porch with him
when a team of baseball players came trooping across the street
they must have been coming back from a game because they were
still wearing their uniforms those neat gray uniforms with red
socks   and i must have been really impressed with them

because i turned to lou who was the nearest adult and asked him
what team they were and lou looked at them and said "the red
sox"   and i got hysterical with laughter because they were
wearing red socks and we both knew they werent "the red sox"
and i thought this was so funny i never forgot it even after he
went away   because one day he went off again and we didnt
hear from him for a while   but then we got a telegram from
california saying he fell off a cliff in yosemite

californias had a disastrous effect on people i knew and i
was scared to death of it   and i didnt know how scared i was of
california   but i never got here

and at the same time i had another view of california a
kind of golden view   because when i was a little older and no
longer living with my grandmother and my aunts but living with
my mother

my mother was a professional widow   one of those
people who made a profession of having been a widow   my
father died when i was very young   and this was a great
misfortune i suppose   but i cant decide whether it was a
misfortune or not   i always thought the great misfortune was
that i wasnt an orphan

but in one of those periods when i was living with my
mother in a state of irritated discomfort

my mother had come from a jewish family
but she had the character of an irish catholic   she was
someone who would have loved to crawl on her knees and push a
peanut with her nose around the fourteen stations of the cross
shed have loved to have been a catholic   and many times i said
to her why dont you convert so you could do penance you could
flagellate yourself you could wear sackcloth and ashes you could
do all these great things that catholics are set up for and jews are
not   you could annoy priests by confessing to imaginary sins
but my mother didnt have the courage of her nasty self lacerating
convictions and she insisted on being jewish in some vague
panreligious way   and she liked to read spiritual books that
proved that all religions were one religion   though she was
really probably only a superstitious atheist trying to cover her
bets   but one of her basic strategies was to deny herself
whatever she could identify as pleasure   and one result of this
strategy was our unfortunate little radio   a little yellow
bakelite radio that used to sit on the nighttable   now that i
think of it   it was kind of pretty   a little rounded yellow
plastic radio with a tiny speaker   but it was dying   for all the
time that we had it   it was dying and i had to sit with my ear to

its little three inch speaker to listen to my favorite radio programs
in order to hear the jack benny show   and it was from the jack
  benny show   that i listened to on our little yellow radio that i
  got my golden image of california   it was from the jack benny
  show that i learned about places called azusa and cucamonga
and to this day i cant imagine anything as wonderful sounding as
azusa and cucamonga   i didnt know what they were like but
    their names rang in my ears beautifully   cucamonga sounded
  more like an animal than a town or a ranch   but whatever it
was it sounded great   and of course the jack benny show made
southern california seem like a kind of golden rural space
small townish and golden   and maybe it was in the 1940s   but
    i know it caused an enormous anxiety in me many years later
  when i was working as a consultant for this very museum at the
  time maurice tuchman was putting on his art and technology
  show   and maurice and i had a falling out about the show at
one point or another because i was one of the cosultants whose
  consultations were not being paid enough attention to   this
  happens among friends and it was a long time ago   but one of
    the things i was doing for the show in my role as consultant was
  acting like a kind of preliminary matchmaker sizing up the
situation at corporations that thought they wanted to take part in
  the show by collaborating with one artist or another   and this
    part of my job was to check the fit between the artist and the
  corporation   so i would go out as a kind of scout to see what the
  real situation at the corporation would likely be if we sent a
particular artist out to work there   and i remember one of the
    artists i was scouting for was ron kitaj who wanted for some
  reason or other to work with the design group at lockheed   and
the people at lockheed seemed to be willing to work with him
so i had to go out to lockheed to look at the situation   and when
    i learned that the lockheed plant was in burbank in the san
fernando valley i was very excited   because i knew from the jack
  benny show that the san fernando was a verdant farming valley
    and i wondered what a high tech aerospace outfit was doing
  tucked into the soft green fields i knew so well   that was back
  around nineteen sixty eight or nine   and because I was looking
forward to this whole adventure i decided to rent a little mustang
    you know those tiny fords with crisp lines that looked like sports
cars but werent   they had these tiny little engines and had
  their weight so badly balanced you had to put sandbags in the
  trunk to keep them from slewing around on a turn   so here i
was in my little mustang and i was about to drive through up over
  one of the canyons   benedict or laurel   to see this

technological marvel of a building tucked into the green
farming valley

now los angeles was a very beautiful city
and it still is in many parts of it a beautiful city in spite of
everything that humans beings have done to it   and these
canyons are among its most beautiful parts

so i drove up the canyon to the crest and
looked down and was totally shaken   mile after mile of little
pastel colored stucco houses laid out one next to the other like
places on a sunken monopoly board lying atlantislike under a
strange grey sea that i realized had to be smog   jack benny had
misled me

now i probably never would have come to california except
for my friend allan kaprow   paul brach was starting a radical
art department down at the university of california at san diego
and wanted allan as a combination artist and intellectual to come
out and anchor it   but paul couldnt persuade allan to come out
to california at this time   and allan suggested he hire me   i
was a poet and critic an art critic and doing doctoral work in
linguistics at the time   i didnt know paul but i knew he was a
serious painter   but id never heard of the university of
california at san diego   as far as i knew san diego was a marine
base   but i asked around and found out it also had scripps
institute of oceanography a hot molecular biology department and
some terrific physicists   and all of these scientists were
standing around with an open checkbook under a palm tree   my
friend jackson maclow told me they also had a great experimental
music department and paul was a charming guy and he was able
to sell me on coming out to run their art gallery and teach art

why me   i was finishing a doctorate in linguistics
im only an art critic and a poet   what do you want from me?
i dont know anything about teaching art   no he said itll be very
good   people will come to your classes they wont know what
youre talking about   youll be talking about art   itll make
them feel better because youre talking about it   so its all right
that they dont know what youre talking about   so i said but
eventually theyll figure out what im talking about and then what
do they need me for   and he said thats when they graduate   i
said oh i see

i had never thought about being a teacher
i was studying linguistics because i felt like studying linguistics
i was interested in it and i liked it   i wasnt looking for a job
im a determined independent elitist and i dont give a damn about
doing anything except what i feel like doing   but what i felt like

doing was thinking about things and talking about them   so I
figured if they dont mind my talking ill talk about whatever
interests me and theyll come to class if they feel like it   and if
they dont theyll go away just like in a european university
     but i didnt know if i could do this because my wife eleanor
the artist eleanor antin   was busy making art in new york as i
was busy writing criticism in new york   but it turned out
fortunately that we were both very bored in new york in 1968
     new york in 1968   i know when you read the art
magazines   if you read the art magazines   youll think that
new york was a wonderful hotbed of exciting art in 1968   it
wasnt   but if you read the art magazines youll believe this at
any time in the world   because thats the job of the art
magazines   to create the illusion that something terrifically
interesting is happening all the time   and it isnt its happening
very rarely   if youre really a veteran of an art scene you go
around desperately looking for something interesting   about one
in a thousand shows is worth looking at   or maybe its really one
in a hundred   its a sad story but we know this   the
members of the secret society that make up the art world know
this   but the art magazines have glossy pictures   nothing
looks better than a glossy picture in an art magazine and they
print these promos   everyone is promoted because thats the job
of the art magazines   its to make the whole art world look more
exciting   thats why they receive their advertisements from all
the galleries and the museums   its to make their whole world
look exciting   so youre bound to think it was a terribly
interesting time in 1968 in new york city   but it was really kind
of boring
     at this particular moment the minimal art which had been
brilliant in the early 60s and which i had written about and
admired had gotten tired   it was becoming a kind of academy by
1968   it had lost its abrasive edge and needed a rest as we
needed a rest
     we also needed a rest from new york   we were native
new yorkers and we were sick and tired of the city   sick and
tired of the intense feelings of the city and one of the things about
new york thats different from southern california is its the kind of
urban space where everybodys very close to everybody else   you
get the feeling that everybody is sitting in everybody elses lap
you have no room and you have no privacy   you cant afford
privacy   so everything is built close   if you made loud love in
your apartment theyd hear you next door   if you have an art
idea and speak about it in a bar   itll be turned into an

artwork by somebody next week before youve finished thinking
about it   thats why everybody in new york is very secretive
when a new york artist gets an idea for an art work he keeps quiet
he probably notarizes the idea because hes afraid someone will
steal his great idea   which is probably that he intends to make a
sculpture thats completely horizontal or build it out of pillows or
swiss cheese   nobody has ever made a sculpture out of swiss
cheese   though henry moore might be assigned primacy in the
genre   but at the same time everybodys also talking to
everyone else about whats the right kind of thing to be doing
whose doing it whose starting to do it and whos no longer doing it
and because everyone is sitting in everyone elses lap everyone is
looking over everyone elses shoulder and wondering whether
theyre doing the right thing   because everyone is listening to
everyone elses conversation   and eleanor was getting very tired
of this and thought it might be nice to get away from it   so she
said   look im busy   why dont you go scout it out
so paul brought me out to visit san diego   now san diego
is the very bottom of california   its almost mexico   which is
exciting of course   but at that time   1968   the only people
who knew that were living invisibly in this part of california
because all the spanish speaking people lived in places that you
didnt immediately get to see when you were brought in to work for
the university   anyway they bring me out here   im flying out
here   and i had to fly out through los angeles   and as the
plane is approaching what i think is los angeles i look down and
see something very strange   i see all these blue gumdrops
little rounded blue gumdrops   and i have no idea what in the
world this is
coming down lower and lower and seeing
them closer i begin to realize theyre swimming pools   with
softly rounded edges and curved like little trays   and it was
strange enough to see them sitting in this tawny sandstone
landscape   curiously planted with the kind of palm trees you
expect to see on the coast of algeria   so you dont really believe
in them   and then just as we land theres a little earthquake
a little earthquake   can you imagine what a little earthquake
is like   the trees shake the earth moves gently under you   i
started to laugh i thought this was ridiculous   so i called elly
and said youve gotta come   ive just been through a little
earthquake the palm trees shook   cars moved one foot each
water spilled over the borders of the swimming pools   who
knows what could happen here   californias the place to be   its
either going to lead america over the cliff or its going to lead it

back   this is the right place to be   now how did i know this
          i guess i knew it from the look of the buildings the
brightness of the architecture and the way people lived in it
every building i saw had a skin over it that looked at first like
concrete   but you can tell its not concrete because they paint it
   and people dont like to paint concrete because they think its
natural like stone   but this is a thin skin they call stucco that
they spread plasterlike over lath and chicken wire and they paint
   it pink or blue or green or yellow or even sand color   and none
of these little buildings ever has a basement   theyre jacked up
on cinderblocks over shallow crawl spaces for the water pipes the
electrical conduits and the gas lines   coming from the east i had
   never seen so many houses without basements   or in many
cases without underfloorings   and when i thought about this i
realized i was looking at a bedouin encampment   this was a
   nomadic group and everybody here was ready to go
          theyre really ready   i said to myself   maybe theyve
got an idea here   theres something about the earth that leaves
us as bedouins and maybe its more obvious here
          now its true i didnt experience this all at the same time
   part of it when we came in   when we moved here my little
   son was one year old   so he wound up speaking with a
california accent which i dont have   but we were in this little
house   first thing we never lived in a house   in new york you
dont live in a house you live in apartments   well some people
do   but in manhattan most people dont   and we were coming
here from living in a newly renovated apartment over a ground
   floor mafia undertaking parlor   which was nice and peaceful
in a lebanese neighborhood that had very good little restaurants
   that all had signs in the window in arabic reminding people that
politics and religion were not discussed here   thats how things
were kept peaceful in this otherwise rather volatile neighborhood
   which was right near atlantic avenue where they had these
wonderful shops like the one run by the sahadi brothers where i
used to go to practice arabic   it was a wonderful place   but
when we were moving to california we knew that we were going to
be confronted with having a house   where would we have it
          paul said ill get you a place in la jolla   and i said not on
your life   i had seen la jolla when i first visited   and la jolla
is very pretty   it was 1968 when i first visited and i was sure
   that i had been returned to 1952   all the women wore white
gloves   i hadnt seen anything like this since the fifties and even
   then living in new york i hadnt seen it very much   and there
were the people who lived in la jolla in rancho santa fe and on

point loma   theyre pleasant people awfully pleasant   as
pleasant as wonder bread   the men wore dark blue blazers with
   brass buttons and cream colored pants with checked shirts and
   they all watched the stock market and played golf and tennis   ˉ
paul   i said find us some funky place in the north county   and
   paul was wonderful   he came up with a little house in a town
called solana beach   solana beach was one of those little towns
   that stretched along old highway 101   and the house he found
us was a little white house surrounded by enormously high
   oleander hedges   in a way this gave us a kind of european
garden walled around by ten foot high oleander bushes in all their
   thorny poisonous beauty   and within the garden was a giant
   pepper tree and orange trees tangerine trees a peach tree   for
   us it was incredibly beautiful   but we didnt know anything
   about house living   one day im walking out of the house and a
neighbor says to me its disgraceful   and i said whats disgraceful
and he said your tree is hanging over my driveway   and i said
its not my tree   and he said what do you mean its not your tree
   and i said i rent it from the person who owns it and this tree has
   been here for years   its been minding its own business for
years   and he said well it interferes with my camper every time
   i pull into the driveway   and i said we could call the owner
and see if hed like to have the offending bough cut off
            but this was all kind of new to me   people living next to
   you complaining about a tree   i could imagine complaining
about parties running late into the night because they mightve
   heard a party late at night   though you couldve had an orgy in
   the garden and nobody wouldve known as long as you kept quiet
because we were sealed off by the tall oleander   but living here
   among the houses of this small town solana beach   the towns of
   this part of southern california line the highway   not the new
highway thats not so new anymore I-5   but the old coast road
   all the commercial buildings are lined up along the coast road
with the houses beginning a block back on either side   the older
   part of town is the west side where the houses get bigger and
   more expensive as they move further west with the prime real
estate   even though some of the houses are kind of shambly on
   the bluffs over the water   and we had lucked out and we had
this beautiful little place in the old part of town even though we
   didnt know whether we were going to stay   but we began to
understand the nomadic nature of the environment soon after we
   got there because a couple with a camper moved into the house
right across the street just a few weeks after we moved in   they
   were a handy couple and they started fixing up things as soon as

they moved in   they put up a new fence they painted the house
they trimmed the trees they changed the entrance   they were
   always tearing something down putting something up   they
   worked like hell and we thought they were really building their
lives   after a little while theyd be able to sit back and enjoy the
results of their effort   but six months later they sell the house
   to a retired couple and theyre gone   it seems they made a
business of buying houses fixing them up and selling them to
   some sucker for more money   or maybe theyre not suckers
   either   because they can live in that house for five years and
sell it to somebody else for even more money
          which is the way that a lot of people acquired capital in
southern california   this is the southern california style   you
buy a house live in it a little while and then sell it and   you can
count on the continuous inflation for your profit   eventually you
   buy houses you dont even live in and sell them for more money
   and finally you become very rich and move to la jolla or rancho
santa fe where you have a golf course at your back and you buy a
   blue blazer and you give up your little camper for a mercedes or a
   bmw and you turn off the country music because youre not a
   redneck any more   so you tune into the top forty or easy
listening stations and you send your children to private schools
   where they learn to be as bland as you
          we saw this happening again and again and we thought
there must be a message here   but we werent prepared to enter
this game of musical houses first because we didnt know if we
   wanted to stay in california and second because we didnt really
   understand it   so when the owner of the little house with the
giant oleanders offered to sell it to us for about sixteen thousand
dollars because he liked us and because we took such good care of
the beautiful garden he had planted and because he had no need
   of it   we said we dont really know   and a woman from
fallbrook bought it   she moved in   chopped down the
oleander so you could see she wasnt having any orgies cut down
   the pepper tree severely cut the fruit trees and hung plastic
   plants on the porch to prove she was a decent citizen   so this
was a california life we didnt understand   but we lucked out
     we had a colleague a writer named reinhardt lettau who was a
professor in the literature department of the unversity   a
   disciple of herbert marcuse   who was a professor in the
   philosophy department back then   and reinhardt like many of
us was against the vietnam war that was raging back then   but
   reinhardt   who was a bit of a hysteric   was against the war in
   a way that made a lot of noise   and in the course of things a

marine recruiting officer came to the campus   and when he was
preparing to make his pitch reinhardt was outraged and went up
   and slapped him on the head with a rolled up newspaper
naturally the television crews were there with their cameras and
reinhardt was featured on the evening news   now reinhardt
   lived in a shambly old green stucco house with a tile roof on the
   bluffs over the water with a grand terrace from which you   could
track the whales or look seagulls in the eye   he lived there with
monique   a strict maoist whose dark hair was severely cut
   straight across her forehead   among posters of lenin and mao
and the uprising in paris of the year before   and this house was
   owned by an elderly lady who lived in la jolla and rented the
   house to reinhardt for about 160 dollars a month   and when
she turned on channel 10 at five oclock that evening they were
playing the reinhardt story   and she had her agent tell him he
   had to get out   not because of slapping the marine officer with
   his rolled up newspaper   but because he was sleeping with
monica to whom   according to channel 10   he wasnt married
"david" reinhardt said when he heard we had to move out of our
little house with the wonderful garden   "this is the right kind of
   house for someone like you   we have to get out but i wouldnt
want it to go to just anybody"   and he sent us to talk to wes
   maurer   the sweet old drunk who ran the philip marlowe real
   estate agency and handled the house for the la jolla lady   the
   deal was clinched when he learned i was a professor at ucsd and
married to elly   the owner likes to rent to uc professors he said
especially married ones
        so we rented the place for 180 dollars a month and we
   stayed in it a long time even as it was falling apart   because we
loved it   though we were eventually paying 200 dollars a month
   for it   and they offered to sell it to us for forty thousand dollars
   though they were willing to take a thousand off the price because
they thought we would have to tear down the house   but we still
didnt get it   we still didnt understand this buying and selling or
   owning of things in this way and we thought it was bizarre   a
few years later somebody did buy it and they tore down the house
   and replaced it with a monstrous white thing that swallowed the
   beautiful terrace creating something that we would never want to
look at again
        but for all of the eight years that we lived there we saw
this kind of movement of people and things   and the feeling i
   had was again that feeling when i saw my first earthquake
   and we had a second little earthquake when we moved into our
first house in solana beach   we had been in solana beach only a

month and there was another little earthquake   our bed skated
gently across the room and our little one year old climbed out of
his crib and crawled into bed with us   and we knew again the
twitch of the skin of this tawny animal california   and i began
to think about this   how california was really like some kind of
animal that is very aimiable patient and long suffering   but
sometimes it gets nervous   sometimes the tawny skin twitches
and the buildings mounted on its back move   and this happens
often enough that whole lives are lived in relation to this or seem
to be   and my sense of this was something i came to realize
gradually after living here for many years

because we got here before all these great subdivisions
had come in and before all of the great highway that connected all
these little towns I-5 had been completed   we lived in the house
on the bluff over the water for many years and from where we
lived you could see the highway intermittently at night or catch
glimpses of it from the lights of cars that occasionally passed
because the old town center that was strung out along the old
coast road 101 was in a sort of valley between the bluffs on the
west and the hills to the east through which the new highway ran
now I-5 wasnt even completed at the time we moved into
solana beach   and south of oceanside it was still a little two
lane road then   but eventually   a few years after we came
they completed it   still there were relatively few cars running on
it   especially at night   at night it was like watching a kind of
eccentrically programmed light sculpture   after 10 pm car
lights would show up once every 5 minutes or so   and if you
went to your front window or stood on the sloping lawn outside it
that we allowed to become a field of weeds   if you stood on this
sloping lawn and looked toward the highway after 10 oclock
you could stand there for five or six minutes   before you saw
two or three cars go by   after 12 you could stand there for
fifteen minutes without seeing a car go by   that was when we
first moved in   but after a while you would see them every two
or three minutes and by now theres no time of the night   even
at two or three or four in the morning its a continuous light show
and things like this have been happening all over southern
california

once there was a little mayfair market at the foot of the
hill leading down from the bluff into town and you could walk to
the market from where you lived   this was a little beach town
and you could walk to the market   though some people might
drive because of the hill or because of the groceries they had to
carry   still we used to walk to the market and back and it was

no problem   but then they built a mall a shopping center in the
hills near I-5   and then everyone had to drive to the market
even if they lived in the hills   because there were no streets in
the eastern part of the town
            all the time that we lived there things kept changing like
this   and i began to have an image of what this was like and i
was beginning to get an image of what the future would be like
the future of malls someday someone is going to be an archeologist
of ruined malls   because what are they going to do with old
malls   supermarkets that no one goes to vacated target stores
abandoned for hotter locations   once a target store goes away
what are they going to do with the building   make an airplane
hangar out of it?   you know these vast horizontal buildings that
house all the goods that anybody could want on the face of the
earth in their reduced forms
            whatever would happen to these weird buildings
            well i found out the other day   i happened to drive by
one of these new malls they built alongside the highway in solana
beach that was an old mall now and not too successful   they just
wiped it out   they bulldozed it out   all the buildings that used
to sell groceries and stereos and computers and bicycles and
running shoes and toothpaste gone   and theyre going to replace
it with another collection of businesses that i guess will be pretty
much like the ones they just bulldozed but newer   and the new
developer will have to sell the deal to some new group of hopeful
people who think they can make a go of it where the old group
couldnt   and what will they put there?   a bowling alley a
frozen yogurt shop a chic boutique a bath center a massive health
food store?   i dont know but its all changing everythings moving
in this way california becomes a paradigmatic part of america
americas nomadic moment   thats the sense of where the earth
stands in relation to you   it knows youre irrelevant as if you
were a tourist here   everybodys a tourist   the indians here
knew it well   they lived very lightly and they moved from one
place to another from the seashore to the mountains   following
their food sources as the seasons changed   gathering shellfish
by the ocean and acorns in the mountains   and they didnt build
very deeply   today californians have a somewhat similar
feeling about the land   theyre not very deeply rooted and they
build almost as lightly as the california indians   but feeling
something is not knowing it   knowing requires something more
and my friend richard had this feeling without knowing it too well
            we met richard not long after we moved here   richard
was one of the most popular gynecologists in the area   he was a

tall handsome man and charming and he had a lovely wife
alexandra   they lived in rancho santa fe   which was the very
    tailored and wealthy part of northern san diego county
because he had a very successful practice he and his friend jack
they were an interesting pair these two handsome young doctors
    both   a kind of study in contrasts   richard was dark with
curly hair he could have been an actor   a movie star if he didnt
have to act   and alexandra was an elegant blonde and blue eyed
    beauty   while jack was blonde blue eyed and boyish and had a
tall and leggy dark haired wife named melissa   and richard
drove a bronze mercedes while jack drove a red corvette   but
    they shared this very successful practice and they were both as
generous as they were successful   once a week they each drove
    down to work at a free clinic in mexico   they took a lot of
charity patients in san diego and no artist or artists wife ever had
to pay for treatment   so their offices and homes were filled with
    the paintings and drawings photographs and sculptures of san
diegos artists
            it was through his interest in art that we first got to meet
richard   i was director of the university gallery back then and id
    used my new york and los angeles connections to put together a
show of post-pop painting   that was back in 1969 and it was a
more or less timely show dealing with the reappearance of
    representation   so it included a wide range of artists of
    different kinds   ranging from straight pop artists like warhol
    and lichtenstein and wesselman to the more painterly styles of
alex katz and sylvia sleigh   and aside from the fact that it was
a little early to dwell on representation for an art world hooked on
the prime importance of abstraction it was a reasonably
    conventional show   but this was san diego in 1969 and the
    wesselman in the show was one of his "great american nudes"
    it was a kind of collage work with the nearly cartoon-like female
figure lying spread legged on a piece of fake leopard skin fur   a
completely sexist beaver view nude   and somehow even before
the show had opened word got out about the wesselman   and
    there were already complaints   not from outraged feminists
feminism hadnt been born in san diego in 1969   it was still
basically a navy town and the city was living in 1959   or more
    likely 1951   so the complaints were from puritans or if not
puritans from people with a strong sense of public propriety
    whatever they did in their bedrooms or other peoples bedrooms
living rooms or jacuzzis   and the complaints were all being
    fielded by the chancellors office before being shunted over to the
    art department where i could handle them   so paul as the

department chairman was a little worried about the opening with
the chancellor coming and all the other uc and la jolla dignitaries
            now our gallery back then was one of the strangest art
galleries id ever seen   it was the only gallery id ever seen
with a black ceiling   it was a long windowless stucco shed that
    had served as the officers bowling alley of camp matthews the
marine base our campus housed before the regents of u.c. acquired
    it in a land swap with the military   but the school did an
architectural remake and spruced up the outside with a lot of
redwood around the entrance and redwood stripping inside   in
fact they got so carried away with the redwood stripping that they
hung some from the ceiling making the low ceiling lower and
    recessing the lighting fixtures up behind it where they
        disappeared into the black ceiling making this the darkest art
        gallery i had ever seen   they completed the remake by covering
the concrete floor wall to wall with mauve carpeting that gave the
place the appearance of a discreet gentlemans club or a high class
funeral parlor   it was the first big show of the season and while i
    was hanging the show paul kept popping in and out between
classes to see how things were going because he was a nervous
guy and as a painter he had lots of opinions about hanging
paintings   but things were going pretty smoothly   id brought
    in extra lights and managed to get a lot more on the paintings
        so you could really see them   though i had the feeling every
time paul looked at the wesselman he would have liked to see it a
lot darker
            the evening of the opening he got there early while my
assistants were taking care of the last details spraying windex on
    the few works with glass over them laying out wine glasses
and he hung out with us till the doors opened and the first few
    people drifted in   but nothing remarkable was really
happening   the wesselman was at the far end of the wall away
from the entrance door and   like most opening crowds the first
few visitors mainly faculty   clustered around the wine table
    generally scanning the room   pleased to see and be seen by
each other and fortifying themselves with a drink before plunging
into serious picture looking   then mcgill arrived
            the chancellor was a husky middle aged guy with brush
cut grey hair who could have passed for a brit general if he had a
    sandhurst accent   as it was he looked like a c.e.o for g.m. or
at&t although hed been the head of a science heavy psychology
department before taking over as chancellor at ucsd   which
    really is a large corporation   and later he got to be famous for
being president of columbia university another large corporation

so i guess he really was a c.e.o.   he came in with a whole group
of people   among them richard and alexandra and jack and
melissa   but unlike the earlier visitors he untangled himself
from the wine table after a few words and a couple of handshakes
   to follow richard and alexandra down the line of paintings
with paul inconspicuously bringing up the rear   and i admit i
was pretty curious so i drifted over too
            they passed the bechtle and the alex katz and came to a
dead stop right in front of the wesselman   richard leaned over
and peered directly between the the spread legs of the great
   american nude   "left median lateral epeziotomy" he said in a
   stage whisper   everybody broke up laughing and that was the
end of it
            now richard was an interesting man   they were an
   interesting couple he and alexandra   richards practice was
very successful and even with his charity work he was living the
affluent life of all good doctors in southern california in those days
   of tax shelters and complicated investments before hmos   and
he and alexandra lived in a spacious spanish style villa on several
tailored acres of san diegos choice north county real estate with a
   swimming pool and a tennis court and servant quarters   they
   belonged to the country club and played golf and tennis   and
though they had no children they seemed to be leading a typical
affluent southern california life
            in spite of all that   they seemed displaced and a little
   remote   maybe it was alexandras cool east coast style or the
occasional faraway look in richards eyes   they had lots of
acquaintances and people they socialized with out of habit or
   convention   but their only real friends were jack and melissa
who also had no children   the two couples were inseparable
   they played tennis and golf together swam together went to the
theater or concerts together and to art openings   and while they
saw lots of other people there was a kind of bond between them
that couldnt be explained by the simple fact that richard and jack
   shared a practice or that melissa and alexandra had gone to the
   same east coast college   the only thing they didnt do together
was travel together   and they had this passion for travel to
   picturesque places   but they would travel separately   so if
jack and melissa went off to japan   or if richard and alexandra
went off to africa theyd arrange to have dinner together at the
home of the returning couple   usually alone but not always
   and after dinner and brandy the guy would bring out the slide
   projector and show the pictures while his wife gave a running
account of the trip   i was never at any of these slide shows but i

heard that the pictures were mostly pretty ordinary if a little eccentric because they tended to show the usual things   a gondolier on the grand canal or a street vendor in the piazza di san marco punctuated oddly by unexplained casual images of people sitting in a hotel lobby or a man walking into an elevator and while the account that accompanied the slide shows was   casual and anecdotal   there was something ritualistic and deeply serious about them   as if through this procession of ordinary little stories one couple was revealing something secret and deep about themselves to the other   something no outsider   could understand   richard and alexandra had been to egypt
                    now i dont know anything about egypt
when i think of egypt i think of ruth st denis looking at a cigarette   ad and inventing egyptian dance   she didnt really invent egyptian dance   she looked at that cigarette ad and seeing an image   of egypt she figured shed discovered the east   this was the perfect los angeles story   it was 1915 and she knew from all the yogis running around los angeles that the east was the site of anti-materialistic spirituality   so she simply decided to push further east because she thought india was more spiritual than   egypt   egypt was just a bunch of pharaohs while india was filled with naked yogis or bodhisattvas in saffron robes   and before you know it she was starting her los angeles art institute in 1915 inventing modern dance mostly by placing attractive nearly   naked people in picturesque poses that she assumed were spiritual and erotic because shed seen them in photos of ancient wall reliefs or in magazine articles on kootch dancers in bangalore and in spite of the absurdity or because of it ruth st denis in true california fashion became a teacher of martha graham and one of the great inventors of modern dance
             i never saw ruth st denis' 1915 cigarette ad   and what   do i know about egypt i didnt get from a pack of camels   so thats what i supposed ruth saw   a camel standing in front of a pyramid and maybe a picture of the sphinx   this is the complete tourist picture and if you go to egypt thats what youre going to see   you may tour the old part of cairo you may go look at the suez canal a buried temple or two and youll certainly look at the   sphinx   but you know that even before you see the pyramids youre going to take a camel ride   someone is going to show you how to ride a camel and someone watching will always take your picture   and i take it that all of these images were in   alexandras slide show of their egyptian trip   during which   richard was completely silent till alex got to the image of the   camel ride   the picture was not of either richard or alexandra

the picture was of a pleasant looking middle aged lady falling off a
   camel that was neither standing nor sitting but halfway up and
halfway down as alexandra explained
         the camel driver told the camel to get down and the camel
got down   the woman climbed on and the camel got up and it
went well   so the driver let the camel walk a little bit   she
took two steps and abruptly sat down   this took the woman by
surprise and threw her off balance so she tried to get off   it also
took the driver by surprise and he ordered the camel back up
   but the woman was still half off the camel   so when he told the
   camel to get back up the woman started falling further and he
ordered the camel back down   the camel dropped down and the
   woman tumbled completely off   in the picture the woman is
toppling off the camel on the way to the second sitdown
         all through alexandras account of this bizarre incident
richard had remained silent staring intently at the slide and he
   remained unusally silent for the rest of the show   when asked
why   he said the picture reminded him of something he couldnt
quite figure out   but by the end he remembered   it was the
camel   after the picture was taken and the woman had fallen off
it was the camel kneeling there   its face he said   it reminded
him of the sphinx
         now this was just the kind of image that flares up in
someones mind for a moment and is almost as quickly forgotten
   and richard never mentioned it again   he probably never
thought about it again because   though he was an intelligent
man he was not an intellectual   he was a doctor   and doctors
are more like artists and most of their intelligence is expended in
   their work   so richards life went on as usual   caring for
patients in san diego or mexico   playing tennis or golf   going
to concerts and the theater and to art openings and little parties
   but one day jack took his corvette and was speeding down to
the clinic in mexico when a truck carrying tiles from tecate to san
   diego pulled out to pass a slower truck and it carried its tiles no
further   the bright red corvette was totaled and boyish blonde
   haired laughing jack was dead
         richard never seemed to recover from jacks untimely
accident   his life changed completely after that   he moved out
of his house and into the servants quarters behind it   he
   stopped going to concerts and openings   where alexandra
appeared alone   he started spending more time at the clinic in
mexico   and even that wasnt enough   for a while he literally
   disappeared   they say he was in an ashram in india   though
im not sure thats true   but when he came back to san diego he

gave up his practice left the house to alexandra and took up an
    entirely new career curiously related to his old one   once he
had helped bring people into the world now he was helping them
out of it   working with mortally ill people and helping them find
  a humanly meaningful dying   and hed been doing this for some
time before we heard of it   and when we did wed been through
the dying of a number of friends
                              weve been through the deaths of a number
of friends recently ellie and i   we were sitting by watching
  kathy acker die   a dear friend of ours and an ex-student
  someone we really loved and we watched her die young and
terribly of cancer   and what do you do in those circumstances
    sitting there you do the best you can   but what was his
  expertise   what did richard do to make the dying more bearable
  more human   and we heard this story
              he drove with his cancer patient out into the mojave
  where they built a little fire and wrapped themselves up in
blankets and camped out for the night   they lay on the ground
  and spent hours singing wordless songs   then they put out the
  fire and just looked up at the stars in the cold night sky   and
  lying there richard began to speak almost to himself in a voice
hardly above a whisper   about how far away these stars must
  be and how long it takes their light that travels a hundred and
  eighty six thousand miles a second and millions and millions of
  years to come down to the earth where it looks so bright to us
  while so many of them must be already dead and may have been
dead for millions of years but their light is still with us and could
  stay with us for many more thousands of years   we have to
    think about our lives that way   the odd thing was that this
cancer patient got a remission of his cancer and had this story to
    tell   meanwhile i dont know where richards gone   but he
  seems to have disappeared from california leaving us to deal with
  its sphinxlike character and its camels shrug

*This work originated as an improvised talk for the Institute of Art
and Cultures of the Los Angeles County Art Museum, given on January
11, 1999 as part of a series of presentations attempting to sketch
"The Image of California."*

The Intercourse of Life: Experiencing "the price" and "the structuralist"

Lou Rowan

David Antin's four books of talk pieces afford us a richness demanding and rewarding the fullest engagement of our minds and senses. Antin's work is continuously and sincerely experimental, and accepts the traditional challenges of experiments in science and philosophy: how to build on the work of one's epoch to answer questions and re-solve problems with which the basic phenomena of existence confront us.

Antin's discourses, a singular oral tradition developed over the last four decades, present a "problem of Homer" in reverse—we know how he produces them, but we hesitate to specify their genre. So let's begin with a working hypothesis: he produces *narratives* whose units of structure are breaths corresponding in turn to the units and sequences of his thoughts. And if we assume that narrative is "projective story," then we can see Charles Olson's repositioning of literature in *us*—in our ears, mouths, minds, breath—as an exact and fitting preface to Antin's enterprise (Olson 240-43). Robert Kelly once told me, "Olson is not a son of a bitch but the father of many bastards." The legitimacy of Antin's genre—its "proper" category—becomes academic when we respond to the energy of a narrative tradition beginning "Call me Ishmael."

"the price" begins with a Babe Ruthian gesture. Antin points us to the far—or maybe the near—bleachers:

> i always thought the idea of the self was surrounded by
> questions   and in fact what i was interested in were   precisely
> those questions   which were questions   i spent a lot of time
>   asking   because i didn't know the answers   for if i knew the
> answers i wouldnt have any reason to ask the questions   and
>   one of the questions   im interested in asking is   what is
> the locus of the source or ground of the self (*what it means* 93)

We can hear echoes of Gertrude Stein in this diction: the verbal repetitions with syntactical changes, the absence of periodic syntax, and the absence of figurative language. Here is Stein announcing her ambition for *The Making of Americans*: "To begin with, I seem always to be do the talking when I am anywhere but in spite of that

I do listen. I always listen. I have always listened. I always have listened to the way everybody has to tell what they have to say. In other words I always have listened in my way of listening until they have told me and told me until I really know it, that is know what they are" (Stein 241).

The act of composition before an audience, Antin tells us, brings urgency, immediacy, weight to his work. The repetitions in his verbal units (for they are not necessarily sentences) have their evident origins in speech, as Stein implies of hers, but their import is deeper than style. Particulate, akin to the words of scientific formulas, of philosophic investigation, they roll and bounce like balls on the inclining planes of their generators' intent. They capture direct observation, creating simple subdivisions of phenomena, so that we can apprehend them directly, without emotional miscues. Like Buster Keaton's deadpan purity, they accumulate action by action to a new way of seeing—the difference of effect, say, between the repeated physics-lab bombardment of *The Bridegroom* and the conventional liberal-critical jargon of "And now, young man, you will progress from matrimonial humiliation to enduring a deliciously convoluted storm of ladies."

Antin's theme—"what is the locus and ground of the self?"—is announced clearly and emphatically, and we're off and running through breathtaking variations. He addresses deconstruction's circumscription of itself; he provides his definitions of narrative and story, retells and comments on a Homeric and a biblical narrative in the light of his definition, retells three stories from his family's lore, taking us back to its roots in Russia, plus a noncommittal Soviet journalist's story—and shows how all these recent stories embody the crucial interactions between *stories* and the implicit or explicit personal *narratives* of their tellers. Then he redismisses deconstruction for its stated irrelevance to his concerns and concludes telling a tale from his mother-in-law's declining years that meets with stunning poignancy the challenge implicit in this intellectual chase: *so show me a story that matters.* All this and more, as they say, in twenty-six pages!

Antin explains the importance of story and narrative to his purpose: "i always thought the idea of the self was surrounded by questions." He proposes that we cannot "maintain a continuous consciousness and have a sense of its boundaries   unless its tested against something that opposes and isnt it" (94). The self "is entirely constructed out of the collision of the sense of identity with the issues of narrative. . . . story is a configuration of events or parts of events that shape some transformation   but narrative   or so it seems to me   is a sort of psychic function   part of the human psychic economy and probably a human universal" (95). And he rounds out this dynamic definition of the self: "now my sense is that the center of narrative is the confrontation of experience   an experiencing subject with the possibility of transformation   the threat of transformation or the promise of transformation . . ." (93-95). This is a definition that makes fiction and story matter as much as we do and that gives them, at core, a vitality toward which we struggle in our daily doings, a vitality surging through Antin's work, enlightening his artistic stance: *I'll do it if it really matters, and I'll do it in an arena and in a format that tests whether it really matters.*

The story concluding "the price," and affording its title, combines for me William Gaddis's satiric comprehension of our economy with Douglas Woolf's droll, inclusive sympathies for its victims. Antin may seem austere in his refusal to create conventional forms eliciting conventional rewards, but he is highly enjoyable to read and to hear. His art is as far-reaching in matter as Musil's in *The Man without Qualities*—another work combining essays with narrative structures and another narrative artist calling himself a poet. And Antin's mini-Kakanias, ranging from Apaches to the State Department, to Harlem, to midlevel AT&T execs, to poets on stage, to professional classes in southern California with redwood escutcheons, are rendered with agile satire and clear-eyed absence of righteousness.

Taking them as a whole, we can compare Antin's four talking books to modern personal epics—an inventor's hybrid, say, between "Song of Myself" and "*A*"—after all, the flower-pun which concludes the latter, "are but us," grounds it in the self (Zukofsky 563). But it's maybe better in this context to see the books as a large novel, developing at a pace as eccentric as any of our lives, whose plot and plottings are the doings and the intellectual enterprisings of its dominant character, David Antin. The artistic discipline of this narrator eschews easy satisfaction, bridles at the emotional/lyrical. He concludes, "is this the right place?"

> how do you know youre through with something?   you know because the phone rang. . . . why not?   now i might say   of this particular discourse   that theres no place at which i can end it without producing a kind of profoundly pornographic poetic effect   which i assure you i can do   i could produce a vast symphonic conclusion   and you might walk out feeling benefited   but i wont do it (*talking at the boundaries* 49)

In fact his art pulls up short to question any received way of apprehending phenomena or of reacting to them. Social customs, maps, sexual issues, academic disciplines, vernacular locutions, genres, literary terms, feelings, vocations—all conventions are hypotheses to be tested. This systematic frustration and reconnection of our expectations is the price we pay for the rewards, the surprise, the insight thrown at us by these experiments. I see the talking books as an intellectually and emotionally stable *Tristram Shandy*—Antin's punctuational pauses indicative of a serenity, a pacing of the breath seeking the clarity of rootedness in our physical and psychic being, while Sterne's dashes signal breathless sallies of avoidance, frantic and funny escapes from the style and from the many meanings of *gravity* in a world newly circumscribed by "laws" of physics that impress themselves upon our brains and bodies in the wars of nation-states and in our interpersonal jostlings.

We can apply Sterne's cosmological self-felicitation and self-categorization to the talking books:

In a word, my work is digressive, and it is progressive too, —and at the same time.

This, Sir, is a very different story from that of the earth's moving round her axis, in her diurnal rotation, with her progress in her elliptick orbit which brings about the year, and constitutes that variety and vicissitude of seasons we enjoy;—though I own it suggested the thought,—as I believe the greatest of our boasted improvements and discoveries have come from such trifling hints.

Digressions, incontestably, are the sunshine;—they are the life, the soul of reading;—take them out of this book for instance,—you might as well take the book along with them;—one cold winter would reign in every page of it; restore them to the writer;—he steps forth like a bridegroom;—and bids All hail; brings in variety, and forbids the appetite to fail. (Sterne 73)

In "the price" Antin's lovers engage the capitalist system, combat the frailties of their aging bodies, stretching the rules of their old folks' facility, blazoning the intertwinings of their hearts and bodies as, in the oblivion of Alzheimers, they don each others' clothing—a pinch and a pull for a tall man and a small woman. The glorious comedy of their affair, its warm detailed eccentricity, recalls Uncle Toby besieged by the Widow Wadman.

And eloquence unites Antin with Sterne. If Antin purges language of what Zukofsky liked to call afflatus (drawing out the word, as if it were an elephant lumbering by), he uses the medium to its fullest, achieving polished, elaborate effects:

because working at language is a lot like working at
sculpture   theres a kind of stubborn material to it
    the language   thats only so ductile or tensile or

strong   and a poet doesnt   create it   though it may seem
    that he does   but being a poet and working with language is a
lot like being a spider and working with silk because the
    language comes out of your mouth much the way thread comes
out of a spider   so that it looks like youve made it   but only in
a   way for as far as   the silk goes   you havent got a choice
the threads are made of exactly the same stuff for each spider of
your kind   and though you can   choose to bring them out
    singly or doubled or plaited into cable   the choices   are
the same for all spiders of your family and there are only a
limited number of structures you can employ for the web
    whose elegant grammar belongs equally   to all of you   and
    while one poet spider may be more precise or more   casual
in stretching the radii or unwinding a logarithmic spiral of the
    chords   and this may be a matter of personal acuity or
taste   its still the same web with the structural limitations of
    its type   like english   or french so the epeira has a sticky
thread that the labrynth spider hasnt got   and the epeira
family can lay out a stark geometric web in a single plane
    perpendicular to the ground   confident that a flying insect
will stick   while the labyrinth spider has to lay out a three
dimensional maze to entangle insects in a web

and like spiders we poets are all beneficiaries and victims of
    our language   there are limits to what we can do with it as
we move around in it   picking up the thread of a discourse
    laying out others   adding adjusting and winding around old
ones . . . (*what it means* 163,164)

The graceful insouciant modulation to upper-middlebrow figurative
vernacular, "thread of discourse," is the move of a collage or jazz artist at his "digressive progressive" finest. We can describe this passage (quoted in part) as akin simultaneously to a "Homeric simile"
(noting its elaborate factuality) and a "metaphysical conceit" (noting its elaborated wit), and we can see it as an extrapolation of
Whitman's "Noiseless, Patient Spider."

For if Antin is avant-garde, it is from amplitude; it is because he
has deployed fully and energetically the resources of all literary
traditions to hand, married them to an omnivorous erudition and
curiosity, grown his art to a nonjudgmental, an unpinched unpreju-
diced fullness, and exercised the elegant courage to let these resources carry him and speak through him.

Elegance: the busy spiders adorn the expository beginning of
"the structuralist," the tale of a modern hero's epic adventures of

discovery. The adventures take us below the surface and to the frontiers of the meaning of language, and this passage projects and illuminates the theme about which and *with* which the whole piece, one of Antin's longest, plays its narrative and intellectual variations.

The hero—and he is one—Anastasius or Nasi is "a small man or a large dwarf." The quality of his career illustrates Creeley's proposition beginning "Mr. Blue"—"That dwarfs, gnomes, midgets are, by the fact of their SIZE, intense . . ." (Creeley 20). Nasi is an expert linguist, translator; he is an original and accomplished painter; he is an athlete; and he's a conversationalist of passion, cogency, and endurance. Nasi endures neither the grotesquery of Creeley's dwarf, of Poe's Hop-Frog, of West's Honest Abe Kusich, nor the broad symbolic weight of the screaming German drumstick. His one impish move is a leap to a party table to give Oscar Williams a well-deserved champagne-dousing. For Nasi would lead his select audience of scholars and poets to understand the ground of language, which is God, and the ground of visual perspective, to which his muse and model leads his painting. In late-night sessions at the Waldorf Cafeteria in Greenwich Village we see the "best minds of my generation" passionately sleep-deprived on Sixth Avenue under fluorescent lighting—scholars of language accompanying Nasi partway on his quest.

For the longing these minds express with ready learning—to wield their academic skills to address, even resolve, issues of weight (like the promotion of peace through a commonality of language)—this longing breaks itself upon the facts of history they know and witness, breaks itself upon the limits and contradictions of their academic formulations, and is broken by the very fragility of its beauty, like the Professor's Babel-like structure of spoons, knifes, forks, saucers topped by minarets of cups, or like Nasi's minimalist Jell-O readymades. For a profundity of "the structuralist" is how fully, with what articulate detail it captures these extra-academic exercises in their brilliance and their knowing world-weariness.

But Nasi, whom we meet climbing ropes and doing flips like a master gymnast, will not relinquish his quest for the essence of language, and he is armed not only with his ready grasp of modern linguistics but also his fluency in twenty-six languages. Nasi brushes aside the dictum of modern academic linguistics that questions about the origins of words are meaningless, that is, outside the game. He writes an epic in the ur-language ("sub-morphemic sememes") through which (he is convinced) we can connect as humans and through which God presents himself. Nothing less than an epic poem will do. He declares to David Antin, an interlocutor with the academic training and the Stein-like passion to listen while talking—and ready to "know what they are"—that his preparation for the epic is "scientific":

> "i am collecting and studying all the possible submorphic
>   sememes from all the languages of the world   the ones that i
>   know and many that i do not know   i am studying them and
>   testing them to see if they are really so   and i am doing this
> scientifically and stucturally but because i do not wish to
> persuade by mere rhetoric   merely to convince the minds and
> not the hearts. . . ." (*what it means* 198)

Nasi cannot proceed toward his masterpiece without "science," which appeals to the "heart," leaving mere rhetoric to the head. Nasi, the ultimate "projective" scholar, is an objectivist (or "objectist" as Olson has it) in his conviction that only the power of facts, of the units of sound-experience, can lead through the discipline of linguistic science to the amplitude and truth of epic. Like most heroes, Nasi must fail, but Antin, an accomplished medievalist, takes us on a noble quest.

In "the sociology of art" Antin evokes an oral society's discourse on pottery-making: "if they say anything at all   which they may not   they say something like 'this is the way to make this kind of pot   first   you get ready   and you sit down   sit down here   no youre not ready   go away   youre not ready yet go think about the clay   heres some clay   take it   go for a walk   feel the clay go feel the clay' " (*talking at the boundaries* 192-93). The prose poems of *autobiography,* which preceded the talking books, show Antin doing something like this handling, walking from, and inviting his narrative material. The book is a discrete series of unrelated mini-narratives, like:

looking into the dark oblong mirror into which a triangle of light had fallen through partially open doors as into a pool of water I somehow became convinced of my identity with that luminous figure. We were both completely empty, devoid of properties and totally lucid. In this state I began to believe I was unreal, and this conviction was confirmed by the fact that I was unable to feel anything at all. It occurred to me that I might get dressed go down to the bar at the corner and get into a quarrel in which I might get hurt and feel pain. But the bar was closed—it was half past three. So I went up to the viaduct overlooking Tiemann Place and looked down over the street below. I thought I might lean over the parapet and place myself in some danger of falling in order to feel fear. This was unsuccessful. I couldn't succeed in feeling anything except the damp cold of the stone I held in my hands. Gradually I eased out further and further till I hung over the street without succeeding in feeling anything when I heard the distant sound of laughing voices further down the Drive. I started to laugh myself choking and coughing and scrambled back over the parapet. (*Selected Poems* 98)

To Antin the "modern" or "post" commonplaces of alienation and psychic displacement are as obvious and as malleable as the potter's clay and can be dealt with in a paragraph—a paragraph epitomizing Musil's Ulrich, whose lucidity and absence of qualities drag him across ranges of mental and physical experiments. There is no rhetoric in the last sentence about what the speaker "realized," but there is indeed a transformation occasioned by "voices and laughter." An actual transformation, unlike the verbal glow superimposed on another Upper West Side event, an occasion of tawdry *sameness:* "Yet high over the city our line of yellow windows must have contributed their share of human secrecy to the casual watcher in the darkening streets, and I was him too, looking up and wondering. I was within and without, simultaneously enchanted and repelled by the inexhaustible variety of life" (Fitzgerald 40).

But if we cannot readily "understand" the transformation in Antin's piece, other than registering that hearing voices and laughter-stimulated laughter and the fact of return—this unwillingness to glaze the facts with rhetorical aperçus, this generosity leaving each of our "senses(s) of identity" free to "collide" as we will with the "configuration of events"—this is an experimental discipline opening the way to the fullness of the talking pieces, where real inquiry and precise thought combine with stories.

And what is the transformation these talk pieces shape? What can they, in fact, mean to the lives of their readers? How can we use them? What happens to us here if indeed, "the center of narrative is the confrontation of experience   an experiencing subject with the possibility of transformation   the threat of transformation or the promise of transformation"? These questions take us happily (I hope) beyond the norms of criticism, as Nasi discarded the norms of linguistics: but let's see.

As he introduces Nasi, Antin avows, "i have a deep distrust of the plausible   and i suspect that what we have most in common is the profound singularity and implausible detail of our generally common lives" (*what it means* 166). The title piece to *tuning* shows an alternative to the plausible misconceptions implicit in "understanding," developing a perceptual and communicative process called "tuning" that allows us a "common going," versus a "common standing." *Common going* impels us to work at shucking our preconceptions of each other. *Common going* discovers "discontinuities," that is, surprises, in the seeming commonplace or "plausible" (*tuning* 125-31).

And if we admit that the very commonplaces of our lives—Antin discusses breathing and walking—*seem* continuous but are repetitiously discontinuous, eccentric, then have we not an agenda, the possible grounds, for an *appreciation* of our common and singular experience—that is, its growth? The *OED* makes explicit what we learn in high school French, that there's a semantic intertwining of *experiment* and *experience* and includes these definitions of *experience:* "To make trial or experiment of; to put to the test . . . to meet with; to feel, suffer, undergo." And further, "The state of having been occupied in any department of study or practice, in affairs generally, or in the intercourse of life." I can hear a modern Sterne galloping with that last phrase, *the intercourse of life.*

A utility of Antin's work, the transformation we suffer experiencing it, is the emptying, draining, shrinking of the preconceptions and prejudices with which we destroy our own—and, worse, others'—experiences. If we can be open to, move with, these speaking episodes of a vitality crucial to our literature, then can we be the better for it? Is that implausible possibility here for us? In the words of Lotto, the instrument of civic and personal financial planning in Antin's native Empire State, "Hey, you never know."

WORKS CITED

Antin, David. *Selected Poems 1963-1973*. Los Angeles: Sun & Moon, 1991.

——. *talking at the boundaries*. New York: New Directions, 1976.

——. *tuning*. New York: New Directions, 1984.

——. *what it means to be avant-garde*. New York: New Directions, 1993.

Creeley, Robert. *The Collected Prose of Robert Creeley*. Berkeley: U of California P, 1988.

Fitzgerald, F. Scott. *The Great Gatsby*. 1925. New York: Scribner's, 1995.

Olson, Charles. *Collected Prose*. Berkeley: U of California P, 1997.

Stein, Gertrude. *Selected Writings of Gertrude Stein*. New York: Vintage, 1962.

Sterne, Laurence. *The Life and Opinions of Tristram Shandy, Gentleman*. New York: Odyssey Press, 1940.

Zukofsky, Louis. *"A."* Berkeley: U of California P, 1993.

The Theater of Genre: David Antin, Narrativity, and Selfhood

Christian Moraru

> narrative lies at the core of my ideas about the structure
> of the self
> > —what it means to be avant-garde (92)

> the self   itself   is emergent in discourse
> > —talking at the boundaries (10)

> [Prose is] "a cultural and ideological notion"
> > —"Thinking about Novels" (211)

If a genre is "a theater of expectations," as David Antin argues in a commentary on Toby Olson's novels, then that genre marks off "a site of possible operations within which those expectations can be satisfied, deferred, deflected, frustrated or transformed." This theater itself, Antin goes on, "can be regarded as a concrete structure satisfying a particular building code, or merely the promise of a place" occupied by "undreamed of objects" or "unimaginable happenings" ("Thinking" 210). Further, in "the structuralist," a poem from *what it means to be avant-garde*, Antin puts his theatrical-performative concept of genre in historical perspective. "[A] genre," he tells us, "is a theater defined by a history of the performances you remember taking place within it   and any work seeking to play that theater will be judged in relation to the history of performance youve constructed for it" (159).

My essay offers up a few considerations on a certain dimension of Antin's genre poetics—or counterpoetics, to use the better term employed by Henry M. Sayre apropos of Antin's talk poems (Sayre 432). Specifically, what interests me here are Antin's view and practice of narrativity, along the lines the author himself draws above and elsewhere in his work. I will be pursuing narrativity, that is, not as a traditional building code that keeps, for instance, metaphoric inflections of discourse at bay, but as a multigenre strategy of summoning the unexpected and the unimaginable, the unpredictable and the uncanny—ultimately, as a modality of tracing the dynamic, culturally controlled production of the self. Revealingly, Antin has both developed and reflected on this modality in his poems. As Hank Lazer has aptly observed, "An investigation of narrative lies at the heart of Antin's considerations of what it means to be a poet" (124). Following critics such as Lazer, Marjorie Perloff, and Antin himself, I want to take a closer look at the practical results of this investigation—at the theoretical inquiry into narrativity as well as at several poems growing out of this inquiry—and see how they bear on Antin's poetic genealogy of selfhood, his invariable project. To reconstruct Antin's narrative model, I will focus primarily on Antin's texts from *talking at the boundaries* (1976) and, to a lesser extent, *what it means to be avant-garde* (1991).

Antin works out this model, I would like to suggest, *across and against* the classical tripartion of genres. More to the point, he effects a performative (onstage) conjuring up of life's strangeness and multifariousness, which are evoked essentially by narrative means as his performances reel out sumptuous, long-winded narrative flashbacks.[1] It is equally worth noting, though, that these prose-based protocols of discourse also function like metaphoric structures as defined by most theories of metaphor. Namely, in spite of their prosaic and realistic appearances, they overflow preset categories of objects to shed light on the unknown, on the terra incognita of the self's unique experiences. As Paul Ricoeur insists in the preface to the first volume in his series *Time and Narrative,* such "illumination" may occur both through metaphoric language and plot. "The productive imagination at work in the metaphorical process," Ricoeur maintains, "is thus our competence for producing new logical species by predicative assimilation. It 'grasps together' and integrates into one whole and complete story multiple and scattered events, thereby schematizing the intelligible signification attached to the narrative taken as a whole" (x). Moreover, the French philosopher notes, since metaphor is a staple of poetic discourse and plot an utmost feature of narrative, the two genres appear "closely bound up with each other" within "one vast poetic sphere that includes metaphorical utterance and narrative discourse" (xi).

Antin's post-Aristotelian view and enactment of narrativity are not incompatible with Ricoeur's phenomenology of genre and other, more recent—one might say postmodern—attempts, in criticism, literature, or the arts, to break away from the tripartite scheme classical poetics has handed down to us.[2] But the American poet takes a step further, I think. He declines to rehearse the distinctions between fact and fiction and poets and thinkers, respectively, as we learn in an interview with Larry McCaffery (41-42). Nor does Antin differentiate between prose and its storytelling repertoire, on the one hand, and poetry and its tropological arsenal, on the other.[3] In effect, he proposes in the same interview that "Narrative action

may be similar to the way metaphor functions in some kinds of poetry—the difference being that storytelling is grounded in an event
more widespread, common social practice" (41). Furthermore, he
mentions the development of Wittgenstein's style and thought—an
enduring influence which Antin has often acknowledged[4]—to remark that the very language of the *Notebooks, Zettel,* and *Philosophical Investigations,* whose texture itself constitutes a
metalinguistic meditation, becomes "enchanted with the subversive
tendencies of language and its multiple discourses." Notably, this
enchantment obtains through narrative and metaphors that increasingly come to shape Wittgenstein's later work (50-51).

But, cutting as he does across established genre boundaries to do
away with arbitrary and, as theorists such as Gérard Genette have
argued in a broader context, apocryphal classifications (65), Antin
introduces a new one. There is no clear-cut term to describe it since
Antin's synchretic "performances"[5] straddle the traditional divi-
sions between genres, representation modes (fiction versus nonfiction[6]), discourse types (literature versus criticism; psychology and
philosophy versus aesthetics and, again, literature), expression
forms (writing/textuality versus speech/orality/"improvisation"[7]),
and relevant terminologies. For lack of a better word, I would like to
call this distinction phenomenological, much though the author
might resent such an attempt to rein this distinction in conceptually.

This classification principle is most clearly brought to the fore,
simultaneously theorized and applied, as Lazer has keenly
observed (124), in "the price," a piece performed in San Francisco in
1986 (*what it means* 92-119). "Poem-rap" (Alpert 188) and critical
essay at the same time, the text expounds Antin's notion of selfhood
in a discourse lodged at the crossroads of all the domains, forms,
and paradigms listed above. It starts off, in point of fact, with a typically phenomenological move, with that sort of self-reflective opening protocol that speaks eloquently to the phenomenological legacy
of the poststructuralist mode of inquiry and even of certain forms of
cultural analysis, such as identity studies (i.e., Foucauldian and
cultural-materialist critiques of the notion of disembodied subjec-
tivity). Thus Antin publicly owns that the self, the actual object of
his performative thinking out loud or questioning and the very notion of question(ing) are intimately tied together. Now, this realization alone would give the lie to the critics contending, as Antin
ironically paraphrases them before long, that he "had not enjoyed
the benefit of   french deconstruction   which should have dis-
abused [him] of [the] illusion of . . . the unitary self" (93). Quite to

the contrary, Antin owns. "i always thought," he says,

> the idea of the self was surrounded by questions   and
> in fact what i was interested in were   precisely those
> questions   which were questions i spent a lot of time
> asking   because i didnt know the answers   for if i
> knew the answers i wouldnt have any reason to   ask the
> questions   and one of the questions im interested
> in asking is   what is the locus of the source or
> ground of   the self   so when i thought of the title
> for this talk as "where are you?"   what i had in mind
> was to look for the place where the self   or what i
> take to be the self   has its ground (93)

What Antin envisions here is something far less nebulous than the ontological concept of *Grund,* which Heidegger and others after him have employed to probe the essence of poetry and its illumination of the foundations of being. In the poem under scrutiny the "ground" designates the place from which the self somehow emerges, comes or is brought to the fore, into the open, or discourse. Again, to philosophers like Heidegger, this stands out as an utmost feature of poetry as a particular form of language; yet Antin prefers to call this process narrative. It integrates the self as structured identity and self as becoming or "identity in-the-works," so to speak, trading upon—while declining to solve—the Parmenides-Heraclitus dilemma of classical metaphysics. Thus, on the one hand, the unrelenting disclosure of the self warrants a sense of identity or coherence-granting continuity within the same individual entity that we refer to by calling him or her by the same name throughout his or her life. On the other, we see this identity undergo experiences so different—so "differentiating"—that they threaten to unravel the fabric of the entity they are meant to weave (94). Consequently, it might be more appropriate to talk—again in a fairly Wittgensteinian[8] tone—about one's selves rather than one's self as much as there are so many (different) ways of talking about the same self or "I" (*what it means* 162-63).

To put the matter otherwise: for Antin, the identity and the self are two different things. The latter is the broader category, springing, as Antin specifies, out of a "collision of the sense of identity with the issues of narrative" (95). It is at this juncture that, the obvious "overlap" notwithstanding (Lazer 126), the poet puts forth the demarcation I was talking about above, one which sets off *narrative* from *story*. "i would like to distinguish," Antin continues,

> between two things   one i would call narrative and the
> other story   and as i see it theyre related   but not
> the same   story is a configuration of events or parts
> of events that shape some transformation   but
> narrative   or so it seems to me   is a sort of psychic
> function   part of the human psychic economy and probably
> a human universal   at least we identify it with being
> human   and it involves a particular paradoxical
> confrontation
>
>   consider the possibility of being confronted by a
> potential transformation   think of some thinking mind
> some subject   some experiencing human being even a
> very elementary one
>   at some point this being encounters the
> possibility the likelihood of transformation . . .
>
>   now my sense is that the center of narrative is the
> confrontation of experience   an experiencing subject
> with the possibility of transformation   the threat of
> transformation or the promise of transformation (95)

This is not the only place, in "the price" or elsewhere, in which Antin originally parts company with critics and thinkers on aesthetic and philosophical issues. It is, though, one of the most consequential. For, I would argue, it theorizes with clarity, against structuralism and rather along the lines of poststructuralist thought, narrativity as understood and practiced by Antin. According to this under-standing and practice, narrative is the subject's internalization of his or her potential change, human mind's confrontation with the alienating-annihilating possibility of "JE est un autre." In discourse (Antin's discourse included), such a possibility translates into a phenomenology of continuous development, flux, growth, crisis, and change, in a word, transformation. While story suggests completed cycle, closure, *structure,* narrative stands for—and, again, brings about—*structuration,* repeated reconstruction (grounding) of selfhood in the wake of decisive critical moments and in socioculturally specific contexts. As Antin specifies,

>   what narrative at its core celebrates or ritually
> reenacts is this grounding of self   over the threat of
> its annihilation . . . and here is where my distinction
> between narrative and story comes in
>   because i would hold that a story is merely

the configuration of events or parts of events that
   shape a possible transformation   a temporal
configuration of events that marks the passage of one
   articulated state of affairs into a significantly
different one   which when it engages the desires and
    fears of an experiencing subject represents the
   external shell or surface manifestation of a possible
narrative   but it is the engagement with the
   possibility of change that is the fundamental issue
                       because any event that is of
any significance at all must change you (98-99)

In view of this forthright statement Antin's whole work strikes me as an ongoing narrative meditation on the self, which is to say, a ceaseless interrogation of metamorphosis and "becoming-Other" grasped as the inner logic and inescapable drama of being. Of course, "the price" itself, so to speak, is paying the price for this vision, along with numerous other poems by Antin—as many splendid illustrations and celebrations of change. For, to be sure, change—and being, selfhood therewith, ultimately— "comes at a price" (99). And so does the poem, the "price" for which is Antin's postmodern balancing act or relentless negotiation of structure and structuration, story and narrative, identity and self. Notably, various personae of Antin's narratives run the risk of disintegration as they evolve: "the degree to which [a significant event] changes you is the degree to which it is a threat to your existence" (99), the author himself acknowledges. But, if this prospect is real, can then the text itself, no matter how we choose to call it—poem, narrative, performance, "talk poetry" (Altieri 13), and so forth—avoid the same mortal danger, i.e., dissolution, amorphousness? Traditional poetics would probably give us a skeptical answer here. But Antin's performative, antiprescriptive, transgressive discourse hints at something else. It seems to me that Antin's innovative take on narrative as a category different from story as well as other literary forms, operates as an integrative, coherence-building principle of his performances/texts rather than as a centrifugal force. Paradoxical as it may seem, narrative—vehicle and symptom of existential change and difference—works to provide Antin's own narratives with continuity and flow. In this sense, "the price" itself is once again an example.

I use the word *example* advisedly, I hasten to add. Antin develops his theory of narrative by narrative means, through concrete examples—what he calls "thinking by way of example" (111), and a very explicit thinking at that.[9] In doing so, he acts out the venerable truth that oral cultures have for long been living by: knowledge is as manageable in narrative as in abstract categories (Ong 140).[10] Thus, in Antin, theory—in principle, a model that formalizes, conceptualizes knowledge—is shaped as narrative. Accordingly, to instantiate his model of the self as a "social construct" (98) growing out of the "series of accommodations" (adaptations and mutations) the self has to undergo, the author resorts, indeed, to the example of a "famous russian journalist" (99) who went through momentous "accommodations," personal as well as collective. Thus Antin's character "came to terms" with himself and more or less the entire twentieth century of Russia and its successor, the now defunct Soviet Union: the Bolshevik revolution, various leaders and dictators "from kerensky to brezhnev," and the collective nightmare they have been responsible for. Only "coming to terms"—survival as moral and political compromise, Antin suggests—entails paying a dear price. And both the self of this writer—and a spokesperson for the former Soviet Union to boot—and this self's narrative chronicle bear out such a transaction. Realistic, pragmatic, or simply "cynical," this antiheroic self is endowed, Antin points out, with a "shiftiness" that enables it to "fold itself around whatever comes without tearing   the mensheviks the bolsheviks the constitutionalists the bolsheviks again the leninists   and in the end the stalinist imperium" (101).

No doubt, there is a *story* here. Yet it does not quite honor the self. This is a dismaying account of successively aborted narratives, of "narrative crises" and "situations" (102) that the self's survival instinct warded off, denied, or forgot, and, in so doing, failed the test of responsibility, as the character's writings testify. In "what i am doing here," the opening piece from *talking at the boundaries,* Antin is very adamant about this relation between self-perception—one's sense of one's own personality, that is—and *ethical,* "self-interrogating" memory, which staves off the temptation of "selective" recollection. "[T]he only way   that i can conceive of myself   as a personality," Antin states in an important confession, is "by an act   of memory   by an act of interrogation of my memory   which is   also talking   the self   itself   is emergent in discourse   in some kind of discourse   it is probably available   but it comes up under dialogue   and the dialogue   is   conducted with it   and then the self emerges   even though the self   may not have been there until you called upon it" (10).[11]

To go back to "the price," a somewhat similar albeit far less self(-)incriminating case than the Russian writer's provides the author's father-in-law. As a young boy, we learn, he helplessly witnessed the execution of a soldier whom Trotsky sent to death for having "commandeered" a herring. "whenever he [the poet's father-in-law] tells that story," Antin writes in another definition/enactment of narrative,

> he comes to the edge of a narrative in which he stands
> at the brink of a terrible transformation   which if he
> chooses to experience could prove horrifying   and
> which he characteristically deflects with a laugh   but
>   by repeatedly approaching and resisting the
> transformation that entering this narrative would force
> on him   what he approaches in this story   at least in
> its repeated tellings   is very much like narrative as i
>   have defined it   but it is a narrative of the
> narrative situation   of the threat and terror of a
> narrative which could if experienced transform my
> father-in-law's self beyond his own recognition
>
>   and yet at the same time if i am right   his
> continued resistance to this threat is a fundamental
> self constituting act (105)

Revealingly, the father-in-law's story is interwoven with its telling. They cannot—and should not, Antin insists—be kept apart. The delivery does not distort the tale;[12] in fact, it actually makes the delivered episode be what it is, mean what it does, for the teller, the characters, as well as for the audience. In and through the very act of storytelling, the storyteller takes up not only a narrative position but also an ethical stance. Unlike the Russian writer, who in his stories chose to ignore crisis and thereby the narrative constitution of his self as inflected by certain critical moments in his life, the father-in-law confronts such moments in his story. And again, the story bears out this personal engagement, through a unique dynamic of discourse and story (history), to recall the structuralist terminology.

One should bear in mind, though, that Antin takes aim precisely at this terminology and the formalist mind-set couched in it. Here is his critique, which merits extensive quotation:

> now this act of confrontation is almost entirely
> absent   from the accounts of narrative given by the
> structuralist thinkers like propp or bremond or lévi
> -strauss or todorov or roland barthes   because they
> are fundamentally externalists concerned with the

articulation of story as a kind of abstract and
generalized social production   and while they sometimes
illuminate elegant symmetries in the shapes of plots i
  dont think they are really relevant to a study of
narrative at all   mainly because they begin from texts
  instead of tellings   and even if they come out of
tellings they come out of more or less ritualized
  occasions that tend to obliterate the narrative centers
  that arise from human social experience   but stories that
  arise from ordinary social occasions are always
  narrative   because they arise out of a   circumstance
in which you are talking and trying and failing to make
some kind of sense

    and the stories that they have collected are
usually nobody's telling and often a kind of synthesis
of several people's tellings   or else they treat them
as nobody's telling   where nobody is trying to make
any particular sense (110-11)

Antin rebuts above an entire tradition of "folklorism" (111), formalist ("morphological") poetics (V. I. Propp), and its heir, French structuralism. He calls this objectivist or neopositivist line of thought
"externalist." Opposed to it is, one might say, his "internalism,"
which interlocks the tale, the telling, and its cultural-historical context, and the teller in a single discursive apparatus. Intriguingly,
this apparatus is both a subject *in* Antin's text—as inscribed in the
book I am quoting from—and its shape. For the text is, after all, the
"(tran)script"—"notations" or "scores"[13]—of an oral performance on
which Antin delivered ("told") it, even though, it goes without saying, "whatever winds up on paper is never exactly like whats in the
air" ("the price," *what it means* 124). Theme and form are, here as
elsewhere in Antin, the two faces of his Janus-like talk poem. Accordingly, change, which narrative represents, fashions not only the
selfhood of his characters, whose metamorphoses he feeds into his
work, but also this work itself. The latter lights up an autobio-
graphic space where the reader witnesses how the author's own life
has been in its turn more or less molded by these metamorphoses.
Doubtlessly, Antin's talk poems commemorate—in both senses—
transformation. They orchestrate a phenomenology of inner becoming, of self-acknowledged crisis, change, and growth, unfolding as
they do a poetic panorama the main instruments of which are, oddly
enough, narrative as well as dramatic: narrative in that Antin's
"poems" basically consist of stories told mostly in denotative lan-

guage, and dramatic in that the author delivers his "stories" by performative means, *coram populo*.

"the river," which, appropriately enough, follows "the price," is in point of fact change itself, a Heraclitean, "ongoing enterprise" (*what it means* 123) as much as a poem *about* change. Its inevitable flip side, stability—identity features that remain unaltered while the self evolves—is also present throughout the poem but chiefly in its latter half, which tells another story of the poet's father-in-law. "the river" raises the "question of beginning" (126) and answers it by meandering through a few narratives exemplifying the leitmotif of "beginning," which the author reiterates verbatim at strategic moments. Actually, Antin uses the plural "beginning*s*" rather than the singular, and the distinction is noteworthy. The poem recounts, among other things, a series of "starts" in the author's and his father-in-law's life as so many occasions for the people involved to experience narrative at decisive turns in their lives: the speaker's decision to move to California and teach in San Diego or the father-in-law's decision to emigrate to the United States following traumatizing experiences in Hungary. In part the poem gains its consistency from the organizing presence of the symmetrically deployed leitmotif (126, 134, 142, 153), the latter being part of the explicit commentary on the narrative episodes featured by the poem.

In a deeper sense, though, the piece is held together by an undergirding narrative phenomenology in the sense specified above; it shows how people face out dramatic transformation and thereby deal with who they are or are about to turn into. Change— or the possibility thereof, at least—may be brought about by experiences such as voluntary relocation, hasty self-exile, the learning of a new language and its use in one's writing, a new career, one's discovery of a new artistic talent, and so forth. These may be solemn exploits or anecdotal moments, such as the comic encounter between one of the poet's co-workers and her tattooed date in "what am i doing here" (*talking* 8). In retrospect, however, all these turn out to be *meaningful* and memorable. They are worth "remembering recording representing," to quote the title of another poem from *talking at the boundaries*. As such, they prompt narrative self-representation and self-understanding, a fundamental sense of identity which, again, Antin's stories do not "reflect" mimetically but "constitute."

NOTES

[1]Marjorie Perloff has made the important point that *"narrative* (but not fiction) is an integral feature of the talk poem" in Antin, comparing his typical "story" to Cage's *koan* (*Poetics* 330). In my essay I will trade upon the distinction Antin draws between narrative and story.

[2]"The history of genre theory," Gérard Genette contends, "is shaped throughout by these fascinating schemes that both inform and skew the oftentimes heterogenous reality of the literary field and claim to discover a natural 'system' while, in fact, they lay out an artificial symmetry consisting of illusory categories" (49; trans. mine). Also see Antin, "The Stranger at the Door" (233-35) for a similar position on "genre membership" (235).

[3]In "the river" Antin tells us that, failing to convince his New Directions publishers not to promote his work as poetry, he "tried to convince them to put [him] in the prose section as well" (*what it means* 125). On the other hand, Antin "insists that [his talk poems] are not prose, which is a much more frozen thing" (Hornick 8). In the talk poem "is this the right place" Antin also submits that "writing is a form of fossilized talking   which gets put inside a can   called a book . . . or maybe we should say a frozen food container called a book" (*talking at the boundaries* 45-46).

[4]In her distinguished book on Wittgenstein and the twentieth-century poetic avant-garde, Perloff also lists Antin's work among the "growing body" of contemporary "Wittgensteiniana" (6).

[5]"There is," Jerome Rothernberg writes in his essay-manifesto on the "poetics of performance," "an unquestionable and far-reaching breakdown of boundaries and genres between 'art' and 'life' (Cage, Kaprow), between various conventionally defined arts (intermedia and performance art, concrete poetry), and between arts and non-arts (*musique concrete,* found art, etc.)" (640). See Perloff, *Poetics* 288-339, for an analysis of John Cage's and David Antin's "poetry of performance." Also see Lazer's essay on Rothenberg and Antin.

[6]Here is Antin's response to a question about the distinction between "writing and thinking": "I'm not interested in any forms where distinctions between 'fictionality' and 'factuality' can be clearly formulated. . . . 'Fiction' is a label that positions all the works grouped under it too straightforwardly in the domain of the imaginary and the untrue, or at least the contrafactual, and takes away its stakes as human experience. I don't want anybody to be sure whether what I say is a lie or a truth, whether I remembered it, heard it, imagined it, dreamt it, or invented it. I'd like the boundary between fact and fiction to be as unstable in my work as it is in my experience. Yet at the same time I have a strong desire to get at something I would call reality, however indeterminate that may be" (McCaffery 41).

[7]See Antin's conversation with Hazel Smith and Roger Dean, "Talking and Thinking" *passim* for a discussion of his work as "improvised poetry."

[8]In his detailed review of Perloff's *Wittgenstein's Ladder,* Antin teases out the "narrative implications" of the Wittgensteinian reflections on the "idea of personal identity" (149) from *The Blue Book.* He notices the impact of such implications both on what the philosopher has to say and on the

saying or telling itself, on "the process of narrativization" uncovered in *The Blue Book*. Specifically, Antin notes that Wittgenstein asks how many persons we are dealing with in a "man whose memory on the odd days of his life consists only of his experiences of the odd days, while his memory on the even days consists only of his experiences of the even days, and asks if we have here one person or two" (149). Of course, this situation could be complicated ad infinitum—each day corresponding to a different person—but the argument remains essentially the same: first, identity is determined by narrative; and second, one's sense of a *coherent* identity, the "story," depends on how one deals with narrative "tests," with crises and moments of potential transformations.

[9]Resulting from this logic of the "exemplifying" discourse is a real problem for Antin's critics. As Charles Altieri comments on Antin's "postmodern" metaphor of "tuning," there is at times hardly any need to "explain" Antin's ideas since the author does the explaining himself in his talk pieces (Altieri 13). This also places them in the tradition of "meditative poem" (Garber 220).

[10]Walter Ong follows, on this score, Eric A. Havelock's works on Homer and Plato.

[11]Memory, Antin states in an interview with one of his critics, "is central to all human concepts of the real, including science, history, and personal identity. It is an effort to create a continuum which makes self possible" (Hornick 7).

[12]See Scholes and Kellogg's critique of the "common misconception" regarding the "corruption" of the original story through its oral delivery (23).

[13]"these talks," Antin describes the relation between oral performance and textual rendition in his work, "are not 'prose'   which is as i see it a kind of 'concrete poetry with justified margins'   while these text are the notations or scores of oral poems   with margins consequently unjustified" (introductory note to *talking at the boundaries* i).

WORKS CITED

Alpert, Barry. "Postmodern Oral Poetry: Buckminster Fuller, John Cage, and David Antin." *Early Postmodernism: Foundational Essays*. Ed. Paul A. Bove. Durham: Duke UP, 1995. 188-206.

Altieri, Charles. "The Postmodernism of David Antin's *tuning*." *College English*. 48.1 (1986): 9-26.

Antin, David. *talking at the boundaries*. New York: New Directions, 1976.

——. "Talking and Thinking: David Antin in Conversation with Hazel Smith and Roger Dean." *Postmodern Culture* 3.3 (1993).

——. "Thinking about Novels." *Review of Contemporary Fiction* 11.2 (1991): 210-16.

——. *what it means to be avant-garde*. New York: New Directions, 1993.

————. "Wittgenstein among the Poets." Rev. of *Wittgenstein's Ladder: Poetic Language and the Strangeness of the Ordinary,* by Marjorie Perloff. *Modernism / Modernity* 5.1 (1998): 149-66.

Garber, Frederick. "The Talk Poems of David Antin." *North Dakota Quarterly* 55.4 (1987): 217-38.

Genette, Gérard. *Introduction à l'architexte*. Paris: Éditions du Seuil, 1979.

Hornick, Lita. *David Antin / Debunker of the "Real."* Putnam Valley, NY: Swollen Magpie, 1979.

Lazer, Hank. "Thinking Made in the Mouth: The Cultural Poetics of David Antin and Jerome Rothenberg." *Picturing Cultural Values in Postmodern America*. Ed. William G. Doty. Tuscaloosa: U of Alabama P, 1995. 101-39.

McCaffery, Larry. "Matches in a Dark Space: An Interview with David Antin." *Some Other Frequency. Interviews with Innovative American Authors*. Philadelphia: U of Pennsylvania P, 1996. 36-58.

Ong, Walter J. *Orality and Literacy: The Technologizing of the Word*. London: Routledge, 1982.

Perloff, Marjorie. *The Poetics of Indeterminacy: Rimbaud to Cage*. Princeton: Princeton UP, 1981.

————. *Wittgenstein's Ladder. Poetic Lanauage and the Strangeness of the Ordinary*. Chicago: U of Chicago P, 1996.

Ricoeur, Paul. *Time and Narrative*. Vol. 1. Trans. Kathleen McLaughlin and David Pellauer. Chicago: U of Chicago P, 1984.

Rothenberg, Jerome. "New Models, New Visions: Some Notes toward a Poetics of Performance." *Postmodern American Poetry. A Norton Anthology*. Ed. Paul Hoover. New York: Norton, 1994. 640-44.

Sayre, Henry M. "David Antin and the Oral Poetics Movement." *Contemporary Literature* 23 (1982): 428-50.

Scholes, Robert, and Robert Kellogg. *The Nature of Narrative*. London: Oxford UP, 1966.

David Antin:
The Hermeneutics of Performance

Hélène Aji

> well now we have a problem
> with our overlong career of literalism   overlong
> and singleminded   its been so long now that many of
> us find it hard to understand the terms of any other
> possible career
> > —David Antin, "the sociology of art"
> > (*talking at the boundaries* 178)

The *prolegomena* to David Antin's poetic work are, if not well-known, at least fairly simple and straightforward. Like many poets who preceded him and like many poets of his own generation, he grounds his enterprise on the assumption that the death of literature is imminent, that the poet has to fight against forces of reaction and return to an academic and stultified past, eventually that apocalypse is at hand if the true voices do not manage to make themselves heard. Polemic and discussion start when it has to be decided which voices are true and which are not, what is reactionary tapping into the past and what is fertile borrowing and learning from the past, whether literature is a dead body on which only vultures feed or a live corpus able to help renewal and original creation. Antin addresses the question in a way that contradicts Donald Wesling's antithetical definition available in his article "Difficulties of the Bardic": literary criticism must come to terms with the dual nature of language. Language is at the same time the sublimated medium of literature and the common instrument of daily communication. For Antin, this dichotomy is not relevant, and the core of the matter is not to understand a difference between two species of language, but, on the contrary, to understand that language is of one kind and to work out all the consequences of this understanding. One first apparent symptom of Antin's assertion of the necessity to erase all limits, all boundaries, is to be found in his own description of his personal trajectory:

> when i agreed to come here   to indiana   barry
> alpert didn't have a title for what i was going
> to talk about . . . i was no longer   so

>   clearly a poet   a linguist   an art critic
>   all of which i had so clearly been   and . . . my
>   work was therefore no longer so clearly a poem a
>   criticism an investigation but somehow   lying
>   between them   or on their borders (*talking at the*
>   *boundaries* 55)

David Antin refuses to be submitted to any desire to classify and order; in the same way as he does not want to be called a poet, he does not want to abandon the status of a poet. The same goes for his position as a critic, in a stronger way still since he considers it an important function of poetry to examine and criticize whatever surrounds it. He in fact posits himself on the margin, as an outsider, someone precariously poised on what he calls "the fringe," away from the "white light" of celebrity, acceptance, and recognition, out of the reach of such sinister types as the businessmen he meets for lunch, as similar and interchangeable as goldfish in a bowl, with nondescript names such as Mike and Sam, Tip and Top (*what it means* 3-29). At the same time he carefully stages the performance of his poems and polishes his image, building himself into this outlandish figure of a gigantic bald bard, randomly propelled into the lecture halls of universities but also willingly exposing himself to the limelight. This ambivalence governs any appraisal of David Antin's work, since I do not think that the poems can be taken solely at face value, simply for the principles they expound or the way those principles are exhibited. In the end Antin's poetic mode might very well correspond to the title of one of his recordings: it is ruled by a "principle of fit," with the double meaning of the word: the poem would be this product of a crisis situation and the artifact made to adapt to some demand.

At the roots of Antin's present poetic practice, one may find common points with poets such as Gary Snyder, particularly in their insistence on the primitive heritage and on the oral and aural nature of poetry. Basically, they assert the necessity to claim a literary corpus too little taken into account because unwritten or presented only under the second-hand form of a transcription of spoken events by outsiders. They consider that books contribute to the institutionalization of a certain number of texts, thus excluding other texts for the arbitrary reason that they cannot circulate as easily as best-selling printed matter. If some poets, such as Jerome Rothenberg, resort, as a consequence, to collecting those texts to make them known or to imitating them so as to make them new, Antin chooses another way, since his intake from primitive poetic modes is more conceptual and contextual than thematic or even formal:

> if poetry was a
> kind of talking   and it had to be if there was no
> writing   then a poet was someone who could talk
> when the time came   could remember other
> talking   and could tell the important things
> how they had happened and why   and what might
> have happened if these things hadnt happened in the way
> they happen to have happened (*talking at the boundaries* 185)

Thus Antin lays emphasis on the questionable nature of our relation to the world, particularly to the earth. The necessity to reverse this relation and to understand that our environment is not to be bent according to our desires, but that we are the ones supposed to attune ourselves to its demands is not an original idea of Antin's. However, it has serious consequences for his poetic practice and does not stop at an ecological claim for more respect for nature. In this matter the input of primitive societies is paramount, but Antin's way of interpreting it and applying it to his own modes of dealing with what surrounds him in specifically poetic terms modifies whatever previous reading of primitive myths has been done so far:

> basically weve been a hardware society while theyve
> been a software society   they were the people who
> programmed and were the people who shoved   thats a
> difference in the way of tuning   they were tuning
> themselves to the earth and we   if we were tuning
> were trying to compel the earth to tune to us
> which is hardly a way of tuning (*tuning* 177)

What Antin learns from the primitives is that poetry is essentially a narrative mode, that it loses its meaning and importance as soon as this aspect of direct transmission of a story is forgotten, as soon as the context of poetic delivery is made unimportant by the use of mobile books, eventually as soon as the oral dimension of this transmission is lost. At the same time this narrative emerges as a response to the world and as the result of a productive as well as integrative activity. Creating a poem appears then as an activity closely related to the ancient practice of myth-making:

> from these first men   stupid   insensate and
> horrible beasts   all the philosophers and
> philologians should have begun their investigations of
> the wisdom of the gentile nations   and they

> should have begun with metaphysics which seeks its
>   proofs not in the external world but within the
> modifications of the mind of him who meditates
> it in such fashion the first men of the gentile
> nations children of nascent mankind created
>   things according to their own ideas but they in
>   their own robust ignorance did it by virtue of a
> wholly corporeal imagination . . .
>   for which they were called "poets" which is
> greek for "creators" hence poetic wisdom the
> first wisdom of the gentile world must have
> begun with metaphysics not rational and abstract
>   like that of learned men but felt and
>   imagined . . .
>
> and the stories they knew to be lies they called
>   them "fables" and "legends" and sometimes
> "myths" because myths merely meant stories the
> word myth means a story it comes from a greek
>   verb an interesting verb *mutheomai* means to
>   tell to talk originally what it meant was
>   to talk when someone gets up and starts
> rapping in an epic (*talking at the boundaries* 158-59)

This passage from *talking at the boundaries* is fascinating because both logically and semantically it links the myths of the past to Antin's actual poetry and establishes a parallel between hackneyed etymology and original thought, thus underlining the possibility of finding in the familiar the seeds for an unfamiliar poetic practice. Indeed, for Antin, the primitive poet is a figure that allows him to undo and redo fundamental definitions, including the very definition of the primitive, which he rejects as an operative term because of its derogatory connotations of cultural simplicity and lack of sophistication. This work on definitions is a ramification of a more systematic and apparently schoolbookish work previously engaged in *definitions*, a collection presented as a schoolboy's exercise book in which the poet declines the possibilities for words or expressions in an attempt to shift any univocal conception of language and move out to the field of free association, which, as we shall see, is a major feature of Antin's talk poem. For instance:

> deteriorate * become-or-grow worse * impair degenerate . . .
> jump-out-of-the-frying-pan-into-the-fire skirt-Scylla-and-
> fall-into-Charybdis (*definitions* 21)

Indeed, whatever Antin says about myth and myth-making is not new; but the way he takes into account all the aspects of primitive practice to list the major features of his own practice adds an edge to his more general considerations. Namely, Antin insists on the perceptual origins of primitive metaphysics, on the absence of rationalization or abstraction, on the possibility of constructing abstract discourse, but also on the necessity to conceive it as one plausible (or implausible) lie among others, on the supremacy of talking not only as a mode of transmission and communication, but above all as a creative process; his definition of myth as "rapping in an epic" is then climactic and essential in the sense that it implies the physical presence of the poet, a certain amount of spontaneity, the telling of a narrative at least partially improvised, and a philosophical meditation on the world at the same time as a chain of lies. The clash between reflection and fiction, between philosophical impulse and compulsive narration, between theoretical assertion and practical adaptation is what gives Antin's poetry its elusive multiplicity and ambiguity, since it contains the mixed elements of a poetics and of a poem. Truth and lies, reality and fiction, the written and the oral are then notions that collapse in front of what could be deemed Antin's poetics of performance.

Actually, what seems to happen is the basic refusal of any dogmatic stance; instead of generating a new poetic dogma, Antin wants to give evidence of the absurd and arbitrary nature of any preconceived theory that would consequently find its field of application. Contrary to what may have been done by Alain Robbe-Grillet for the nouveau roman, there cannot be, for Antin, a manifesto for a *nouvelle poésie* that would subsequently be translated into a poetic practice; the poem is manifesto enough in itself, but its motley character implies deciphering, sorting out, interpreting, in short, engaging in a whole range of activities which depend at the same time on the poet, on the critic, and on the public. A corollary of this is the idea that writing functions as an obstacle to this perennial work of actualization and that somehow once a text is written it becomes immutable, sacred in the sense that it cannot be touched or modified.

> writing is a form of fossilized talking   which gets
>   put inside of a can   called a book   and i respect
>   that can   its a means of preservation   or
>   maybe we should say in a frozen food container called
> a book   but on the other hand if you dont know how
> to handle that frozen food container that icy block
> will never turn back into talking   and if it will

never turn back into talking it will never be of use
to you again (*talking at the boundaries* 45-46)

Thus writing is apparently for Antin the imperfect remedy to a problem of conservation of the text, and its major imperfection is the fact that the printed text is an object, a commodity to be exchanged and circulated, but not to be changed nor adapted. It is barren as ice and paradoxically dated, outdated even as it gains perenniality. Actual communication and ongoing creation are seen as threatened by the book industry, and more specifically Antin's poems are shown as distorted by the necessity to write them down. Indeed, as Henry M. Sayre puts it, "oral poetry is rejecting not so much the text itself as the logocentric and quasi-metaphysical attitude toward the text which invests with priority and ultimate authority" (180). Constituting the poem into an item in a book is denounced by Antin as a painful, disturbing, dissatisfying compromise; to him, the page conveys a partial and misleading image of the original poem, the one produced through talking. Antin questions the shape of a book, its organization in pages, the possibility in reading to repeat the same passage over again as many times as wanted, the fragmenting of the text into units that are not motivated by the very nature of the text but by exterior factors (How long can I read at once without something or someone interrupting me? Shall I stop out of habit at the end of a page so as to be able to resume more easily? If the text does not retain my attention, will I just discard it?). All this is impossible as long as the talk poem has not yet been transcribed and printed, turned into a written text:

now the book itself   can be considered a
package a kind of care package so to speak   right
      i mean i do my talking here and i take my imperfect
recording and i transcribe it in the hope of finding
      what in it was the real thing   the real action
      and i try to get it into the book in such a
way that its still intelligible when it goes into this
rectangular object with covers that you open   like
this   and which is partitioned arbitrarily by those
      things they call pages
                                    there are
no pages when i talk   you dont turn anything at
      all   that is   i turn you turn but we dont turn
      pages   someone doesnt bring down a screen in front
      of me every few minutes and   then let me continue

again (*tuning* 55-56)

The conflict lies in the final necessity to transcribe, to transform the spoken text into a written text so as to preserve it. Without ever questioning the logic of this process, Antin underlines its faults, the risk of fixing a text and consequently of a fixation over this text and the danger of moving from talking to reciting, from reciting to writing, from writing to repeating and ending the processes of original creation:

> that making poems   talking poems   could start
>   dying   and people could start trying to remember
>   somebodys good talking   and therefore reciting
>   and from reciting   its not too far to trying
>   to save it in writing   but we know all about that
>   about how writing is about anxiety   trying to
>   hold something still (*talking at the boundaries* 192)

This outlining of the process of poetic creation as Antin sees it may lead to considerations of another characteristic of the written text which makes him wary of books and publishers:

>   the whole problem of our literate and literal
>   culture has been   to some extent   the problem
>   of the totally dislocated occasion   that is in this
>   case the book   which goes out into a distributional
>   system unknown to us (*talking at the boundaries* 56)

According to Antin, the book turns the text into an object, a commodity that can be transported, bought, sold, in short, that can be divorced from its maker without any loss being felt. In his rebellion against an illusion that the text is no more than that, Antin is postmodern in the sense given by Terry Eagleton; instead of merely protesting the transformation of the work of art, and the literary text in particular, into a commodity, he asserts this transformation and tries to find a way out by accepting it as a fact and by fighting the reification of the text by making it into an event. Whereas modernists, Pound for instance, protested against capitalism as the intrusion of money and commerce into the field of art, Antin, as a postmodern poet, shows that art can escape this reification precisely by working with it, reifying everyday life and everyday language.[1] Thus the process already started in *definitions*, which aimed at debunking ready-made phrases, is pursued in his overall action aiming at debunking the act of poetic creation and the status of the poet. Working in his "associative monologue"[2] both along the paradigmatic and syntagmatic axes of language, Antin demonstrates the possibility of renewing and revitalizing the very definition of poetry.

This might, no doubt, explain his antagonistic relation to Harold Bloom, who is seen as the apostle of tradition as the ongoing degrading imitation of the great texts of the past and of poetry as the sentimental expression of exceptional ego:

> and the first question that anybody asked me as we
> were standing around the punch bowl was what do you
> think of harold bloom?
>   i said im sorry   i dont think of harold
> bloom   they said but could you think of harold
> bloom?   i said i could think of harold bloom
>   i could think of harold bloom if i wanted to
>   you want me to? all right   i'll try   they
> said what does harold bloom have against you?   i
> said   its not personal   they said   but he
> seemed so angry (*what it means* 47-48)

Antin proceeds by explaining that the root problem is in Bloom's appraisal of time. Of course, for Antin this feature is not exclusive to Bloom, but appears clearly in the critic's vision of literature: the past is considered with nostalgia whereas the future is pregnant with dreams unfulfilled; however, the present remains empty, unoccupied and unexplored. It is this very occupation of the present that governs Antin's poetic practice. Yet Antin's presentation of the poet never implies a staging of the development and constitution of an individual; the poem offers itself as a chance conjunction of varying elements that constitute the apparently random flow of discourse. As Sherman Paul underlines it in *So to Speak,* Antin radically modifies the very nature of the poem, which becomes a "relational event" in which the poet meets his public, in an attempt to find the conditions of "real living."[3] In fact, what Antin is constantly working on throughout his talk poems is well beyond the questions he asks in the poem; there is an underlying question about the coincidence of time and space which crystallizes into the nodal point of presence. This question was already investigated in *definitions:*

> you are there and i am here
> is it a corollary of the fact that two things cannot
>   be at the same place at the same time
> that two things can be at two different places at the

same time
you are there and i am here and i see you
but you are changed
two things at the same place at two different times (8)

And Antin keeps exploring the modalities of presence through each poem. The repetition of the process over and over again corresponds to successive attempts at tackling the mystery of presence and at approximating its potential, but perhaps unreachable, resolution. Moreover, another problem underpinning this reflection on time and space is raised by the effective passage from mere concomitance to a situation of actual communication. It is in this process only that Antin becomes a performative poet in the double sense of voicing and of enacting his ideas about poetry at the same time.[4] "It is talking, rendered as an ongoing process of mutual thinking, as an articulation of differences leading to ever greater definition and making ever finer distinctions–or at least showing such definition and distinctions that offers the surest way to go on" (Comens 190).

These words, in Bruce Comens's conclusion to his work on Pound, Williams, and Zukofsky, herald Antin's postmodern tactic. According to Comens, there is a difference between modernism, which tries to find an overall strategy that could deal universally and generally with the world, and postmodernism, which concentrates on local attempts at coming to terms with the fragmented nature of the real. Obviously, the term *local* is to be taken, as concerns Antin, both in a spatial and in a temporal sense. However, I think that locality is also to be conceived as a form of action; for Antin, it opposes the delocalization due to the book, and it opposes the disembodiment engendered by the practice of reading a text instead of witnessing and listening to its production. In this perspective the notion of performance includes the whole process of production and reception of the text: simultaneously, in the present, the poem is generated and received, and the modifications that arise from this mode of creation are multidirectional. Indeed, Antin claims that his method of premeditation followed by improvisation allows for the intervention of the public into the genesis of the poem. If there is a preconceived idea at the origins of the poem, the desire not only to talk, but to talk about something, then this desire is complemented and finalized on the spot, in the setup of the poetic event. In this respect the staging of the process of creation acquires a major role: not only does Antin decide to talk to a number of people, but he also decides to do it under specific conditions. In a scientific manner that recalls his days as an engineer, Antin always gathers the same elements for the repetition of a similar experiment; the success of this experiment depends on what varies more than on the constants (a lecture hall, a group of people, most often intellectuals, a tape recorder). Of course the variants remain implicit, and although Antin sometimes gives clues such as a particular event in his life or a precise anecdote, this is not sufficient to explain the absence of rumination and the emergence of a text and a body of work that constantly moves forward. For this reason I find it rather disquieting that some people tend to see in Antin's poetry an avatar of the collage technique. Thus Jerome Rothenberg: "In the face of multiple chronologies, many poets turn to synchronicity (the simultaneous existence of all places and times) as a basic organizing principle. As a method, a process of making the poem, this becomes 'collage': not history but 'the dramatic juxtaposition of disparate materials, without commitment to explicit syntactical relations between elements' (D. Antin)" (105). Although Rothenberg is here quoting Antin verbatim, he borrows his words to use them in a different context, since they are words about avant-garde works and about collaging for Antin and not words about his own work. In "what it means to be avant-garde," Antin underlines the fact that he does not believe he belongs to the avant-garde. If one word is to be applied to his talk-poems, it is more than the term *collage,* it is the adjective *dramatic:* he stages the unpredictable, preserving it from the temptation of thinking and elaborating in advance. To this extent, Antin belongs to this "interesting phenomenon" alluded to by Marjorie Perloff in *The Dance of the Intellect:* "We are now witnessing, at least in America, an interesting phenomenon. Minor poets continue to write neo-Romantic lyric; in this context, the attack on television and the media as the enemy can be seen to be a kind of defensive nostalgia. At the same time, a new poetry is emerging that wants to open the field so as to make contact with the *world* as well as the *word*" (181).

This new poetry, to which I think David Antin belongs, could then be characterized as a hermeneutic process: as it explores the world and tries to gain a better understanding of its components and of their dynamic relations, it also explores the possibilities of language. Antin's specific typography, his use of phonetic spelling, his economy of punctuation, which replaces most markers with blank spaces, make all this culminate in a definition of poetry as "uninterruptible discourse" (*talking at the boundaries* 23), as the unbroken chain of a threefold movement of the mind:

remembering
recording
representing
(*talking at the boundaries* 93)

NOTES

[1]See Eagleton: "Postmodernism, confronted with this situation, will then take the other way out. If the work of art really is a commodity then it might as well admit it, with all the *sang froid* it can muster. Rather than languish in some intolerable conflict between its material reality and its aesthetic structure, it can always collapse that conflict on one side, becoming aesthetically what it is economically. The modernist reification–the work of art as isolated fetish–is therefore exchanged for the reification of everyday life in the capitalist marketplace. The commodity as mechanically reproducible exchange outs the commodity as magical aura" (392).

[2]Marjorie Perloff's words, 147-48.

[3]See Paul: "The talk-poems are also dialogical because, in Buber's sense, he meets us. Reality–perhaps the poems represent this reality, too–reality, real living, is meeting. The poems are relational events (Buber's phrase)" (21).

[4]See Paul: "Doubly performative: a poet speaking, demonstrating his declaration, enacting his ideas" (35).

WORKS CITED

Antin, David. *definitions*. New York: Caterpillar Press, 1967.

———. *talking at the boundaries*. New York: New Directions, 1976.

———. *The Principle of Fit 2*. Washington: Watershed Tapes, 1981.

———. *tuning*. New York: New Directions, 1984.

———. *what it means to be avant-garde*. New York: New Directions, 1993.

Comens, Bruce. *Apocalypse and After: Modern Strategy and Postmodern Tactics in Pound, Williams and Zukofsky*. Tuscaloosa: U of Alabama P, 1995.

Eagleton, Terry. "Capitalism, Modernism and Postmodernism." *Modern Criticism and Theory*. Ed. David Lodge. London: Longman, 1988. 385-98.

Paul, Sherman. *So to Speak: Re-Reading David Antin*. London: Binnacle Press, 1982.

Perloff, Marjorie. *The Dance of the Intellect: Studies in the Poetry of the Pound Tradition*. Evanston: Northwestern UP, 1996.

Rothenberg, Jerome. *Pre-Faces and Other Writings*. New York: New Directions, 1981.

Sayre, Henry M. "The Object of Performance: Aesthetics in the Seventies." *Georgia Review* 37.1 (1983): 169-88.

Wesling, Donald. "Difficulties of the Bardic: Literature and the Human Voice." *Critical Inquiry* 8.1 (1981): 69-81.

The Art of Thought:
David Antin, Improvisation, Asia

George Leonard

Considering David Antin's improvisations, his talk poems, will lead to insights not only about Antin, but about improvisation itself. Comparing Antin's aesthetics with certain Asian artworld practices, we glimpse a central difference between the historic aesthetic values of the Western and East Asian high artworlds.[1]

Antin Performing a Talk Poem

By their nature, Antin's talk poems are intimate, therefore somewhat exclusive events, and the reader may not have attended one. Let me sketch the experience.

You're sitting in the intimate audience that poetry readings draw, most likely in a mundane academic setting: industrial carpet, beige drapes, ten or fifteen rows of sturdy, coffee-damaged desks or chairs. Antin sits to one side while an introduction is read. He rises without fanfare, stoops to turn on a cassette tape recorder placed in front of him. His opening remarks are (typically) undramatic: "don wellman wrote asking me if I would write something   do something for an issue of a magazine he was putting out" ("radical coherency" 177).

For all the banality of the setting, David Antin is no banal figure—and that matters to the performance. Anyone sophisticated enough to be in this artworld audience is finding him a resonant image. Well in his sixties, he is nonetheless a powerful physical presence—Picasso-bald, built like Jackson Pollock, slouching like the 1950s Brando, dressed in a faintly Kerouac retro style, he evokes an earlier (and, to the hip audience, inevitably purer, less mercantile) artworld: the Cedar Bar, Happenings, New York in the fifties and sixties. He stands (literally stands) for a time before American artists were widely popular or domesticated into academia—a world which chic art directors now photograph for *Vanity Fair* in black and white to suggest integrity: "JACKSON POLLOCK WORE KHAKIS." David Antin too is much photographed and in the photos looks most himself in a white T-shirt, jeans, and a Garrison belt.

Yet—for all the Brando look of him—Antin has been in academia for decades and was a brilliant academic gamesman, longtime chair of his own department. U.C.—San Diego built him a building for it. He is one of the most educated American poets, a linguist who speaks several languages and has translated books from French, a poet/philosopher whose work is connected with Wittgenstein's. (John Cage, struggling to characterize him, said finally, "David's very . . . *smart*.")

But, physically, *there is that look*. Onstage, that matters, and it matters more each year. Antin, in the aimless contemporary artworld, has grown into the stature of an icon—*not of the past,* for his whole presence speaks of health and power—but of a healthy survival *within the present* of a long and genuine American artworld tradition. As books appear with titles like *What Was Postmodernism?*—past tense—and the American artworld awakens, cotton-mouthed, from its dogmatic French slumbers, the presence of a sustaining American tradition—in the flesh, talking to you—is exciting. David Antin, after all, not only helped establish pop art; a quarter century ago he wrote the seminal essay "Is There a Postmodernism?"[2] Present tense. He was tired of pop. Now he has wearied of postmodernism. By this act today, in front of you, creating anew, he *embodies,* literally, a deeper American tradition that has outlasted all of it. It is a reassuring thought.

This now iconic figure, standing quite close, can see you as well as you can see him, which is both interesting and alarming. (The first time my wife saw Antin, in a videotape, she said, alarmed, "My God . . . so tough!") He begins to talk, and, as you watch, he watches you too, "tuning" in on you (so central a goal, he has made it the title of one of his poetry collections). Speaking, watching you, improvising the poem while he studies you, he is trying, through his speech, to "tune" your instruments together with his, all your minds, together, "a fundamental human act," as he works to create a kind of rhythmic communion that the whole room joins in, "a common space" (*tuning* 167). Think of tuning forks resonating together. For the next hour, tuning in/on/with you, Antin improvises his new talk poem—*your* personal talk poem, being created in a kind of sensory dialogue with you, his face, his body language responding to your faces, your body language in a kind of weaving dance.

The poem is, you discover, a regular story, but at times it rises to an intensity of metaphor and takes on a hypnotic cadence that is more than prose; not unlike the moments in African American poetic oratory when a speaker, on topics sacred or secular, gets into the Spirit, finds a rhythm beyond mere speech. One of Antin's best poems, "the river," gets there almost at once. It begins:

> coming into a space like this   obviously a very
> friendly space in that it has a very warm tone to it
>   in a way thats almost disconcerting for a poet
>   mainly because what youre used to is the randomness
> of the road   the notion that youre going
>   somewhere and you don't know where that is or what its
> like   and you're going to go do your talking poem
>   talk poem   talk piece   do your piece of talking
>   which is a piece of talking   because essentially
> your talking is an ongoing enterprise   at least my
>   talking is   an ongoing enterprise that I try to
>   relate to my thinking
>   because talking for me   is the
> closest i can come   as a poet   to thinking
>   and i had wanted for a long time a kind of poetry of
> thinking   not a poetry of thought but a poetry of
>   thinking   since getting so close to the process of
> thinking was what I thought the poem was ("the river" 123)

The tape recorder in front of Antin picks this up, and later, in a book, the audience will find the text, printed as above (or close to that). The best critic of modern performance art, Henry Sayre, has pointed out that Antin "privileges neither speech nor writing and uses each to undercut the other" (207).

Casually as the performance began, it ends in a dramatic climax. Typically, the story takes an unexpected turn, there is a revelation and, in the "Aha!" experience which spreads across the room, all instruments are at last in tune: a moment of understanding, agreement, and communion.

Such is an Antin talk poem. But why are there such things?

We enjoy seeing David Antin in person, surely, but why is it better that he create a new work in front of us, instead of doing the more normal thing everyone else does—read a work he has had time to revise and perfect? Why would we be disappointed if we came to think (erroneously!) that Antin had memorized his poem and simply performed it? Actors do that. We're not disappointed in them. The complex reasons we value this unusual experience—a David Antin improvisation—and what we value about all such experiences, will occupy the rest of this essay.

Let me start by pointing out the highly personal tone of my critique so far. My deliberate centering on the poet and his presence and the audience's contact with him is unusual in Western aesthetic criticism. In East Asian aesthetic criticism, however (of a calligrapher, for instance), it would be the norm. And that's part of the answer.

The Experience of Improvisation:
Contradictions and Anomalies

When we experience an improvisation, what exactly is it an experience *of?*

Improvisation is so familiar that we fail to realize how strange it is that we value it. The very same people who admire Flaubert for his five years of effort revising endless drafts of *Madame Bovary* shift some gear and admire David Antin for refusing to revise, for submitting a first draft. Why? Not only do artists like Antin refuse, somehow they refuse *on principle* to make the work as good as it could be. Then the same people who value *Madame Bovary* the more for its polish, seem to value the improvisation for its lack thereof. The audience does not merely *excuse* the improvisation. They savor the *lack.*

This apparent contradiction is only apparent. What audience and artist value about improvisation is an experience the Western aesthetic has traditionally scanted, but one which East Asia thought central to the art experience. (Hereafter, for brevity, I'll simply write *East Asian* as shorthand for the high cultural tradition of Han-ethnicity Northern China and postsinicized Japan and Korea.) It was made literally canonical by Hseih Ho's "Ku Hua P'in Lu" (late fifth century C.E.) (Siren 219-20). Western aestheticians are largely unaware how very different the Asian artworlds have been. The current Western artworld values Asian art, but for Western reasons; just as it values Yoruba work for Western reasons.

East Asian aesthetics will reveal what we too experience when we experience improvisation. The center of attention shifts from object to artist. We forego the greater aesthetic satisfaction we could gain from a revised, perfected object or from a memorized performance, because we believe ourselves to be gaining even more value from experiencing *the making of art*—that is, by experiencing creative human thought itself, the forward motion of the human mind, what Thomas Kuhn has described, in cultural history, as the work of the scientific "revolutionary."

To make so enormous a topic manageable, we need, for improvisation, a kind of *Brown v. Board of Education,* a test case stating the issues with unusual clarity. And so we came to see David Antin do a talk poem.

Refining the Term *Improvisation*

What, however, did we really see?

What *is* improvisation? Is it a genre, something like landscape or oratorio or sonnet? No, for while landscapes and oratorios and sonnets exist in one art (or, with metaphoric stretches like calling a Turner a grand opera filled with arias of paint, in two or three arts, at most) improvisation occurs in all the arts, without any metaphoric stretching at all. One finds it routinely, and importantly, in jazz *and* painting *and* dance. As we start to include improvisatory stand-up comedy and public speaking in the list, we realize there are few places in life where improvisation isn't known. I'm forced to call the term a mere designation, for I know of no genre which matches this. The only explanation is that improvisation is not inside *any* of the arts. Rather, they are sometimes inside *it.* Improvisation is a phenomenon which, to paraphrase Hopkins, plays in ten thousand places, the arts among them.

Antin and his best critics begin by carefully separating improvisations from spontaneous or automatic writing and even from superficially similar aleatory art, like John Cage's *4'33"* and Allan Kaprow's Happenings.

First, is there anything *materially there,* like color in a painting or sound in a sonata, that causes us to identify an Antin poem as an improvisation? How is an improvisation different from this essay's first draft? Is there any material difference between the two, anything we could literally point to? If a student puts off writing her paper until the night before it's due, I might give it a low grade, saying it's "still rough" or "needs work." If the student replied, "That isn't a rough draft, it's an improvisation, and I can't, on principle, revise it," is there something *in the work* she could point to, to support her claim?

In San Diego, in 1997, Antin graciously tried to answer that question during a taped interview about his life's work and goals, which lasted five full days. The transcript fills five hundred double-spaced pages. Listening to Antin speak and observing him at work during that five-day, marathon improvisation gave me the insights which, after three years' reflection, have crystallized in this essay.

In 1997 Antin started by showing how works routinely designated improvisations are not casual, aleatory, nor even first drafts. Antin took the time to read into the tape transcript a long quotation from Charles Hartman's book comparing Antin's methods with Charlie Parker's: "Probably the most prolific and inventive improviser in jazz was Charlie Parker, whose impromptu chorus on a familiar tune could become a jazz standard in its own right." Once, Parker's solo break on "Night in Tunisia" startled his fellow musicians so much they forgot to keep playing. Yet Hartman cites Thomas Owen's "voluminous" research showing how Parker "built" his improvisations "out of a little store of about a hundred motifs which

Owens catalogues in all their variations." Antin too not only invents, but reuses and recombines (here Hartman quotes Steven Fredman about Antin) "elements, stories, ideas . . . arranged musically like a succession of riffs rather than being spontaneously invented. . . ." (78)[3] Antin felt this distinction vital to any understanding of improvisation. During the five days of interviewing, this was the only time he read a critic's text into the record.

A week after the interview, I unexpectedly verified Antin's practice for myself. Antin performed a brief talk piece at a celebration in honor of his close friend and longtime U.C.—San Diego colleague Allan Kaprow's seventieth birthday. It's relevant to note that Kaprow is, of course, the inventor of the Happenings. I was startled to recognize a long "set of variations" which I had heard Antin do for the transcript.

Improvisation, then, is not mere spontaneity or automatic writing. Antin can be said to improvise *with* materials without having to *create* all the materials then and there. Combining is also improvising.

Antin, Cage, and Flaubert

This means that Antin's improvisations are not only art, but very much art *works,* very much composed. That firmly separates Antin's improvisations from fully aleatory art, of which the most famous example is John Cage's 4'33".[4] Although Cage and Antin admired, respected and encouraged each other, grouping the two together only confuses us about each.

Antin's compositions are nothing like Cage's Zen acceptance in 4'33". In the suggestive new language being created for evolutionary cladistics, the purported link between Cage and Antin, despite their superficial resemblances, is only convergence: bats and birds both fly, but they descend from different clades, different lineages.

Indeed, Antin's clade, far from being Cagean, runs directly back to Gustave Flaubert. Antin "endured arduous training in preparation for a novelistic career," Barry Alpert long ago reported. Antin even published "one highly-finished Flaubertian story, 'The Balanced Aquarium,' in the *Kenyon Review* (of all places)" (666). In the transcript, Antin recalls, in his youth, writing *several* novels before deciding the novel didn't suit him.

Alpert must have discarded this fact as anomalous, for he goes on, like Marjorie Perloff later, to trace Antin's affinities with Cage. Criticism imagines Antin leaving the novel, which he did, but only in the sense that birds are not the dinosaurs basal to their lineage.

Antin, invited to comment on that idea, protested. His work was *not* Flaubertian. "if there's anything i know it's flaubert! i tried to escape flaubert." He searched for improvisatory techniques not only in jazz but in "all the world's forms—in flamenco, in ragga music, the sitar and tabla variations." (He did not, for the record, search China or Japan.)

Yet—while Antin is surely not Flaubert—in one important way, Antin's work never *stopped* being Flauber*tian*. In the 1997 transcript Antin viscerally describes the way, like a running back hunting for daylight, he plunges, in the talk poems, to the right, to the left, trying to get to that moment when he finally says it right.

> see a lot of my work has to do
> with the notion of poetry as thinking the notion that you can get
> at poetry as thinking and the only way that you can get at any-
> thing as thinking is to think and what happens i i can find my
> way to think and once i start thinking its not exactly conversa-
> tional because im busy thinking and im sort of locked on trying to
> get towards meanings and open them up and try to find my way . . .
> once i start doing that this peculiar kind of concentration takes
> over and there is very little backing away from the stuff i mean i
> may circle it i may move around in it i may rethink something i
> may shift gears but im constantly working at it as if i were
>   as if i were a running back and the play was designed to go off
> tackle and no hole opened up off tackle and I had to find an open-
> ing and i look for a little daylight and im kind of moving from one
> place to another but i have to move fast but it doesn't feel fast
> because im constantly looking over the line for the opening
> through which you move one quick move and you get through[5]

Antin believes his effort is closer to Charlie Parker's than to Flaubert's, but his effort retains every important character of Flaubert's search for *le mot juste* except for two. Antin gives himself only one chance; and he takes the considerable risk of letting us watch him search. That is certainly not Flaubert, the arch-reviser, but it is in the direct Flaubertian line.

Nothing could be more foreign to the mature John Cage's practice and above all to what Cage put forward as his overriding goal—getting the artist's heroic personality out from between the audience and the world, so that the audience finally learns it can take the world straight (Cage 431). "Waiting for a bus we're present at a concert. Suddenly we stand on a work of art, the pavement." For instance, Cage lambastes Varese for allowing his "personality" to intrude in his music. The mortal sin of Western art, its ultimate failure, Cage argues, has been the romantic Western artist misusing art, not to lead us to contemplate the world, but to exhibit his artistic personality. All Cage's creative and novel uses of the Zhou Dynasty classic, *I Ching*—uses which have little to do with the *I Ching*'s original purposes in eleventh century B.C.E. China (Schwartz 390-403)—aim at removing the heroic Flaubertian artist from the stage. Antin, precisely opposite, takes center stage to give us *David Antin Tonight!*

The Problem Returns

Yet we are still stuck with our original problem. We have only delayed it.

Let us accept Antin's planned first drafts as improvisations; let us accept his partially rehearsed first drafts or even certain kinds of second drafts as improvisations; we still eventually reach the moment David Antin and I reached, looking at a talk poem he was unhappy with. The moment crystallized for me the larger aesthetic issue concerning improvisation and turned my attention to Asia for a solution.

The University of Chicago Press had a (legal, not aesthetic) contract with Antin to publish his collected essays and talk pieces, in the form he chose. When we were discussing a certain piece, he was plainly disappointed with it. The suspense had failed. Antin saw that all this particular piece needed was some pruning in the middle, yet he decided to decline publishing the piece in the Chicago collection rather than make the simple cut that would improve it.

While I had to admire Antin's ethics, I also had to wonder what he was being ethical about? Antin had spotted how to make what *he* believed would be an aesthetic improvement to the object. He didn't refuse on aesthetic grounds but on *ethical* grounds. He said he had an "understanding" with the audience. The piece was assumed to be an improvisation and, if revised, would no longer be. It would be aesthetically superior, but something more important would be lost.

"If the piece is better," I asked him, "then the audience is happy, and what is unethical about that? What are we trying to do here, anyway?" If their primary enjoyment of his improvisation, I wondered, was not their enjoyment of the best object possible, what exactly *were* they enjoying? They could only be willing to overlook the Antin improvisation's lack of all the formal qualities the fully revised, fully Flaubertian work had, because they were obtaining some greater kind of satisfaction from it. But what could that be? Granted, for Antin, *improvisation* did not mean spontaneous writing and submitting rough drafts. Granted, his talk poems were subtly polished, were art*works,* not Cagean chance. *Improvisation* still meant Antin deliberately abandoning, after one or at the most two drafts, the effort to give the audience the best object possible. What did the audience get from him that could ever make up for that?

The East Asian high cultural aesthetic tradition has an answer. Antin's refusal, while unfamiliar in the West, would have been far more familiar in an Asian artworld setting. From a calligrapher, for instance, it would be routine. That artworld illuminates what the West actually values about improvisation: a Confucian-humanist admiration for human prowess combines with a Taoist and Buddhist desire to share in the moment of enlightenment. (I rely on the reader to interpolate mentally the blizzard of phrases like *predominantly, in most instances, with notable exceptions, but not in the south,* that an undergraduate would demand I say. Otherwise the next section will be impossible to present in less than a volume. That will have to be this essay's contract, then, between writer and audience.)

The Western Tradition of the "Ideal" Object

Our problem has now put us in a position to break some new ground and notice a large and significant difference in orientation between Western and Eastern artworlds. As Thomas Kuhn writes, insights begin with anomalous facts, and ours has been the Western audience's odd agreement to accept improvisation, although the agreement automatically means getting a lesser art object.

I have spoken of Flaubert, for his revisions are proverbial, but in that respect Flaubert belongs to the oldest Western high artworld tradition of the arts. If any art historical statement is uncontroversial and supported by a consensus, it is the following: the doctrine most characteristic of the Western artworld from Aristotle's time to 1800, and at intervals since, has been the "Ideal." Let me briefly summarize Erwin Panofsky's history of the tradition in his classic history, *Idea.*

Plato had provoked this theory, really a defense of the art object's right to exist, by arguing that it had none. Plato argued that the ordinary world was itself an imitation of an idea/ideal, as a bed was an imitation of the perfect bed in the craftsman's mind. Art objects, then, were just an imitation of an imitation, a "third remove from the truth." What was the use of the stuff? Plato is no simple philistine. Plato, who would even ban most Greek myths from his ideal Republic as immoral, derogated the art object so that he could suggest, a moment later, that political and moral uses would redeem the otherwise third-rate thing.

Aristotle's rebuttal to Plato's attack (which satisfied the West so well it was repeated and refreshed down to Sir Joshua Reynolds's *Discourses)* started the "Ideal object" discourse, and granted the art object a dignity apart from its Platonic use as a mere teaching aid. Art objects, he countered, were sometimes no simple imitation of mere real things: the best *partook of the Ideal.* The artist combined the scattered excellences of the world into a perfected object better than any mere real thing. The Christians, as Panofsky shows, then had (like Marsiglio Ficino) no trouble adapting that doctrine to suggest an Ideal object's superiority to a world marr'd by sin.

Object-Centered Art and Artist-Centered Art

During the 2,300 years between Aristotle and its last great celebrant, Ingres, the Ideal object dominated the Western aesthetic discourse. After all, if the art object didn't offer you better than you could find in the real world, why bother with it? The artist's role became, inevitably, perfecting an object to the best of his ability. That had been my question to Antin. His declining to revise seemed, to my Western-educated sensibility, an abdication of the artist's primary responsibility. Western aesthetics, in the course of mounting the ideal defense, turned all its attention on the object. Western aesthetics is *object-centered.* In *Idea* Panofsky never questions that, but (it startles me to realize) it is an almost accidental by-product of the "ideal" discourse.

Historically, Asian aesthetics is *artist-centered.* We are scarcely aware that it is because the West is so object-centered that much of Asian aesthetics barely seems like aesthetics to us at all. Its criticism, often to our bewilderment, centers on the artist—on gaining contact with the artist and sharing his experience. (It would falsify Asian history to write "or her experience.")

Western aestheticians, obsessed with the object, have been embarrassed by, or have regarded as naive, the East's interest in reading the object for the artist. "It is commonly believed in China," the respected scholar Chiang Yee writes, in a 1973 book published by Harvard University Press, with an introduction by Sir Herbert Read, "that calligraphy expresses the personality of the writer. . . ." Well and good, but we are unprepared for the intensity of the Chinese scholar's interest in conjuring up the ancient artist, or the hero-worshipful tone. "The calligraphy of Su tung-P'o suggests to me a man fatter, shorter, more careless in nature than Mi Fei, but broad-minded, vigorous, a great laughter-maker and a great laugher . . ." (11-12). Such criticism is quite typical, and extends to painting as well, which was not really a separate art. So extensive an aesthetic orientation could stem only from even deeper cultural predispositions. As I will show, that interest wells naturally from deep cultural orientations in Taoism, Buddhism, and Confucianism.

East Asian Aesthetics in Relation to the Cultural Predispositions

I deliberately subtitled this essay "David Antin, Improvisation, *Asia*," rather than "*Asian aesthetics*" because improvisation takes us deep into Asian culture itself. One of the great principles of aesthetic analysis, and one of the reasons aesthetics matters philosophically, was often expressed by John Ruskin thus: "Tell me what you like and I'll tell you who you are." When we discuss aesthetics, we discuss precisely *what a culture likes,* and that is invariably revealing.

Chinese culture finds its "axial age," as Benjamin Schwartz and all others agree, in the 500s B.C.E.(2, 16-39); its preeminent expression, by Han times, is Confucianism, as the West terms the writings of the *ru jia,* the scholar school. (For a book-length discussion of these points, see my essays in *The Asian Pacific American Heritage.*) As the great Asianist William Theodore de Bary has relentlessly pointed out, when Asian dictators like Singapore's Lee Kuan Yew claim that so-called Asian values are anti-individualist and demand the subjection of the individual to the group, they falsify tradition. The Confucianists *(ru jia)* are concerned with the perfection of their activist sage, the *chun tze,* who is to the family what the flower is to the root. If the family didn't produce him, de Bary even argues, they wouldn't be interested in it. If the root sends up no flower, what's the point of it?[6] East Asian aesthetics bears de Bary out.

The Taoist countervoice to the worldly, humanist Confucian worldview emerges by the 200s B.C.E. But Taoism only disputes the nature of the hero sage, not his centrality. The collections associated with the names Lao Tsu *(Tao te Ching)* and Chuang Tsu are almost notoriously indifferent to the group and—in their concern for the sage's self perfection—willingly pay the price of his withdrawal from society. "Heaven and Earth have nothing to do with *ren* [human compassion and benevolence]. . . . Being truly wise has nothing to do with *ren*. To the Sage, the people are like the straw animals we burn during sacrifices." [7]

The Taoist is confident the inspiration his life affords the group more than compensates, socially, for his withdrawal. That's a given. If he "holds fast enough to the Silence," then, amazingly "the Ten Thousand Things of Life will all be acted on by him" (*The Way* 143). The modern West, by now almost unconsciously committed to the

Hegelian sense of history as impersonal forces and tides, "history without names," is constantly at a loss to deal with how effective certain individuals can be—the Gandhis and Gorbachevs and Martin Luther Kings. Asia has made cultivating such figures its central concern. Before German high romantic history, of course, the West had no difficulty believing that "history was the biography of great men." The East, before German romanticism in the form of Marx overwhelmed it as well, assumed so. Taoism and Confucianism primarily quarreled over what his nature was and how to produce him. (Again, it would utterly falsify both to add "or her.") Buddhism, when it finally arrived in China, only strengthened this orientation. It was creatively misinterpreted through China's experience of Taoism. Its most characteristic Chinese form, Ch'an, scraps the scriptures, despises language, and relies instead on an intuitive "direct transmission" between heroic "patriarchs" and *roshis,* "Masters," who radiate instruction through their very beings.[8]

The *Chun Tze* as Artist

This is why, although the West has been interested in the object, the Asian artworld, flowing out of its society's values, Confucianist, Taoist, and Buddhist, has—contrary to the West—inevitably been interested in the *chun tze* as artist. I deliberately paraphrase Thomas Carlyle's phrase "the Hero as Artist," for Carlyle's hero-worshipping aesthetic (very much a lone voice in the West) is the closest Western aesthetic to this position.

Western aesthetic criticism is uncomfortably aware that even the Chinese interest in Line and Form is not formal, but graphological. To us, it almost looks like handwriting analysis. Michael Sullivan acknowledges this aesthetic: "Not only is a man's writing a clue to his temperament, his moral worth, and his learning, but the uniquely ideographic nature of the Chinese script has charged each individual character with a richness of content and association the full range of which even the most scholarly can scarcely fathom" (185). The Chinese painters, Conrad Schirokauer adds, differ from the West "in that they conceive of their art in terms of calligraphy: both painting and calligraphy served the purpose of writing down on paper or silk the ideas the gentlemen had in their minds. . . . [C]alligraphy was prized as a revelation of the lofty character of its cultivated practitioner. . . ."[9]

Around 500 C.E., Hseih Ho gave this already ancient aesthetic its classic formulation. Hseih's epigrammatic Six Canons of painting (more literally, Six Laws, *liu fa*) were, Michael Sullivan reports, "so significant for the whole history of Chinese Painting" that "much—perhaps too much—has been written about [them]" (88). Mai Mai Sze, in the book based on her Bollingen lectures, devotes the better part of several chapters to Hseih Ho, since his principles "had existed long before his time," and his Six Canons "with slight modifications . . . were accepted as and have remained the general standards of painting and art criticism" (38).

Mimesis is respected ("Conform with the objects to give likeness") but it is only canon 3. Canons 1 and 2, which Sullivan, Sze, and Yee rightly consider primary, concern the famous *chi yun*, "spirit resonance," and its expression through the "bone manner use of the brush."

During the Sung Period five centuries later, those two principles were being explained, by Kuo Jo-Hsu, as entirely *traits of exalted character*: "the Spirit Resonance *(chi yun)* must be inborn in the painter. It can certainly not be acquired by skill or dexterity, nor can anyone arrive at it through months and years of study, it is secretly blended with the soul, one does not know how, yet it is there." Kuo, in the tenth century, summarized the five centuries since Hseih Ho: one experienced the *chun tze* artist's *chi yun* through learning how to read his line. Spirit resonance

may also be perceived in the styles of people's signatures. . . . [These] preserve the nobility and meanness, the adversities and successes (of the writer). How could calligraphy and painting fail to reflect the high or the low *chi yun*? Painting is (in this respect) quite the same as calligraphy. Master Yang said: "Words are sounds of the heart-mind (*shin*), calligraphy is painting of the heart-mind; both reveal whether the man is a superior character or of a low kind." (qtd. in Siren 76)

The classical East Asian canons or principles, Osvald Siren concluded, do *not* refer to Western formal qualities, what we mean by line, but really describe "virtues or merits depending *on the painter's character* as much as on his training and mastery of the means" (76).

Artists in the Christian West are routinely anonymous until the early Renaissance, frequently anonymous thereafter, and powerful critical schools up to the present day deride any attempt to proceed beyond the work to the artist. In sharp contrast, the Chinese by the Tang Dynasty are as interested in reading the artist's personality in the work as Thomas Carlyle would be. John Cage's fantasy (an enabling fantasy, which led to great work) of the self-effacing Oriental Artist is simply Orientalism. Certainly, the names of famous objects' makers have been lost, but that is entirely different from the idea of anonymity.

We don't talk about it in the West, but even trained art historians

often approach art this way too. We may not admit it, for we have
been taught that such interest is subartistic. Nonetheless, standing
in front of van Gogh's *Starry Night* at the Metropolitan Museum,
feeling the passion of the slashing lines, I am thrilled to be sharing
in his ecstasy before nature, his powerful *chi yun* resonating in me.
I even feel, in his painting's presence, awed and physically closer to
him, as if it were a holy relic. I was taught not to have such impure
feelings or, at least, not to admit them in print! Yet East Asian aesthetics believes that that ennobling contact with the painter-sage,
my spirit resonating with his, is precisely *the* great experience in
art.

The Asian artworld's hypothesis about that experience's importance to us, even if we are (as I am) embarrassed to admit it, is a
falsifiable hypothesis and can be tested. If we really react only, or
most importantly, to the object and are not seeking contact with
that moment of thought, it should make no difference to us when
that van Gogh, say, is proven a forgery. Not a molecule of the object
changes. The Western aesthetic must predict that we merely shrug,
remark on the death of the author, perhaps, and enjoy the object as
ever.

In fact, the discovery so completely destroys our interest in the
object that our aversion for such fakes puzzles Western aesthetics.
Books are written about the "problem." It's only a problem for Western aesthetics. In the Eastern artworld it is assumed that the
greater part of one's experience was that experience of the *chun tze*
as Artist. Once that is lost, and one experiences not van Gogh re-
ceiving the Vision but some sly fellow coldheartedly deceiving you,
of course the best is lost, no matter what pigments remain on the
canvas. The Asian aesthetic predicts we turn from a fake in disgust,
exactly as we do, despite the lack of change in the object.

One *reads* the art, more than looks at it, and one reads it to draw
closer to, and be ennobled by, the heroic *chi yun,* spirit-resonance of
the *chun tze* who produced it, to experience with him the movement
of his mind in creation, the supreme moment of the most unique
human ability, which, in East and West, has often been regarded as
the paradigm of the highest human abilities in all fields. That aesthetic follows inevitably from the cultural consensus about the
power of a *chun tze*'s redemptive presence and moral example.

That first moment of inspiration is erased, lost, by the act of revision. It is even lost if too much preparation is allowed. So the audience not only permits Antin to do without revision, they would be
upset if they discovered he had revised and was merely reciting.
That would be somehow fake. They've come to experience the sacred
moment in which the *chun tze* becomes a *chun tze,* in which the sage

becomes sagely by reaching his inspiration. In the moments that Antin calls tuning, they vibrate with him, like smaller tuning forks taking on the resonance of a larger one: *chi yun,* spirit-resonance. The audience willingly trades the (relatively minor, to this way of thinking) aesthetic improvements the *object* could acquire if Antin were permitted to write the poem beforehand and recite it to them. They can gain those perfections only by losing their contact with Antin's moment of vision and the *chi yun* flowing out from it. So Antin and the calligrapher refuse, on principle, to revise a work even though the object would improve, formally. They both would rather throw it away.

The Object Isn't What the Audience Is After, but the Experience

That possibly explains why China, in sharp contrast to the West, made the (to us) puzzling choice of calligraphy as its high art. "From the merchant who hoists up his newly written shop sign with ceremony and incense, " Michael Sullivan observes, "to the poet whose soul takes flight in the brilliant sword dance of the brush, calligraphy is revered above all other arts" (185). Calligraphy reveals the sage's personality as no other art can, so high artists, seeking to reveal their spirit-resonance, ultimately gravitated to that art.

That art then gravitated to media, which displayed the improvising moment by forcing the work to be, of necessity, an improvisation: silk, and above all, rice paper. The West, valuing the revised, perfected object, abandoned egg-based tempera for oil painting as soon as it was perfected in Jan van Eyck's lifetime, precisely (it is always said) for its revision possibilities. Rice paper permits no revision; does not even permit hesitation. Writing with a brush on rice paper is like writing with a felt tip pen on a paper towel: nothing can be erased, but if you become cautious and slow down, the paper instantly absorbs ink from the brush and creates an ugly cloud around the line.

Ut pictura poesis: as in calligraphy, so in poetry. Poetry, considered the highest verbal art, often claims to be, in the East, improvisation. Chinese criticism from the Tang dynasty on, traditionally describes the poets as gentlemen seated at drinking parties, firing off the poems in improvisatory contests. The written texts of poems themselves seek to further this impression, noting dates, times, occasions. Whether such notes are strictly true or not, the ideal is improvisatory. Japan carries the idea even further, for its highest poetic form, haikai (which we now irrevocably call haiku) evolves from the closing lines of improvisation contests.

Japan, through the influence of Ch'an Buddhism (Zen) carries the aesthetic to its extreme in many arts. I am tempted to argue that we see the continuation of this aesthetic even in their ceramics. The high art sometimes literally bears the fingerprints of its maker, and in its irregularity and its refusal to hide the marks of creation it brings the artist firmly to the audience's mind and, indeed, to its hands. This Japanese valuing of the artist's performance, above any object, culminates in the tea ceremony, like Soin's at Daisen-in, an improvisation of motion, talk, taste, enacted by a master.

In the mature Tea Ceremony we encounter an art form the West barely has terms for—and it is our closest parallel to Antin's talk poems. In both cases, the occasion is a *ceremony*. There is a master. There is no script, but the master improvises on top of what Antin calls a planned set of variations. The audience sits intimately with the sage, and his talk is a kind of tuning, with the ultimate goal a moment of communion, of *chi yun,* in which the audience's spirits resonate with the Master and with each other. [10]

The Art of Thought

The Eastern tradition, then, explains to us better than the object-obsessed Western tradition can, what we value about improvisation. The experience of an Antin talk poem is as much of Antin as it is of the poem, the chance to watch the poet/philosopher think.

In natural history museums, of late, it has become popular to expose the work areas, to let the public experience, with the paleontologist, the excitement of seeing the animal appear in the stone. The Stanford Linear Accelerator conducts tours in which one watches the scientists search for ever-smaller pieces of the atom. When one enters the hollowed-out hill where the gun sits, how extraordinary it would be if, at that moment, you were present when a new quark or gluon appeared.

David Antin takes the tremendous gamble of opening his laboratory to the viewing public. The public understands the contract, and willingly lets Antin forego either preparations or improvements significant enough to turn the experience into a dull reenactment, however more concise or polished. They want to be there when the electron smashes the atom and the particles spew forth. "The fine delight which fathers thought," Hopkins wrote of that moment, "the strong spur"—he takes a powerful image from glassblowing—"live and lancing as a blowpipe flame/breathes once, and quenched quicker than it came/leaves yet the Mind the mother of immortal son" (67).

We seek in improvisation to experience, with David Antin, the instant of that miraculous lancing flame. The improvisation is the art of thought itself, and that is why (unlike the landscape or sonata) it can exist in all artistic media. We find it in the arts of speech, music, visual arts. One could add the laboratory tour. The interest isn't in the medium; it is in the human thought encountering the medium—any medium—and lancing it with flame.

NOTES

[1] I use *artworld* in Arthur Danto's well-known sense, to mean "the historically ordered world of artworks enfranchised by theories." For a discussion of the term see Leonard, *Into the Light* (197).

[2] See also Antin's influential "Modernism and Postmodernism: Approaching the Present in American Poetry."

[3] See also Fred Garber for a chapter, "David Antin: the Boundaries of Talking." Stephen Cope, this issue's editor, adds: "Hank Lazer's essay on Antin and [Jerry] Rothenberg, 'Thinking Made in the Mouth' in Lazer's *Opposing Poetries,* vol. 1 (Northwestern, 1996) is one of the more interesting that I've encountered, and touches on the social aspect of Antin's talk practices. Michael Davidson deals with Antin in his essay 'Technologies of Presence' (alongside Ginsberg, Laurie Anderson, and Steven Benson) in a fairly intriguing way also, discussing a talk piece Antin delivered over the radio a few years back, and the effects this shift in venue had on the work itself, as well as its (now disembodied, now distant) audience. That's in *Ghostlier Demarcations: Modern Poetry and Material World* (U.C. Press, 1997), 206-12, also reprinted in *Sound States,* ed. Adelaide Morris (Iowa: U. of Iowa Press, 1997)." Citation from a letter to the author.

[4] For a full consideration of John Cage and *4'33"* see Leonard, *Into the Light* 117-93.

[5] Unpublished transcript by Stephen Cope of 1997 David Antin interview with George Leonard.

[6] 1997-1998 letters, de Bary to Leonard, and New York interview transcript with Leonard, August 1998. I'm grateful to Professor de Bary for inviting me to attend a three-day conference revising the Asian Studies canon for de Bary's standard editions of the works at Columbia University Press.

[7] Lao Tsu, *Tao te Ching,* chapter 5. Translation mine.

[8] Zen was a "special transmission outside the scripture" from the *roshi* or Master. See "On the Buddha's Raft" in *Into the Light* (146-74).

[9] While considering the high artworld, let us pause to record—with some amusement—that the Asian high artworld, like the Western high artworld, battles a longstanding popular tradition—and it's the same popular tradition! First, artists East and West must contend with political people who rank their works strictly by their tendency to promote virtue. Second, uneducated people simply value the paintings by how closely they resemble the objects they purport to represent. ("While the common people . . . ob-

serve most reverently the likeness of the shapes, I avoid such vulgar and common points" Li qtd. in Siren 230.) On a slightly higher level of sophistication—the level of Philostratus' *Imagines*—the Asian popular tradition glories in man's ability to counterfeit nature, mixed with nervousness about whether Frankensteins and Golems might accidentally come to life this way. This and that painter reportedly painted the eyes in last, for fear of being watched; one man sticks a pin in his painting of a lover, and the woman herself immediately feels pain there, so perfectly has he captured her soul in paint. We even find in the East the same social nervousness toward poetry which underlies Reynolds's *Discourses,* for, as in the West, writing was educated, white-collar work, while the painters, who worked more obviously with their hands, seemed to many just glorified craftsmen. ("Chen Ssu Wang said: 'The art of literary composition was started by scholars; the art of painting by men of skill" [222].)

[10]See "Tea," by Kakuzo Okakura, in Leonard, *Asian Pacific Heritage* 219-29. For the Tea Ceremony, the most relevant work is Soshitsu Sen XV. In 1964 Soshitsu Sen succeeded his father as the hereditary Fifteenth Grand Master of the Urasenke School of Tea. An audience that has experienced an Antin talk poem is well equipped to understand this book and why the Tea Master's work is considered art. The Master's serving of the tea breaks the fourth wall between artist and audience as little else can; the tea enlists two more senses in the event, through its scent and its taste. I thank Kyoko Tanaka for taking me to a Tea Ceremony at Daisen-in, and Y. F. Du for showing me Chinese versions in Southern China and Beijing. Almost nothing's been written about the Chinese Tea Ceremony, which vanished under Mao and is being reintroduced in the form of luxury teahouses from Taiwan.

WORKS CITED

Alpert, Barry. "Post-Modern Oral Poetry: Buckminster Fuller, John Cage, and David Antin." *boundary 2* 3 (1975): 665-81.

Antin, David. "Is There a Post Modernism?" *Romanticism, Modernism, Postmodernism*. Ed. Harry R. Garvin. Lewisberg: Bucknell UP, 1980. 127-35.

———. "Modernism and Postmodernism: Approaching the Present in American Poetry." *boundary 2* 1.1 (1972): 98-133.

———. "radical coherency." *OARS* 1 (1981): 177-91.

———. "the river." *what it means to be avant-garde*. New York: New Directions, 1993. 123-53.

———. *tuning*. New York: New Directions, 1984.

Bary, William Theodore de, ed. *Confucianism and Human Rights*. New York: Columbia UP, 1998.

Cage, John. *I-VI*. Cambridge: Harvard UP, 1990.

Garber, Frederick. *Repositionings: Readings of Contemporary Poetry, Photography, and Performance Art*. University Park: Pennsylvania State UP, 1995.

Hartman, Charles O. *Jazz Text: Voice and Improvisation in Poetry, Jazz, and Song.* Princeton: Princeton UP, 1991.

Hopkins, Gerard Manley. "Thou Art Indeed Just, Lord, if I Contend." *Gerard Manley Hopkins: Poems and Prose.* Ed. W. H. Gardner. Baltimore: Penguin, 1953. 67.

Kuhn, Thomas. *The Structure of Scientific Revolutions.* Chicago: U of Chicago P, 1970.

Leonard, George J. *Into the Light of Things: The Art of the Commonplace from Wordsworth to John Cage.* Chicago: U of Chicago P, 1994.

———, ed. *The Asian Pacific American Heritage: A Companion to Literature and Arts.* New York: Garland, 1999.

Panofsky, Erwin. *Idea: A Concept in Art Theory.* 1924. Trans. Joseph J. S. Peake. New York: Harper Icon, 1968.

Sayre, Henry. *The Object of Performance.* Chicago: U of Chicago P, 1989.

Schirokauer, Conrad. *A Brief History of Chinese and Japanese Civilizations.* 2nd ed. New York: Harcourt Brace, 1989.

Schwartz, Benjamin I. *The World of Thought in Ancient China.* Cambridge: Harvard Belknap, 1985.

Sen, Soshitsu, XV. *Tea Life, Tea Mind.* New York: Weatherhill, 1979.

Siren, Osvald. *The Chinese on the Art of Painting: Translations and Comments.* New York: Schocken, 1963.

Sullivan, Michael. *The Arts of China.* 3rd ed. Berkeley: U of California P, 1984.

Sze, Mai Mai. *The Way of Chinese Painting: Its Ideas and Technique.* New York: Random House, 1959.

The Way and Its Power [Tao te Ching]. Trans. Arthur Waley. New York: Grove, 1958.

Yee, Chiang. *Chinese Calligraphy: An Introduction to Its Aesthetic and Technique.* Cambridge: Harvard UP, 1973.

Talk Poem as Visual Text:
David Antin's "Artist's Books"

Marjorie Perloff

David Antin is primarily known as a brilliant *talker,* a performance artist or improvisator whose talk pieces belong, in the words of Michael Davidson, "somewhere among a standup comedian's rap, a storyteller's fable and a formal lecture."[1] Antin has been compared to Lenny Bruce and to Spalding Gray:[2] indeed, he has himself insisted on his commitment to "talk" rather than "writing," as, for example, in the headnote to "what am I doing here?" (1973), where he declares, "if robert lowell is a poet i don't want to be a poet   if robert frost was a poet i don't want to be a poet   if socrates was a poet ill consider it."[3] Socrates, in this scheme of things, because, in Antin's view, his is a form of "talk" that epitomizes the "thinking capacity of language," and hence "poetry as inventive thinking."[4]

But unlike Socrates, whose "talk" is known to us only through its written representation by Plato, Antin transcribes his own talks in a highly particularized format: unjustified left and right margins, lowercase letters, spaces (usually five or six characters) between phrases, and the absence of all punctuation except—intriguingly—the question mark. An Antin transcription, as Davidson points out, "is in no sense a replica of the talk itself. Antin freely edits and modifies the talk so that it becomes a representation, not a mimesis, of speech."[5] The printed text is usually somewhat longer than the original talk (Antin tends to add and amplify), and years may elapse between performance and publication. Indeed, some of my own favorite Antin talk pieces—notably, "The Poetry of Ideas and the Idea of Poetry" (on Wittgenstein and Marx) delivered at the West Coast Humanities Institute at Berkeley in 1984—have yet to be transcribed and published. However "improvisatory" the talk, in other words, the written transcript is nothing if not calculated. As Frederick Garber noted acutely, the refusal to justify margins or use punctuation may well be calculated to "undo the immobility" of standard prose, but "the spaces on the page, whatever their status as counterparts to the pauses in the performance, never go out of being, never cease to make their statements against the discomfiting lies of fixity, even as they are, themselves, irrevocably fixed" (79).

There is, in short, nothing casual or improvisatory about the placement of the words on a given Antin page. Indeed, one could argue, Antin's talk pieces, beginning with "Talking at Pomona" (1972), exhibit a form of Concrete poetry or, more accurately "Concrete prose" in the tradition of Gertrude Stein's prose or such "Concrete" works as Haroldo de Campos's *Galáxias*, with its not-quite-verse, not-quite-prose page-long constellations, where repetition, punning, spacing, and unjustified margins create a tense visual field.

Such attentiveness to visual layout is hardly surprising, given that Antin's early Fluxus-related texts were designed with the care one usually associates with artist's books. *definitions* (Caterpillar, 1967), for example, designed by the poet's wife, the artist Eleanor Antin, is a graph paper spiral-bound notebook, in which typographical layout, handwritten addenda, and ink diagrams like "Owl and Rat," an astronomical drawing that "illustrates" part 2 ("the constellation") of the found-text sequence called "The Black Plague" (see figure 1) combine to create a parody textbook.[6]

In part 3 of *definitions* Antin takes the sequence of propositions that deal with pain (#244 ff.) in Wittgenstein's *Philosophical Investigations*—a series itself made up of short disjunct visual units on the page—and rearranges them so that key phrases like "what is the grammar of pain" and "the future is hidden from us" stand out on the page as isolated units. Further: the vertical lines of the graph paper act as dividers, so that we have effects like the following (*definitions* 31):

| he might | not see c | ruelty as | cruelty | cruel |ty blindn| ess |

Another book whose visual design is integral to its meanings is *Code of Flag Behavior* (1968), with its pseudo-American flag (red and white vertical candy stripes with blue insert on white field at bottom right) on the cover (see figure 2), its red and white frontispiece pages followed by the title page with blue lettering, and its internal spacing, as in "the marchers":

by walking together   they will not feel all alone
their keynote was joyful   lending an aspect to their ardors
that drizzle will not dim   in spite of their protest

and then the shift to capitals a few lines further down:

ALL YOU NEED TO MAKE LOVE   IS THE LOVERS
ALL YOU NEED TO MAKE PLAYS   IS THE PLAYERS
ALL YOU NEED TO MAKE JOYS   IS THE JOYFUL[7]

And a third—perhaps the most striking of the "pre-talk poem" volumes—is the 1972 *Talking*, which Antin designed himself. Here the outside and inside front and back covers are based on his own photographic piece called "30 days of the News." As Antin tells it:

I had set myself the task of photographing every day for 30 days a scene near a newspaper dispenser in such a manner that you could read the headline of the day while seeing the weirdly contrasting San Diego environments to which this news was being reported. The covers consist of my layout of the contact prints. This "daily" photo work went with the "dailyness" of the text pieces—especially the daily November Exercises.[8]

The resulting images (see figure 3) anticipate such later sequential photoworks as Robbert Flick's Wilshire and Pico Boulevard series, and, as Antin suggests, these images are absolutely in sync with a text like the opening "November exercises," in which the exact times of observation form a column placed to the left of the text margin, giving us entries like the following, in which sober documentary notation and Wittgensteinian definition come together in an absurdist mix:

(12:15 PM) She kept her head and he lost his. She telephoned the fire department and he drove up over the curb into a tree. Otherwise the whole house might have burnt down.

(12:17 PM) When the rain lets up the drug will wear off.

(12:20 PM) When you blow up a building you make it smaller.[9]

The later pieces in *Talking* resemble Cage's lectures in *Silence* (1962) in their use of different typographic fonts, boldface, and italics for emphasis. And the final piece, "Talking at Pomona," which was to be the first of the talk poems, is a forty-two page tour de force, there being no paragraphing or pauses between units, no periods or commas, no justified margins, but internal spacing throughout, so that the page looks like an all-over abstract painting (figure 4).

In his widely cited essay "Some Questions about Modernism," published roughly at the same time as this first talk piece (1974), Antin remarks that Gertrude Stein's portraits like "Ada" or "short stories" like "Miss Furr and Miss Skeene" are more properly to be considered as "language constructions":

They were presented in a "prose" format—with capital letters beginning what look like sentences, periods closing them and periodic paragraphing.

. . . prose is a kind of concrete poetry with justified margins. It is essentially characterized by the conventions of printing and the images of grammar and logic and order to which they give rise. But whatever it looks like, a characteristic passage from "Miss Furr and Miss Skeene" is poetry in any intelligent sense of the word." (emphasis mine)[10]

And Antin goes on to quote the following passage from "Miss Furr and Miss Skeene":

There were some dark and heavy men there then. There were some who were not so dark. Helen Furr and Georgine Skeene sat regularly with them. They sat regularly with the ones who were dark and heavy. They sat regularly with the ones who were not so dark. They sat regularly with the ones that were not so heavy. They sat with them regularly, sat with some of them. They went with them regularly, went with them. They were regular then, they were gay then, they were where they wanted to be then where it was gay to be then, they were regularly gay then.[11]

"This," says Antin, "is a traditional phrase poetry in spite of the illusion of punctuation, with its seemingly orthodox commas and periods, that at times seem almost appropriate but then become as irrelevant as flyspecks randomly distributed over a musical score. Stein's language is as difficult to contain within the page punctuation conventions of 'prose' as *Beowulf* or the *Iliad*, which were maddeningly punctuated even in scholarly editions. . . . In a profoundly traditional sense, this is a very elegant prosody; but it is a prosody immanent in English intonation, not the arbitrary conventions of meter" (15).

Prosody in what sense? Despite its "prose costume," Antin argues, "Miss Furr and Miss Skeene" is clearly "poetry" in its collocation of "shared recurring words that are systematically placed and displaced in the slightly varying pitch curves of the different length phrases and sentences" (15). Indeed, read aloud, the passage's rhythmic repetitions suggest lineation:

> They sat regularly with the ones who were dark and heavy.
> They sat regularly with the ones who were not so dark.
> They sat regularly with the ones that were not so heavy.
> They sat with them regularly, sat with some of them.

What Antin doesn't say, concentrating as he does on dismantling formalist (specifically Jakobsonian) notions of "poetry" as an "arbitrary, conventional, overstructured phonological arrangement" (16), is that Stein's prose is not only as phonologically structured as is most "poetry" (i.e., verse), but that it is also highly formalized visually, that, in other words, it really *is* concrete poetry with justified margins. For although, in Stein's case, the number of words per line can vary considerably according to page and font size, the words "dark," "heavy," and "regularly" and "gay" inevitably stand out, as do "they," "them," "there," and "then." Indeed, visually, "they" and "them" (the "dark and heavy men," who were also "not so dark" and "not so heavy") merge with the "there-then" landscape of Helen Furr and Georgine Skeene, a there-then that will be over by story's end. The proper names, moreover, catch the reader's eye as soon as s/he scans the page in question, the oddly spelled *Furr* and foolishly rhyming Georgine Skeene standing out graphemically in the largely monosyllabic visual field.

Later in the essay, Antin takes up the issue of metaphor versus metonymy in poetry, disputing Jakobson's now classic discussion.[12] "The idea of 'contiguity,' " Antin suggests, "doesn't seem sufficient to explain what happens when the notion of 'color' is situated in the context of 'wine,' " since wine is not only red, white, or rosé, but characterized by a complicated set of social contexts. Port, for example, is not referred to as "red wine" even though that's what it technically is, because port fulfills a specific social function as part of an after-dinner ritual. Metonymy is thus a question of context as well as of contiguity: " 'Forks' will evoke 'knives,' 'spoons,' 'food,' 'tables,' ashtrays,' 'air conditioning,' and 'The Light Cavalry Overture' or anything else through a chain of proximal connections that is not blocked by other contexts or lack of energy in the interpreter" (21).

Not just contiguity as such but *contiguity in context:* although Antin doesn't cite Wittgenstein here, his is clearly a Wittgensteinian reading ("The meaning of a word is its use in the language") and an extremely useful one for revising the Jakobsonian definition of metonymy. "By context," Antin has remarked recently, "what I mean is that when the word 'red' hits the word 'wine' the lexeme pair triggers a set of associations with remembered images or narrative scenes—tastings in Provence or in the Napa Valley, lunches on the Lido, advertisements in the *New Yorker,* whatever. Forming the invisible linkages of the metonymic chains . . . are sets of potential narratives our memories can provide, that support or block certain connections."[13]

But there is a further complication. When Jakobson associated metaphor with poetry (as the figure par excellence of similarity and hence image-making), metonymy with prose, he was thinking of the "realist" prose of Tolstoy and Chekhov. "Following the path of contiguous relationships," he writes, "the Realist author metonymically digresses from the plot to the atmosphere and from the characters to the setting in time and space. He is fond of synecdochic details. In the scene of Anna Karenina's suicide Tolstoy's artistic attention is focused on the heroine's handbag" ("Two Aspects" 111). Metonymy, Jakobson further notes, is not confined to verbal art: cubist painting, he argues, is a system of metonymies as is, for example, Eisenstein's film montage (see "Two Aspects" 111). But, observing as he did a strict separation of the genres and artistic forms, Jakobson has nothing to say about the graphemic—almost ideogrammatic—metonymies that operate, not only semantically or visually, as Jakobson suggests, but also ideogrammatically within *writing* itself, thus furthering the process whereby the larger metonymic connections (many of them also absorbing metaphoric elements into the narrative) are laid out.

The notion of a graphemic metonymy seems to be inherent in Antin's discussion of poetry as the "language art":

"Prose" is the name for a kind of notational style. It's a way of making language look responsible. You've got justified margins, capital letters to begin graphemic strings which, when they are concluded by periods, are called sentences, indented sentences that mark off blocks of sentences that you call paragraphs. This notational apparatus is intended to add probity to that wildly irresponsible, occasionally illuminating and usually playful system called language. Novels may be written in "prose"; but in the beginning no books were *written* in prose, they were *printed* in prose." ("Some Questions" 27)

The implication is that when, as in *Finnegans Wake* or in the "prose" of Stein's portraits and fictions, this "notational apparatus" is not observed (whether or not the right margin is justified), we move in the direction of the poetic. And not only is this a matter of semantic relationships but of the material text as well. Take the passage from "Miss Furr and Miss Skeene" cited above and you will note that the visual contiguities produced by eye rhyme (e.g., "there" / "were"/ "where"), reinforced by the heavy stressing on "then," followed by a pause, reach a crescendo in the last sentence, which may be diagrammed according to the following paths:

*Repetition and near repetition of **then***: **They** were regular **then**, **they** were where **they** wanted to be **then**, where it was gay to be **then**, **they** were regularly gay **then.**

*Repetition and near repetition of **were***: They **were** regular then, they **were where** they wanted to be then, **where** it was gay to be then, they **were** regularly gay then.

Rhyme: **They** were regular then, **they** were where **they** wanted to be then, where it was **gay** to be then, **they** were regularly **gay** then.

*Alliteration of **w's** and **g's***: They **were** regular then, they **were** where they **w**anted to be then **w**here it **w**as **g**ay to be then, they **w**ere re**g**ularly **g**ay then.

And in the visual constellation of the paragraph itself, "Helen Furr" and "Georgine Skeene" stand out as different, not only semantically but visually: Helen Furr's "u" is the only "u" in the passage and the double "r" of "Furr" is an oddity; Georgine Skeene is equally "different" for bearing a name that rhymes so foolishly, especially in the context of the surrounding low-key monosyllables.

How does this kind of structuring work in Antin's own talk pieces? The poet misleads us a bit when, in the headnote to *talking at the boundaries*, he writes:

> *these talks were worked out with no sense of a page in mind*
> *the texts are not "prose"   which is as I see it a kind*
> *of "concrete poetry with justified margins"   while*
> *these texts are the notations or scores of oral poems*
> *with margins consequently unjustified*

Read against the discussion of Stein's prose in the *Occident* essay, this declaration, regularly cited in discussions of Antin's talk pieces, is somewhat puzzling. In the very example before us, "mind" rhymes with "kind" in the line beneath it. Coincidence? More important, Antin here falls back into the dichotomy between oral and written, verse and prose, that he himself has so regularly abjured. "Notations or scores of oral poems" are clearly not the same thing *as* those poems. Indeed, if there were no difference, why, living as we do in the age of tape, CD, and digital reproduction, transcribe for the page at all? And why take months—sometimes years—to do so and then put the texts between two covers?

Consider the case of one of Antin's finest talk pieces, "the death of the hired man," which is not included in his three talk poetry collections but was published in the catalog *Siah Armajani: A Poetry Lounge*, edited by Michael H. Smith, who curated the poetry series held at Cal Tech's Baxter Art Gallery in the spring of 1982. This catalog has introductory material, photographs of the participating poets for the series (the others were Jerome Rothenberg, Jerome J. McGann, Clayton Eshleman, Oscar Mandel, and Richard Howard), a biography and exhibition record of the conceptual artist Armajani, as well as twelve photographs of his "poetry lounge," many of them interspersed with Antin's text. Part catalog, part artist's book, *Siah Armajani* is thus a strikingly interactive work, in which a visual artist, Armajani, is positioned between two poets: his contemporary, David Antin, and the "Great American" modernist poet Robert Frost, lines from whose "Mending Wall" are stenciled on the individual desks, and whose text is printed in its entirety preceding the artist's biographical and bibliographical materials. The setting and occasion give Antin a chance to lay out, in a particularly compelling way, his poetics, especially his resistance to certain kinds of poetic artifice and his attachment to metonymy as structuring principle.

Armajani's installation transforms the space of the Baxter Art Gallery into a pseudo-New England schoolroom (or church or meeting house) with rows of little wooden desks and benches (figure 5), hinged knotty-pine bookcases along the walls, some rectangular, some crisscrossed and hence more decorative than useful since they hold almost no books (figure 6), knotty-pine doors and shelving, and a lectern with a cratelike vertical wood panel, oddly separating "teacher" (or preacher) from his audience (figure 7). "Armajani," writes the curator Michael H. Smith, "sees transformation as a process that depends on how the user chooses to view or participate in the installation. Some come to read and listen to poetry. Some come to see, walk around, and touch sculpture. . . . The choice is the user's."[14]

But as Antin observes near the beginning of "the death of the hired man," the choice is not quite the user's: "one thing I didnt expect   that went beyond all my expectations /   was   robert frost that robert frost should be here /. . . . [and] that the entire poem 'mending wall' would be / stencilled line for line across all the desk tops / separating the people on the benches from me up here/ at my pulpit" (*Siah Armajani* 19-20; see figure 8). The irony, of course, is that Frost epitomizes precisely the qualities Antin doesn't like in what he calls "genteel" verse: "if robert frost was a poet," he had earlier declared in his introduction to "what am I doing here?," "I don't want to be a poet" (*talking at the boundaries* 1).

I have discussed elsewhere the performative mode of Antin's talk piece, as well as its use of digression to pinpoint the relationship of Antin's own "death of the hired man" to Frost's (in the well-known poem by that title).[15] But here I want to concentrate on the poem's visual text as it operates in its particular context. We might note, to begin with, that Frost's forty-five line poem is reproduced on page 9, facing the photograph of the South Gallery (see figure 8), so that we have it in mind before we read about Armajani or begin to read Antin's own poem. Here is the opening:

> Something there is that doesn't love a wall,
> That sends the frozen ground-swell under it
> And spills the upper boulders in the sun,
> And makes gaps even two can pass abreast.

> The work of hunters is another thing:
> I have come after them and made repair
> Where they have left not one stone on a stone,
> But they would have the rabbit out of hiding,
> To please the yelping dogs. The gaps I mean,
> No one has seen them made or heard them made.
> But at spring mending-time we find them there.
> (*Siah Armajani* 9)

Whereas Armajani's installation (with its state-of-the-art fluorescent lighting and fake hinges) is a pastiche of the New England schoolroom, Frost's poem purports to be the real thing: a dramatic monologue spoken by the poet-farmer who wants to break down the walls, not only between farms but between human beings, wants things to be *natural*. But as the eye takes in Armajani's installation on the left and "Mending Wall" on the right, it may well strike us that the print column which is Frost's poem is no more "natural" than is Armajani's "schoolroom." There is nothing natural, after all, about the poem's meter—iambic pentameter—which is scrupulously followed throughout, the only deviation coming when the neighbor speaks—"He ónly sáys, 'goôd fénces máke goôd neíghbors' "—a line of eleven syllables rather than ten, with a feminine ending, the pattern repeated in the poem's last line, "He sáys agaín, 'Goôd fénces máke goôd neíghbors.' "[16]

From a visual standpoint, "Mending Wall" is a vertical rectangle, a fully "walled" form. Each line begins with a capital letter, most lines are endstopped, and punctuation functions normally, as it would in prose. Frost's syntax is especially curious. On the whole, the poet tries to capture the colloquialism of natural speech (e.g., "We keép the wáll betweén us ás we gó"), but he evidently cannot resist inversions for special effect, as in the famous opening, "Something there is that doesn't love a wall." As Antin puts it in "the death of the hired man":

> though not only have you never heard anyone speak it you
> can't even imagine anyone speaking it in precisely that way
>   because you suspect quite rightly that something called
> meter has turned an english sentence back on itself to make it
> sound more poetical more important and quaint   something
>   there is for sure that goes around turning over english
>   sentences like "i let my neighbor behind the hill know" into "i
> let my neighbor know beyond the hill" which is too bad
>   because if there was something wild and whimsical in
>   this poem that didn't   respect walls you might suppose it
> wouldn't respect meter either (*Siah Armajani* 24)

Here Antin is doing no more than taking at face value the formalist rule that form equals content, that the *how* is inextricable from the *what*. Why, he asks, does a poem that purports to dislike walls, "that wants them down," create walls of its own by inverting word order so awkwardly? And why, one might add, pad lines with filler, as in

Nó ône has seén them máde or heárd them máde

or

Befóre I buílt a wáll I'd ask to knów
What I was wálling ín and wálling oút.

What is the difference between "I'd ask to know / What I was walling in" and "I'd ask / What I was walling in"? There seems to be no good answer except that that fifth foot has to come from somewhere.

Antin is especially amusing about Frost's "elves" in the following passage:

Something there is that doesn't love a wall,
That wants it down. I could say "Elves" to him,
But it's not elves exactly, and I'd rather
He said it for himself.

Antin responds, "there is no way that robert frost could have said / elves to him   he could not and would not have said / elves to him because if he had ever said elves to / him he would never have been able to face his neighbor /   again across any wall at all   and of course that's / exactly what robert frost wanted to continue to do/   to face his neighbors across his wall and be taken / for a new england farmer   sort of" (*Siah Armajani* 25).

Frost's "elves" have an interesting relationship to the objects in the Armajani poetry lounge. The bookshelf hinges, for example, hinges that Antin analyzes at length in a hilarious sequence, turn out to be fake, in that "the joined things prevent the joint from / moving," Armajani having assembled separate pieces of wood and "hinged / the two loose ends together to form a hanging 'v' from / which you couldn't budge them if you tried   because / the length of each wooden flap prevents the other one   from moving" (*Siah Armajani* 27). "These hinges," then, "are not hinges / at all but images of hinges   or synecdoches that /   as individual hinges expend all their energy calling up / the class of hinges of which they are merely representatives" (*Siah Armajani* 27).

Not hinges but the images of hinges, not a bench but the image of a bench—Armajani has created, not a New England schoolroom or Quaker meeting house but a witty simulation that helps put the *faux* poetry of Robert Frost in perspective:

> this room is beginning to tell us something
> about the contemporary state of poetry   or armajanis
> beliefs about it   which may not be so far off the mark
> an image of a slightly foolish teacher preacher followed   by
>   an uncomfortable audience from which he is divided by
> fragments of robert frost (*Siah Armajani* 30)

Armajani, says Antin, "is / not a folk artist hes a gallery artist who imagines folk or craft and various workmanlike properties" (*Siah Armajani* 43). As such, his installation provides a nice context for evaluating the metaphoric language "hats" worn by Frost and his fellow poets of the early century—poets like Lizette Woodward Reese, Bliss Carman, and William Vaughan Moody.

In a comic disquisition on Frost's "Death of the Hired Man," with its "modern people," Mary and Warren, and its hired man Silas, "a refugee," Antin reminds us, "from english literature," (i.e. George Eliot's *Silas Marner*), Antin has this to say about Frost's language field:

>   hes doing it in a   wooden
> literary language he offers as spoken american   that runs a
>   register from fake folk   "he thinks young wilson a likely lad
> though daft on education"   to 1907 short story talk "harolds
>   young college boys assurance piqued him" through palgrave
> poetical "part of a moon was falling down the west" or "as if she
>   played unheard some tenderness that wrought on him beside
> her in the night" to arrive at the parlor gnomic about home
> "I should have called it something you somehow havent to
> deserve"   that clinches it   and just about the time that mary
> convinces warren to take him in they find the old mans dead
>   now whats dead?   It's the language of this poem that's
>   dead   (*Siah Armajani* 39-40)

And this gives Antin the opening to launch into his own "hired man" story which is about a poor old drunkard named Joe Brizo, who performed odd jobs for Antin's mother-in-law Jeannette, when she ran her Catskill hotel—a "hired man" who fortunately doesn't die at the end of the poem: David, sent on a mission to check on noises that frighten Jeannette, finds him asleep and smelly in the linen closet, and "the next morning he was gone" (*Siah Armajani* 48). Antin concludes:

> now I could have killed him off in the story
> slowly or quickly it wouldn't have been too hard   i
> could have given him a heart attack or pneumonia
> something terrible could have happened   but I was
> thinking of him in terms of what had happened to
> the hired man and that level of escalation I dislike so
> intensely in robert frost   and that's where joe brizo comes in

That's where Joe Brizo comes in. Antin's own poetic text enacts metonymically his need to reject the metaphoric language of a Robert Frost, a language fragmented and reassembled in the *faux*-folk setting of Armajani's installation. Juxtaposition is all. If we read "the death of the hired man" as part of the photographic/poetic collage which constitutes the catalog, Antin's own seemingly digressive metonymic composition, part essay, part narrative, with its complex network of repetitions and permutations, emerges as a sort of latter-day Popean "Essay on Criticism," a delicate plea for common sense, whether in the writing of poetry or the architecture of poetry lounges.

And here the visual dimension of Antin's text figures in. The form of "the death of the hired man" is the perfect equivalent for its meaning. For starters, the printed text is played off against both the image of "Mending Wall" and the photos of Armajani's installation, so that we "see" alternate conceptions of the poetic. For another the page itself, with its jagged margins, spaces, and "all over" appearance (no punctuation, capitalization, paragraph break) becomes a metonymic field. Consider page 24 (figure 9).

At the top, three lines from "Mending Wall" remind us of how poetry officially looks. The first five lines of Antin's "score" begin, perhaps coincidentally, with a metrical run, specifically three iambic feet: "there ís what í would cáll. . . ." It almost seems like a continuation of Frost's "where théy have léft not óne." But of course the passage quickly shifts gears in the direction of what seems to be actual speech—speech heightened, however, by its repetitiveness. "disastrous"/ "disaster," for example, appears five times in the first five lines. The reader's eye, traveling down the page, links "disaster" (surrounded by white space in line 4) to "disaster of his time" right beneath it, and then "debris" in the line below that. Throughout the page, the spacing foregrounds certain phrases—"something there is that doesn't love a wall," for example, the "wall" then related by spacing and visual contiguity to "want," which in turn connects to "why," "where," "which" and "what." Again, within the visual field peppered by these monosyllabic particles, "frost" stands out as does "neighbor," together with "apple trees" and "pines." "his pines" near the bottom of the page, spatially invokes the phrases "here pines" (a diagonal) or (reading from bottom to top) "what pines."

One cannot, in any case, read easily from left to right and top to bottom; rather, one scans the entire page picking out words that are foregrounded by spacing: on page 25, such a word would be "farmer," isolated and repeated a number of times. On page 36, "charlemagne" and "blaise cendrars" stand out, and on page 37, there is "shortstop," a reference to the poet's son "blaze [for Blaise Cendrars] antin" who was playing shortstop on the team, and had also been "born a california child"—a phrase prominently spaced, "dark as an arab" and "a wizened little baby."

A whole imagist poem might be made of epithets for Blaze:

> golden california child
> dark as an arab
> wizened little baby
> the little bastard
> the kind of kid wholl run off at sixteen
> the name of the twentieth centurys most cheerful poet
> blaise cendrars
> a blaze with all the light and somewhat less heat
> (*Siah Armajani* 37-38).

But of course Antin has no interest in deleting the discursive material in which these phrase are embedded in his "talk," discursivity being, in his scheme of things, an essential part of poetic investigation.

In the preface to his *Selected Poems* (1991), Antin remarks on the role the book plays in a gathering of poems:

for me [the poems have] been changed by time and by the way they've appeared in books. Books have a very definite appearance. My books anyway. Because I tried to make them that way. And in spite of the fact that there is a sense in which the work of poetry is an ongoing process, a book is a *self sufficient object, obdurate even,* as it gives decisive shape through selection and ordering to a cluster of attitudes and ideas, enclosing them in a definite space and time. [my emphasis][17]

Antin is of course referring to the pre-talk works here, but I think his remarks apply to the talk pieces as well: these too, after all, come to be collected in books, whose "selection and ordering . . . encloses them in a definite space and time." I do not mean to play down the role *speech* plays in Antin's work; obviously its careful simulation is integral to his poetic processes. But I do want to suggest that a text like "the death of the hired man," far from being only a "score" that transcribes prior speech, is also a material, visual object and hence deserves a kind of attention we have not yet given it.

NOTES

[1]Michael Davidson, review of *tuning, New York Times Book Review*, as reproduced on book jacket of *what it means to be avant-garde* (New York: New Directions, 1993). Cf. *boundary 2* 3 (Spring 1975), Special Issue: *The Oral Impulse in Contemporary American Poetry*, passim, where David Antin is classified, together with Jerome Rothenberg, as an "oral poet"; Charles O. Hartman, *The Jazz Text, Voice and Improvisation in Poetry, Jazz, and Song* (Princeton: Princeton Univ. Press, 1991), 76-94. In my own *Poetics of Indeterminacy: Rimbaud to Cage* (1981; Evanston: Northwestern Univ. Press, 1999), 288-339, I also foreground the performative aspects of Antin's work.

[2]See Maria Damon, "Talking Yiddish at the Boundaries," *Cultural Studies* 5.1 (January 1991), 14-29; Steve Fredman, *Poet's Prose: The Crisis in American Verse*, 2d. ed. (Cambridge: Cambridge Univ. Press, 1990), 137.

[3]Antin, headnote to "what am I doing here?," *talking at the boundaries* (New York: New Directions, 1976); hereafter cited parenthetically. I reproduce Antin's spacing and lack of punctuation exactly as is.

[4]Antin uses this phrase in an E-mail to me, 16 September 1999.

[5]Michael Davidson, *Ghostlier Demarcations: Modern Poetry and the Material Word* (Berkeley: Univ. of California Press, 1997), 208. Cf. Frederick Garber, "David Antin: The Boundaries of Talking," *Repositioning: Readings of Contemporary Poetry, Photography, and Performance Art* (University Park, PA: Pennsylvania State Press, 1995), 78-82; Garber notes that each talk piece has three versions: the original spoken one, the taped, and the visual. The visual, he suggests, is not fully prose because of the unjustified margins and spacing.

[6]David Antin, *definitions* (New York: Caterpillar Press, 1967), hereafter cited parenthetically.

[7]David Antin, *Code of Flag Behavior* (designed by Barbara Martin with the poet; Santa Barbara: Black Sparrow Press, 1968), 15.

[8]Antin, letter to the author, 1 September 1999.

[9]David Antin, *Talking* (New York: Kulchur Foundation, 1972), 12.

[10]Antin, "Some Questions on Modernism," *Occident* 8, new series (Spring 1974): 14; hereafter cited parenthetically. Strictly speaking, this piece is an interview with the *Occident* editors, referring to Antin's own "Modernism and Postmodernism: Approaching the Present in American Poetry," *boundary 2* 1.1 (Fall 1972): 98-133.

[11]Gertrude Stein, "Miss Furr and Miss Skeene," *Writings 1903-1932*, ed. Catharine R. Stimpson and Harriet Chessman (New York: Library of America, 1998), 307-12.

[12]Roman Jakobson, "Two Aspects of Language and Two Types of Aphasic Disturbances" (1956), *Language and Literature,* ed. Krystyna Pomorska and Stephen Rudy (Cambridge: Harvard Univ. Press, 1987), 95-114; hereafter cited parenthetically.

[13]E-mail to author, 16 September 1999.

[14]Michael H. Smith, introduction, *Siah Armajani: A Poetry Lounge* (3 March through 25 April 1982) (Pasadena: Baxter Art Gallery at California Institute of Technology, 1982), 5; hereafter cited parenthetically. In the citations from Antin, line endings are marked by a slash mark (/) and I follow his own spacing and lack of punctuation.

[15]See Marjorie Perloff, "Postmodernism and the Impasse of Lyric," *The Dance of the Intellect: Studies in the Poetry of the Pound Tradition* (1985; Evanston: Northwestern Univ. Press, 1994), 192-96. For Frost's "Mending Wall" and "The Death of the Hired Man," see *Complete Poems of Robert Frost* (New York: Holt, Rinehart and Winston), 47-55. The two poems are respectively the first and second poems in *North of Boston* (1923).

[16]A ´ designates a primary stress, a ˆ a secondary stress.

[17]Antin, *Selected Poems: 1963-1973* (Los Angeles: Sun & Moon Press, 1991), 13.

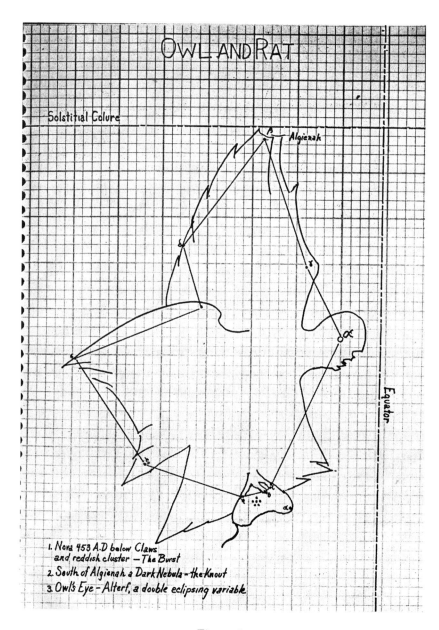

Figure 1

Figure 2

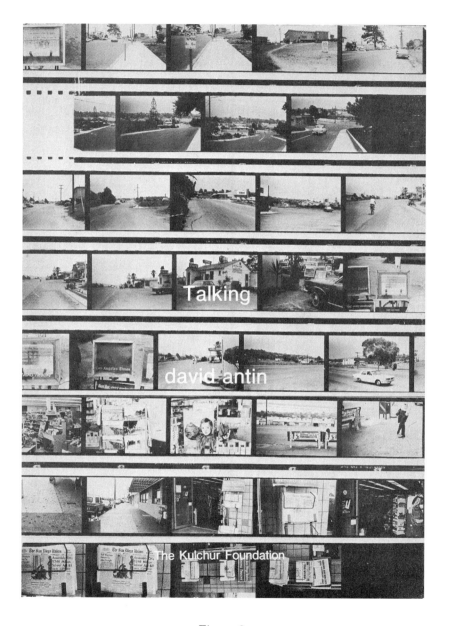

Figure 3

Talking at Pomona

what i would like to talk about   really   is a subject that probably doesnt have a name

   if i were to give it a name it would sound kind of pretentious   and it might be

misleading   so   let me begin by reminiscing slightly   last quarter   we have a

   trimester system that has quarters   it is an absurd system   i set about to ask myself

out loud   with a group of students   who were ostensibly concerned with art

   what we could do to make a discourse situation in art   meaningful or comprehensible

      now that sounds a little vague but what i really wanted to know was this   how can

you think about making art   and i use the word art as an undefined at the moment

      how can you talk about it in such a way   that   it will lead to making more art

      and the making of more art will itself be rewarding rather than a diminishing return

      now how do you set about looking at art making   as something that will be

valuable to do   and the value of which will increase as you proceed to do more of it

   im afraid this sounds like an absurd thing to say because people who normally come to a

143

Figure 4

Figure 5
Photograph by Grey Crawford

Figure 6
Photograph by Grey Crawford

Figure 7
Photograph by Grey Crawford

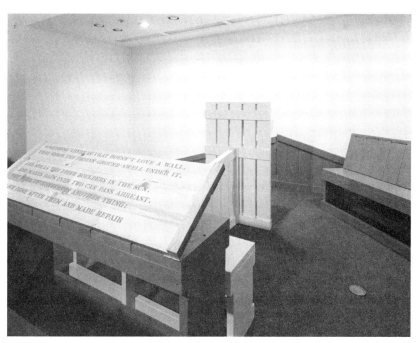

Figure 8
Photograph by Grey Crawford

the work of hunters is another thing
i have come after them and made repair
where they have left not one stone on a stone

there is what i would call a disastrous poetical language
    in robert frost and i dont understand it or why it had
to be so disastrous   because it wasnt a personal
        disaster   perhaps it was a national disaster or a
disaster of his time   but somewhere in the poetical
    debris of such a poem there will be one line that will
make sense   in the way frosts letter talked of
        making sense and you wont want to dismiss it   the
sound of a voice saying over and over again as if its
    speaker had just discovered its meaning something
like   "good fences make good neighbors"   which
    is not equalled but supposed to be by "something there
is that doesn't love a wall"   though not only have
        you never heard anyone speak it you cant even imagine
    anyone speaking it in precisely that way   because
        you suspect quite rightly that something called meter
    has turned an english sentence back on itself to make
it sound more poetical more important and quaint
        something there is for sure that goes around
turning over english sentences like "i let my neighbor
behind the hill know" into "i let my neighbor know beyond
    the hill" which is too bad   because if there
was something wild and whimsical in this poem that didnt
        respect walls you might suppose it wouldnt respect
meter either   so you dont take it too seriously
        and thats too bad because frost   as the poet
        appears to identify himself in speaking for the
force against walls   "that wants them down"
        or represents himself at least as knowing more
than his neighbor about walls and their limitations
        so he keeps bugging him "why do they make good
neighbors   isnt it where there are cows   but
    there are no cows here   my apple trees will never
get across and eat his pines   before i built a wall
    i would ask to know what i was walling in or out"
        to which his neighbor doesnt respond   just
answers with that line that might have come out of a

24

Figure 9

Between a Rock and a Hard Place: David Antin's Art Writings

Henry Sayre

Between a rock (the "concrete") and a hard place (the "abstract"), between the object (in itself) and its description (or reception), between the image (visual) and its meaning (whatever is not visual—written, spoken, thought, imagined): this is the terrain of David Antin's art writing. We can find him traversing this landscape all the way back, in the years leading to the 1967 publication of *Definitions,* an early book of poems written between 1963 and 1966 that he made by working with "prefabricated and readymade materials, recycling texts and fragments of texts, enclosing valuable and used up talk and thought and feeling, hoping to save what was worth saving, liberate it and throw the rest away" (*Selected Poems* 14-15). In the following lines, lifted from Wittgenstein's *Philosophical Investigations* (sections 243, 300, and 368, in reverse order), Antin meditates on the being stuck between word and image, that state of inadequacy:

i describe a room to someone and get him to paint a picture of it
the chairs i said were green he paints red   where i said
yellow he paints dark blue   that's the impression he gets of
the room   i say "thats right   that's what it looks like"

the image of pain

yet we can imagine a language in which a person could write down
or give vocal expression to his inner experiences and feelings
it is not our language ("The Black Plague: Part III," *Selected Poems* 89)

The last five words are not Wittgenstein's but Antin's, and they complicate Antin's project exponentially. Wittgenstein's words are themselves objects—"prefabricated and readymade materials"—fragments of writing containing thought and feeling, perhaps worth saving, worth remembering. They *define,* at some level, what Wittgenstein called "the language-game," the very game Antin is playing in *Definitions.*[1] And yet definitions always fall short. They trivialize experience. As Antin described his work in the much later talk poem "the sociology of art," writing is a process of "trying to find some way of bringing meaning out of a mind and into a place" (*talking at the boundaries* 185). He is trying, that is, to stake out some territory between a rock and a hard place. And it is never very easy.

By early 1966, as *definitions* was taking form, Antin was writing about art. The first piece to appear in a national magazine was about a series of shows by Robert Morris that had taken place over the previous three years, but it focused, particularly, on a show of nine simple polyhedrons at the Green Gallery in New York in the spring of 1965. Called "Art & Information, 1: Grey Paint, Robert Morris," the piece appeared in *Art News* in April 1966. With the possible exception of *Arts Magazine, Art News* in those days was the best, certainly the most serious, of the art magazines, and it hosted a formidable stable of art writers. Vito Acconci, Amy Goldin, John Ashbery, Michael Benedickt, Suzi Gablik, Jill Johnston, Fairfield Porter, Gerritt Henry, and Carter Ratcliffe all contributed in the late sixties and early seventies, and Antin's contribution on Morris inaugurated what the editors (Tom Hess and Ashbery) envisioned as "a series of articles on new concepts in the arts of the mid-1960s" ("Art & Information" 23). The stark simplicity of Morris's work posed the "logically primary question of *What is it?*" (23). Which question Antin carefully began to answer in exhaustive, even excruciating detail:

A long low wedge about 2 feet high; a bulking inclined plane rising nearly 6 feet from the ground; a long, reclining triangular column looking like a square beam split neatly down the diagonal; four squat pillbox shapes, flat on top with two sloping sides; a warped, square beam that rises queerly 2 inches off the floor a the center of its long dimension; and a large, split ring glowing with milk-white light from its two air gaps. (23)

The work, he says, is "simple and impassive," "quite beautiful," and "clearly sculpture," since "it occupies space," but "the concerns of contemporary sculpture are curiously absent" (23-24). The pieces "exclude ordinary ideas of formal composition and interrelation of parts. There are no parts. They seem to defy analysis" (24). They are not "environments," since they "were conceived as individual pieces and were not conceived as a set of interactions with a particular gallery space" (24). Speaking of a set of four mirrored boxes that had been shown at the Green Gallery in New York in 1965, Antin comments on the way that they exist as "negative forms . . . invisible sculpture" (56). The color of almost all the other work is "grey . . . a neutral hue that removes objects from all alien contexts" (56). This color—or noncolor, like the color of glass in a mirror—helps Morris detach his objects "from subject matter," although the work carries with it "the ghosts of subject matter": "the absent reference, the absent context. That's what's ghostly about it. A ghost can be defined as the presence of absence" (57). His pieces are constructed, in other words, "out of what is not there" (57).

What attracts Antin to Morris's work—and it has been a lifelong attraction, culminating in his eloquent defense of Morris's career in the catalog to his 1994 retrospective at the Guggenheim Museum ("Have Mind, Will Travel")—is the way in which the work avoids, precisely, definition. He can describe "what it is" literally—"a low wedge about 2 feet high," etc.—but its interest lies in what it is, figuratively, which is what it isn't: "It's an art of sudden materializations and dematerializations. Now you see it, now you don't" (56). It is an art not of illusion, but elusion.

And it presents us with a language problem. That is, when we move from the object itself to a description of it, we move from one system of representation to another, and the systems are not symmetrical. The situation is comparable to the kind of interlingual dictionaries that Antin describes in "duchamp and language":

<blockquote>
that is to say
you take the great french-english and english-french
dictionary its two volumes will not translate into each
other   the one most obvious thing about these two volumes
is that they are not reciprocally arranged so that the
pages of the french convert into pages of the english
and the pages of the english into pages of the french entry
for entry   the french translates into the english   in
that part of the dictionary   in such a way that if you
got a fluent bilingual french and english speaker and
handed him the english and asked him to translate the
english entries   he would wind up with a set of french
entries that did not correspond to the original french
entries in any very regular fashion   and his entries
would not be wrong at all (101)
</blockquote>

In the same way, the movement between the art object and our writing about it is an exercise in translation. I have resisted reproducing the works by Robert Morris described by Antin in "Art & Information" precisely to make this point. Assuming the reader does not already know what they look like, imagine reconstructing them based on Antin's rather detailed descriptions. In fact, as a reader, you have already had to reconstruct them imaginatively, and you have probably not done so with any sense of satisfaction or adequacy and a certain amount of frustration over the fact that I haven't reproduced them. In this sense art writing is a kind of bilingual dictionary, in which the reader moves back and forth between the image (reproduced) and our writing about it.

But there is writing and there is writing. Antin attributes to Duchamp an interest in the mechanics of language that is very much his own. By the second decade of the twentieth century, Duchamp had come to conclude that the painting of the time "had cut itself off from the kind of linguistic significance that made art what it was" (105). In impressionism, in abstract art—"the kandinskylike color psychologism or gestural drawing-generated psychologism out of art nouveau" (105)—even in cubism in its most hermetic stages just before it returned to an engagement with words in collage, art had tried to divorce itself from language:

> and for good reason   partly because
> of the trivial grasp of the nature of language that was
>   available   but mainly because the linguistic background
> of a work of art had a tendency to congeal into literature
>   theres a difference between linguistics and literature
>   between language and literature   a literary program for
> an art work very quickly leaves the art work or used to do so
>   very quickly   goes on its own allegorical trip . . .
>   . . . the sort of allegories that
>   underlay salon painting say were quite expectable
>   they could be read out instantaneously in fact they
>   scarcely needed reading at all merely a glance and you
>   knew the game   allegory as it was commonly encountered
>   you read it and were off into your own head   never to
> look at anything in the world again . . .
>   . . . that
> kind of allegory was derived from a commonplace set
>   or shared group of ideas and literary preconceptions
>   you could reduce it to a set of sentences very quickly
>   (106)

Both Antin and Duchamp seek to create a different sort of allegory for the work of art. They are interested in an art of "linguistic significance" as opposed to "congealed literature."

What does it mean for an art work to possess "linguistic significance"? In some sense the project of all Antin's art writing is to answer that question, to arrive at that "hard place." Duchamp's readymades offer him a kind of paradigm:

> what is usually involved in the

readymades say   is an object and its name   the object
may be some simple recognizable utensil   a urinal   a
shovel   or a construction of a sort   like a cage with
small pieces of marble in it and a thermometer   and its
  "name" or the verbal text associated with it   its motto
  so to speak   or poem   maybe "fountain" or "in advance
of a broken arm" or "why not sneeze?"   you have the object
  over here and the poem over there   with a wide gulf
between them   which is a kind of enigma   that is to say
    in some way the words affect the object and the object
affects the words (111)

This interaction between object and words creates a kind of
kinesthetics, "a perpetual motion machine" (114) that oscillates between the material and verbal poles of the readymade. Duchamp's
interest in language—and Antin's—is that it is the stuff that sets
the machine going. It activates the material situation. Any single
reading of a Duchamp work "is too stable for it," because "if any
reading were so plausible that it annihilated the other plausible
readings associated with the work / the work would break down"
(114). It would "disappear into the literature of its meaning" (114).
   Let me give an example, from literature—from *Moby-Dick*, to be
precise. Early in the book, Ishmael arrives at the Spouter Inn and
discovers in the entry

a very large oil-painting so thoroughly besmoked, and every way defaced,
that in the unequal cross-lights by which you viewed it, it was only by dili-
gent study and a series of systematic visits to it, and careful inquiry of the
neighbors, that you could any way arrive at an understanding of its purpose. Such unaccountable masses of shades and shadows, that at first you
almost thought some ambitious young artist, in the time of the New England hags, had endeavored to delineate chaos bewitched. But by dint of
much and earnest contemplation, and oft repeated ponderings, and especially by throwing open the little window towards the back of the entry,
you could at last come to the conclusion that such an idea, however wild,
might not be altogether unwarranted.
   But what most puzzled and confounded you was a long, limber, portentous, black mass of something hovering in the centre of the picture over
three blue, dim, perpendicular lines floating in a nameless yeast. A boggy,
soggy, squitchy picture truly, enough to drive a nervous man distracted.
Yet was there a sort of indefinite, half-attained, unimaginable sublimity
about it that fairly froze you to it, till you involuntarily took an oath with
yourself to find out what that marvellous painting meant. Ever and anon
a bright but, alas, deceptive idea would dart you through.—It's the Black
Sea in a midnight gale.—It's the unnatural combat of the four primal elements.—It's a blasted heath.—It's a Hyperborean winter scene.—It's the

breaking-up of the ice-bound stream of Time. But at last all of these fancies yielded to that one portentous something in the picture's midst. *That* once found out, and all the rest were plain. But stop; does it not bear a faint resemblance to a gigantic fish? Even the great leviathan himself?

In fact, the artist's design seemed this: a final theory of my own, partly based upon the aggregated opinions of the many aged persons with whom I conversed upon the subject. The picture represents a Cape-Horner in a great hurricane, the half-foundered ship weltering there with its three dismantled masts alone visible; and an exasperated whale, purposing to spring clean over the craft, is in the enormous act of impaling himself upon the three mast-heads. (20–21)

The moment Ishmael arrives at its meaning, the work is imaginatively dead. "In fact," it ceases to be of interest. This is a lesson that Melville himself takes to heart. The great white whale means a great many different things in the novel and the wide gulf between it and Melville's (which is to say, Ishmael's and Ahab's and Queequeg's) attempts to define it, that enigma, is the motor that drives the novel.

Antin sees abstract expressionist painting as creating an enigma of meaning similar to Melville's whale or the Spouter Inn painting before Ishmael trivializes it. In a 1971 assessment of the state of abstract painting, he condemns the work of the new generation of postabstract expressionist painters as merely "a set of moves." It lacks, he says, the earlier improvisational theory of painters like Jackson Pollock and Willem de Kooning, who understood "that painting is a depicting or encoding system" ("Déjà-vu" 64):

We do not look at paintings. Nobody does. We read them. . . . In this sense we may suppose that these painters were involved in something of a language game, making marks on a canvas that we may read with some indeterminacy but some agreement. The problem with this sort of painting is not whether you should read it, but how. The difficult question that arises is not so much the connoisseur problem of better or worse, but why some of these paintings appear more interesting than others. What may be needed is some kind of tactful if painstaking analysis of the signaling systems employed by the painters. It would be useful and novel if such an analysis made a point of emphasizing the kind and degree of indeterminacy inherently involved in the decoding. But to return to the point at hand, the agreed upon elements of improvisation for Pollock as well as de Kooning are the elements of a representational signaling system or of several such systems. That is what they had to play with. (53)

Antin's art writing emphasizes, again and again, the kind and degree of indeterminacy involved in his reading of the art work in question. He generally outlines the conventional reading—what we might call the Ishmael reading, the way in which a work can descend into the literature of its meaning—and then tries to restore the work to the enigma of its original undecidability. In "Art & Information," for instance, he begins by citing Barbara Rose's approach to Morris's work as exemplary of "minimal" art, exploiting "*literality, repetition* and *boredom*" (23). Antin finds nothing literal about Morris's work: "If they are literal, you have never seen them before" (24). Nor, despite the fact that "three of the works turn out to be variations, by alteration of dimension, of a single form," are they repetitious: "If it is repetition, what is repeated is not the same. Identical twins don't occupy the same space" (24). And they are anything but boring. They are, for Antin, full of surprises: "Surprise in scale. . . . Surprise in mass. . . . Surprise in position. . . . There is nothing minimal here" (56). Or take the example offered by "Jean Tinguely's New Machine," in an essay of that name that appeared near the end of 1968 in *Art News*. It begins with a patent plan of the machine as presented to the Museum of Modern Art in New York by the artist:

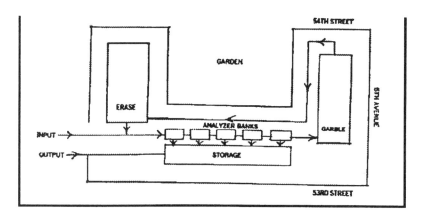

4,578,989
A SELF-STABILIZING
DATA PROCESSING MACHINE
Jean Tinguely, Paris, France, assignor to Museum
of Modern Art, a corporation of New York, N.Y.

Filed Nov. 27, 1968, Ser. No. 567,832

A data processing machine designed to receive an input of data, which is scanned by a series of analyzers for its equivalence with data already contained in one or more of the storage bins of the said machine. The data is scanned in a series of passes through the analyzer banks until all of the identities between the input data and the already stored data are exhausted, after which the input residue is passed through a governor or self-stabilizing system consisting of various erase and garble mechanisms and then passed once again through the analyzer banks. This cycle is repeated until the input data is assimilated to the initial state of the machine. The novelty of the said device consists of a final state or output which is indistinguishable from the pre-input or initial state of the said machine. (20)

The attentive reader will perhaps notice that this curious machine is designed as an exact replica of the floor plan of the Museum of Modern Art before it was remodeled. It is not Tinguely's at all, but an invention of Antin's. Written, according to Antin, "in the language I used to use when I translated German patents into English,"[2] it describes the museum/machine as a giant reductive equalizer which, just as Ishmael subjects the painting in the Spouter Inn to "the aggregated opinions of the many aged persons" with whom he converses, reduces the meaning of art to the level of general consensus. That is, what comes in the machine as input— say, a work of art—is "scanned by a series of analyzers"—say, curators, art historians, and critics—for whatever it shares with the data already in the machine—other works of art. It undergoes various "erase" and "garble" cycles until it is indistinguishable from the other works already in the museum/machine—until, that is, it congeals into the "literature" of art history.

But in its smooth operation, it is not the kind of machine that either Antin likes or Tinguely would make. Tinguely, after all, had made an earlier machine in the "garden" space on the diagram, between the erase and garble areas, called *Homage to New York,* that destroyed itself on the evening of 16 March 1960, refusing, in that sense, to become "input" at all (though the museum rescued a few pieces and occasionally still displays them). Even in its self-destruction, it didn't work right. Tinguely had to saw through a few parts, others flew off dangerously, careening in flames toward the museum itself, and so on. That was its beauty. "Why are we fascinated by machines?" Antin asks:

It is the last refuge of the artistic temperament. If you want a steady, reliable job, you get a dull man [a curator, art historian, or critic?]. But if you want an unpredictable prima donna, get a machine. I have never been to a gallery where all of the machines were running after the day of the opening. Sometimes even then it's too late. So there are records of machines [the legend that grew up around Tinguely's *Homage*]. A fossil or a tombstone. We bring it flowers. Tell us what it did. The interest in machines is to have them surprise us. (23)

For Antin, Tinguely's new museum/machine becomes interesting when it breaks down, when the input is not reduced to the level of the rest, when the erase and garble cycles don't work, when what we get at the end is not the same but different. As he puts it at the end of "duchamp and language": "by building defectiveness into any reading duchamp / ensures the instability of it   so that the pendulum of attention would keep moving   the defects drive his machine" (114). It is the instability of his readings that marks Antin's own art writing. The instability of the reading, in effect, assures the indeterminacy of the work.

In "Jean Tinguely's New Machine," for instance, he erupts into personal reminiscence:

When I was a child during the War—I've always called World War II the War and know better, but I cannot help it—we went to Rockaway and I had lots of time that I spent in penny arcades playing baseball machines. When you put a penny in the slot a small steel ball came out of a hole in the umpire's chest and dropped into the pitcher's hand that was shaped like a bowl. He swiveled releasing the ball toward the plate, which you tried to hit. If it was over the plate and you didn't hit it the umpire's right arm went up for a strike and sometimes when it was not over the plate his left arm went up for a ball but usually it didn't. Though once I got a walk. There was another machine with a gypsy and a mechanical raven, she nodded at you, the raven shook his head and a card came out with your fortune. (22)

What is the relation of all this to Tinguely's "new machine"? Does this reminiscence merely demonstrate "the romance of machines" (22), our nostalgic love for them? Or does it do something more? In fact, it disrupts the character of the prose, the decorum of the space (the "space" of art writing, the space of the art magazine), the objectivity of the "trained eye." It surprises us and thus sets the essay/machine in motion.

And Antin's essay/machine is neither an efficient nor reliable technology. It does not produce a "finished" product, or reading, in the manner of Tinguely's museum/machine, or for that matter, in the manner of the corporation. "It is all very well," Antin reminds us in a review of the spring 1971 "Art and Technology" show at the Los Angeles County Museum of Art, "to imagine the great corporations as immense production machines turning out cars or computers or meat or movies; but it is not so." Corporations don't so much produce goods as "buy and sell related and unrelated other companies at an alarming rate, so that it may be impossible to tell what a corporation like Litton Industries, say, might be producing at any given moment if you have been looking away for a couple of weeks" ("Art and the Corporations" 55). In fact, in the "Art and Technology" show, the museum found itself "in the position of corporate enterprise" (56). Curator Maurice Tuchman in essence acquired two large sets of utterly unrelated "producers"—artists (themselves a hodgepodge of sensibilities) and corporations (competitive and to various degrees uninterested)—and asked them to work together. The problem, of course, is that in acquiring so many unrelated entities, the enterprise was destined to failure: "The larger the machine the more likely it will be to have a great number of sequentially dependent parts. Each of these parts has some probability of failure . . . Result: wipe out" (55-56).

Which is not really much of a surprise. What most machines produce is garbage. At least, sooner or later, it becomes garbage: "The output of machines is staggering," Antin reminds us in "Tinguely's New Machine." "So is the garbage. On a good day if you walk to the Hudson you can see machine art coming down the river. There is Tinguely, fishing" (23). Fishing for what? Rubber boots, old tires, bicycle wheels by the hundreds, the refuse out of which he builds his machines. The output of the Tinguely's hypothetical museum/machine is garbage (garbage in, garbage out). So if the museum is a corporation, it is also a dump. Think of it as a company like Waste Management. It demands that we approach it from an ecological point of view.

In 1970 Antin reviewed an ecological art show at the then new Oakland Museum. Entitled "Lead Kindly Blight," the essay was prefaced by a full-page spread consisting of two photographs: on top, the ruins of Tikal, Guatamala, abandoned about 900 A.D. and covered in dense, lush jungle, and below, the smog-shrouded city of Los Angeles, "ca. 1970, still inhabited" (36). Antin sees the former as latent in the latter. And he wonders what kind of art might respond. What would an ecological art look like? His first example is Douglas Huebler's *Duration Piece, 2: Sand 30' by 4"*, which consists of twelve photographs taken at two-minute intervals of a four-inch-wide strip of sand laid across Route 25 at Plaistow, N.H. It takes a bit of work to arrive at the ecological issues raised by this piece, but they are inescapable. Each photograph shows the entire thirty-foot length of the stripe crossing the road and a view of the road that comprises about fifteen feet on either side of the stripe. Cars appear in six of the photographs. Antin explains:

Suppose the cars are all traveling at 30 m.p.h. This means that they're traveling at 44 feet per second, and they will remain in view along a 30-foot expanse of road for roughly 3/4 of a second. The photographs were taken at 120-second intervals, so that, multiplying by 4/3, there were 160 parcels of time during which a 30 m.p.h. traveling car could have been caught by the camera. It doesn't take much mathematical intelligence to reason that if 80 cars came through in the 2-minute interval (or the 160 parcels of time), that there would be a 50/50 chance of catching a car in the picture. Which is what we have—six cars in 12 frames. That would mean that the cars traveling both directions on route 125 near Plaistow, N.H. come by at a rate of one every 1.5 seconds. . . . What was going on in Plaistow, N.H.? I would say that this is an ecology-oriented work that has escaped from the artist's intention. It is about cars passing a mailbox on a minor road in a nothing state. Is this pollution criminal or tragic? (88-89)

The point is that Huebler's piece is not in the Oakland Museum's ecological art show. Nor are any of the other ecological artworks that Antin describes in the essay—Dennis Oppenheim's *Cancelled Crop,* in which Oppenheim seeded a Dutch field, harvested the grain, and then offered it for sale in a gallery turned silo; a performance by Vito Acconci in which he emptied his four-room apartment week by week for four weeks, transporting each room to a gallery some seventy blocks away, in the process learning how much he could do without; and Eleanor Antin's *California Lives,* a series of portraits of individuals composed of brand-new discount center items arranged as if the subjects had just walked away. Instead, the Oakland Museum show consisted of things like "a red plush-lined *Coffin for the Earth* . . . a block of normally clear cast acrylic resin, the lower half of which had been blackened and filled with an assortment of paper wrappers and matches . . . a painting of a just-having-balled couple lying amid the rubble of their weekend . . . surrounded by real beer cans" (37–38). All in all, the show itself was "pretty refined . . . almost all the sculpture up on bases, nothing to disturb the lovely parquet floors, the neatly framed paintings" (38).

In essence, the Oakland Museum has run the idea of ecological art through Tinguely's New Machine—garbage in, garbage out. In fact, Antin concludes, in the context of the museum, a truly ecological art may be impossible:

The idea of an ecological art is the idea of an art that articulates dependencies, its own conditions for existence or those of the world. Not a statue of an eviscerated seagull or a lament for the California condor. Though these are harmless enough, all that they offer is elegy or taxidermy, which may be all that is possible in the normal context of a museum. . . . At the Oakland Museum, one artist contributed a square-foot block of asphalt through which a single blade of grass poked up. The assistant curator saw me looking at it and said, " I like that one, too. I take it as a sign of hope." But two days in the museum and the grass died. (90)

The implications of this realization—that a truly ecological art "articulates dependencies, its own conditions for existence or those of the world"—are more fully developed by Antin in an essay written a few months later on an exhibition called "The Four Elements:

Earth, Air, Fire and Water" at the Boston Museum. Called "It Reaches a Desert in Which Nothing Can Be Perceived but Feeling," quoting an aphorism by the Russian constructivist artist Kasimir Malevich, the essay presents Antin with an occasion to lament the direction that the history of art, specifically the logic of abstraction, has taken us.

He begins by comparing a 1937 definition of abstraction by Gabo to a contemporary statement by Sol LeWitt describing one of his linear wall drawings. For Gabo, abstraction "has revealed a universal law that the elements of a visual art such as lines, colors, shapes, possess their own forces of expression independent of any association with the external aspects of the world; that their life and their action are self-conditioned psychological phenomena rooted in human nature . . . and organically bound up with human emotions" (38). For LeWitt, the possibilities of abstraction are not quite so grand. He describes his process: "The draftsman and the wall enter a dialogue. The draftsman becomes bored but later through this meaningless activity finds peace or misery. The lines on the wall are the residue of this process. Each line is as important as each other line. All of the lines become one thing. The viewer of the lines can see only lines on a wall. They are meaningless. This is art" (38). In either case, Gabo's "contentless psychologism"(38) or LeWitt's meaningless content, art has reached the desert of Antin's title, a desert in which nothing can be perceived but (the suggestion of) "feeling," whatever that may be. The defining characteristic of this desert it is that is self-absorbed. It absolutely abrogates what Antin considers art's necessity—that is, the necessity to articulate dependencies, the conditions of its own existence in the world—because, precisely, it is inarticulate. For artists as different as Gauguin and Kandinsky, Madame de Staël's famous 1869 declaration that the "arts are above thought" resulted in an expressionist aesthetics which was "prelinguistic and without structural clues to its possible relation to any external reality" (40). It is "disconnected from the rest of life" (40) a "sensory deprivation chamber" (66). Thus, for Antin, "abstraction has declined to an empty and affluent spirituality at the level of consumer goods" (66)—and in this context, it comes as no surprise that of all forms of art, "there is nothing large corporations find more comfortable than decorative abstraction" ("Lead Kindly Blight" 90). But Antin, of course, wants something more. He wants, he says, "a new theory of content" ("It Reaches a Desert" 67).

This "theory of content" must articulate the dependencies and conditions of the work in the world. It must, furthermore, acknowledge the "encoding" and "signaling" systems at play within the work since it is through these systems that the work becomes articulate. Antin wants to do all this, primarily, by acknowledging that "visual art" is dependent on modes of understanding other than the purely visual:

If we are to do something fundamentally meaningful we may have to begin by eliminating the genres that have helped trivialize our art. By this I don't mean sub-genres like "painting" or "sculpture." I mean the distinctions between the arts in general. Is visual information in itself at all capable of producing interesting art? Is acoustical information? Since visualization is not an isolated perceptual sense but a complex mode of interacting with external reality, based on a synthesis of different types of perceptual data, is there any more reason to set out again to invent a "visual art"?(68)

Thus Antin admires Robert Smithson's "earthworks"—from the *Spiral Jetty* to *Incidents of Mirror Travel in the Yucatan*—for their "hybridism," for the fact that in order to achieve "their most effective operation they require support from Smithson's prose" (70). The work is not, in other words, "self-absorbed," even if it is isolated and remote. In fact, in its very isolation and remoteness, it *must* acknowledge its dependencies on other genres to achieve any degree of imaginative necessity.

To move between a rock and a hard place is to move between the visual and verbal and to acknowledge their interdependencies. No work of art exists without both. And it is not simply a question of finding "verbal definitions" for "visual images." That would be dictionary work. In "Art and the Corporations" Antin defines a machine as "the concrete metaphor of technology—the physical embodiment of *the ability to get something from here to there*" (his emphasis, 25). Which is not a bad definition of narrative. Narrative is a technology for getting from here to there, from, say, the visual image to a meaningful articulation of its content. Narrative is very different from definition. Definition consists of substituting one representation or system of representation for another. Narratives, as Antin defined them in a talk-poem called "dialogue," presented in 1979 at the Santa Barbara Museum of Art,

> narratives are a
> fundamental   part of peoples talking they
> are ways of representing in language the unfolding of
> events   and something else   because a representation
> of the unfolding of events may be merely an account   i
> went to the store i selected a pipe a pack of tobacco a
> pouch some matches and a pack of gauloises   i paid for my

> purchases and came to the museum   that's an account not a
> narrative because I had no need for one   a narrative is
> something more it is an attempt to bring the present to the
>   past and let that past unfold there as the present between
> the two of you listener and teller as it is unfolding (13)

For Antin, art writing is a narrative of the process of moving from visual representation to "representing in language." He tries to make present the experience of his own seeing. He cannot see for the listener or reader. He can only tell about what it was like for him to see.

That is why, throughout his career, Antin has returned again and again to the idea of soluble or disposable art. Like conceptual art, which he has consistently championed, the soluble or disposable piece requires narrative because it is nowhere to be seen. It is merely, or especially, legend. In 1969 he curated an exhibition at the University Art Gallery at the University of California—San Diego, which he was then directing, called *Mazes*. It was an installation by Jeff Raskin, a man with degrees in philosophy and computer science and, at the time, member of the school's music department—a man, significantly, used to the idea of eliminating genre distinctions—and it consisted of 2,800 24" x 18 ½" x 18 ½" cardboard boxes of the type used in the moving industry, all arranged to create a series of labyrinths. After the exhibition "the boxes passed from us to Coast Packing, and then to Greyhound Van Lines of San Diego, Dean Van Lines of San Diego, and T. & D. Transfer and Storage of Chula Vista, to all of whom we wish to express our gratitude, not only for giving us the boxes, but also for taking them away" ("Mazes" 20). The show questioned the value of permanence in art, and from an ecological point of view:

Durability? Is that a virtue? There is a building by Sullivan in downtown New York that is now nothing more than a commercial slum. The two most enduring achievements of man may very well be the Sahara Desert and the Los Angeles air pollution. Louis Kahn's Salk building is beautiful and comic, but it is out of the past. It is a mastodon and what we need are sleek disposables. A soluble architecture that we can take down like Bedouin tents in a night and reassemble in a day, so that they will not litter the earth with our garbage. (18)

Almost a quarter century later, in 1992, *Critical Inquiry* editor W. J. T. Mitchell concluded his collection *Art and the Public Sphere* with a piece by Antin entitled "Fine Furs." In it, Antin once again extolled the virtues of soluble architecture:

This is one of the greatest problems of architecture. How to get rid of buildings economically and efficiently that no longer serve their own or any useful purpose and are choking up our streets. . . . The problem is becoming calamitous. A number of years ago I gave a talk on this subject at an architecture school; and it wasn't very popular then, but perhaps its time has come. I suggested that the problem of architecture is not how to make it, but how to get rid of it. The biggest problem in our cities is destroying no longer useful buildings—discarded shopping malls, useless high rises. My solution was soluble architecture—buildings provided with a plumbing system into which you could drop catalytic pills that would cause them to dissolve and run out through their own pipes into the sewer where they belong. (260–61)

"One of the great things about artworks that go away is they remain in your mind," Antin reminds us. "And you can use them" (260). To tell stories, for instance. In fact, for Antin, works of art go away by definition. They exist only in their readings, the narratives we create about them, which, like linear forms, disappear even as they unfold between us. In that sense his narratives are acts of ecology and all the art he writes about is disposable, impermanent—or as good as. It comes and goes like any story, existing only to be told again, in some other place, at some other time, and in some other version of our encounter with it.

NOTES

[1] Antin was playing some language games with Wittgenstein as well. *The Black Plague* can be understood as an attempt to deal with America's relation to blackness in the early days of the civil rights movement, and reading Wittgenstein seemed to Antin analogous to America's disconnection from the realities of black experience. As Antin told me, "Looking at it from a social perspective, reading Wittgenstein is like listening to an autistic person." So, in the days before computers, he copied relevant sections of the *Philosophical Investigations* onto index cards (which accounts, incidentally, for the inaccuracies of Antin's transcriptions) with an eye toward using them in the poem. Before long he had a giant pile, too large to handle conceptually. He took a giant hundred-foot roll of paper towels and began to unroll it through the rooms of the house he was living in that summer in The Springs, on Long Island—around the living room, down the hall, into his bedroom, out again. Next he dropped the index cards onto the paper towels, one per sheet, moving them and rearranging them until they had achieved a more or less arbitrary but satisfactory order. Then he taped them all down, and rolled the towels up again. Writing the poem, he unrolled the somewhat ungainly bundle index card by index card, paper towel by paper towel, incorporating each fragment into the text.

[2] Communication with the author, 17 September 1999.

WORKS CITED

Antin, David. "Art and Information, 1: Grey Paint, Robert Morris."
    Art News 65 (April 1966): 22-24, 56-58.
——. "Art and the Corporations." *Art News* 70 (September 1971):
    22–26, 52–56.
——. "Déjà-vu." *Art News* 70 (Summer 1971): 50–53, 63-65.
——. *dialogue*. Santa Barbara: Santa Barbara Museum of Art,
    1979.
——. "duchamp and language." *Marcel Duchamp*. Ed. Anne
    d'Harnancourt and Kynaston McShine. New York: Museum of
    Modern Art, 1973. 99–115.
——. "Fine Furs." *Art and the Public Sphere*. Ed. W. T. J. Mitchell.
    Chicago: U of Chicago P, 1992. 249–61.
——. "Have Mind, Will Travel." *Robert Morris: The Mind / Body
    Problem*. [Catalog to an exhibition at the Solomon R.
    Guggenheim Museum and the Guggenheim Museum Soho, Janu-
    ary–April 1994.] New York: Solomon R. Guggenheim Foundation,
    1994. 34–49.
——. "It Reaches a Desert in Which Nothing Can Be Perceived but
    Feeling." *Art News* 70 (March 1971):38–41, 66-71.
——. "Jean Tinguely's New Machine." *Art News* 67 (December
    1968): 20–23.
——. "Lead Kindly Blight." *Art News* 69 (November 1970): 36–39,
    87–90.
——. "Mazes." *Arts Magazine* 43 (May 1969): 18-20.
——. *Selected Poems: 1963–1973*. Los Angeles: Sun & Moon Press,
    1991.
——. *talking at the boundaries*. New York: New Directions, 1976.
Melville, Herman. *Moby-Dick*. New York: Bantam Books, 1967.
Wittgenstein, Ludwig. *Philosophical Investigations*. Trans. G. E. M.
    Anscombe. New York: Macmillan, 1953.

Remembering David Antin's "black warrior"

Hank Lazer

In the past I have written about David Antin's work from several different perspectives in an effort to describe and analyze a cultural poetics for his talk poems.[1] In this instance I would like to engage in a more sustained act of close listening. Though I will make some generalizations about the nature and importance of Antin's work—particularly the talk poems—I am determined to remember and speculate about a very specific talk poem, "black warrior," which Antin presented at the University of Alabama on 5 April 1990.

As Antin has published his talk poems with New Directions, each piece is framed by a brief set of remarks that contextualize it, and Antin indicates in many places that often a talk poem bears a specific relationship to the location, to his experience of the audience, and, at times, to his friendship with the person who has invited him (and who may, as I did for "black warrior," also introduce his talk poem). That is, the talk poem is an occasion that is at once site-specific and also more general in its scope of address (as Antin thinks about various interrelated narratives and questions). In "black warrior," for example, Antin begins by saying,

> i'm never sure of what i'm going to
> say   although i have an idea   of what i'm going to
> talk about   usually the idea is provided by the
> situation   to some degree[2]

The talk poem that he presented in Tuscaloosa was not necessarily one of his "best," though what that means and how Antin determines which talk poems to transcribe, edit, and collect is open to discussion.

Antin, somewhat typically, begins "black warrior" by offering a barb directed specifically at the University of Alabama audience:

> i think you had a conference here   where the
> role of the university was discussed   probably by a
> distinguished frenchman   and i imagine   that
> all turned into a discussion of paul de man's youth

                    or heidegger   or whatever

Alabama indeed had been in the news for hosting the conference
where Jacques Derrida, "a distinguished frenchman," and others
met to discuss the nature of a university, and where many of the
world's leading practitioners of deconstruction gathered to deter-
mine a strategy to respond to relevations that Paul de Man as a
young man had written a number of newspaper articles that were
sympathetic to the Nazi cause. This was the first of a series of
Antin's remarks that no doubt annoyed and unsettled the
Tuscaloosa audience.

   Those who felt insulted and who turned away from the talk
missed an opportunity to hear what turns out to be a rather
Derridean performance, though Antin's "deconstructive" gestures,
unlike Derrida's, are accomplished within an improvisational vernacular practice. In "black warrior" Antin undermines the familiarity (or deconstructs the stability and origin) of the term *black warrior* and becomes an advocate for spaces that open up thinking and
art-making to the limitations of knowing. Two other tactical barbs
stand out in my memory of David's "black warrior": his scathing critique of the poetry of Randall Jarrell and Robert Lowell (two poets
revered at that time by the faculty and students in the Alabama
M.F.A. program in creative writing) and his seemingly casual and
approving attitude (expressed in passing in the Carol-story, one of
the talk poem's central narratives) toward a male faculty member's
affairs with coeds (an anecdote that Antin told, unknowingly, to an
audience where the English Department was just emerging from a
flamboyantly exploitive period in which a number of male faculty
members had had affairs with female graduate and undergraduate
students). Perhaps I retain a somewhat distorted focus on the tensions produced by these remarks because I was Antin's (nice Southern?) host and because I was attempting to introduce Antin's work
to an audience that I knew all too well to be quite skeptical of innovative approaches to poetry.

   What I had not counted on was the audience's negative reaction
to the format of the talk poem itself. I think that in the days leading
up to Antin's presentation, they had heard the terms *performance*
and *performance artist* and that they had expected something more
along the lines of Laurie Anderson's voice manipulations, synthe-
sized music, and video pyrotechnics. At the reception after the performance, a few of my students (who had been forewarned about the
dynamics of rejection that would ensue) conversed with him, but
none of the faculty from my home department (the English department) would talk to him. Faculty and students from the art depart-

ment and a couple of independent artist friends from Birmingham (who knew and admired both David and Eleanor Antin's work) spent plenty of time talking to him. I found David's equanimity throughout this entire day's events to be impressive and instructive.

The other strand that I wish to attach to this consideration of Antin's work is his 1998 review-essay "Wittgenstein among the Poets."[3] Beyond critiquing Marjorie Perloff's *Wittgenstein's Ladder: Poetic Language and the Strangeness of the Ordinary,* Antin's essay presents an extraordinary self-portrait. His analysis of Wittgenstein's work offers an analysis of the projects and questions that have occupied him for the past forty years. If you doubt this claim, consider Antin's remark—which deliberately echoes his famous introduction to *talking at the boundaries*—"If Socrates was a poet, Wittgenstein is a poet" (161). To complete the equation, Antin's remark for *talking at the boundaries* is that "if robert lowell is a poet i dont want to be a poet   if robert frost was a poet i dont want to be a poet   if socrates was a poet ill consider it."[4]

Throughout his Wittgenstein essay, I'm struck again and again at elements of self-description present in Antin's analysis of Wittgenstein's work:

nearly all of Wittgenstein's questions and analyses from *The Blue Book* on . . . set in motion a process of narrativization. (151)

all three [Wittgenstein, Stein, and Beckett] were involved in a struggle with the representational capacities of natural language. (151)

The underlying issue . . . that finally culminated in the *Tractatus Logico-Philosophicus* was to create a completely perspicuous way of "picturing" thought, because the problem of language, as he expressed it in the *Tractatus,* was that "Language disguises thought—in such a way that it is impossible to infer from the external form of the clothing the form of the thought it clothes, because the external form of the clothing is shaped with different goals than to reveal the form of the body underneath it." (151)

These particular preoccupations—with narrativization (and its relationship to a manifestation of thinking-in-process), a testing out of the capacities of the demotic (particularly in the realm of the most vexing questions about language and thinking), and how to make thinking manifest (in its contingency and presentness)—are all central to Antin's many years of participation in the language arts.

In his Wittgenstein essay Antin describes the philosopher's practice in a manner that resembles his own:

> All of *Philosophical Investigations* can be said to consist of a *thinking-
> while-writing* that was in all likelihood based on Wittgenstein's own
> *thinking-while-talking*. For whatever else Wittgenstein may have been,
> he was an improvising, talking philosopher, whether he was talking to
> colleagues and friends in colloquia, or to students in lectures, or to him-
> self while he was writing. His lectures were legendary and have been
> described in great detail by any number of his students. According to
> Norman Malcolm, who attended Wittgenstein's lectures in 1939, they
> "were given without preparation and without notes." His commitment to
> improvisation was absolute and quite self-conscious. He told Malcolm
> that "once he had tried to lecture from notes . . . but was disgusted with
> the result; the thoughts that came out were 'stale,' or, as he put it to an-
> other friend, the words looked like 'corpses' when he began to read them."
> (159)

Antin clearly focuses our attention on the importance of thinking-
while-talking, both in Wittgenstein's work and in his own activity.
In doing so, he not only points toward his own kinship with
Wittgenstein, he establishes as well the importance generally of
talking and of improvising as essential to the doing of philosophy.
The particular similarity of Antin and Wittgenstein extends
through thinking-while-talking as the initiating activity of philosophy to a similar reliance on narrativization as central to thinking-
while-talking.[5]

When David stayed at our house for several days during his 1990
visit, I wondered how he would prepare for a talk poem. I had never
seen David do a talk poem, though we had corresponded and conversed, and I had visited him and had listened to a number of audio-
tapes of earlier talk poems. At that point in my hearing of his work,
I had not yet fully understood the consistent nature of the form of
his talk poems, so I had not yet understood how readily David
would be able to keep in mind a series of overlapping and somewhat
homologous questions and narratives. I can verify too that Antin
does not work from notes, that the talking is "spontaneous." I wonder, though, in what sense his talking is not a lecture. Perhaps that
question too bothered Antin's 80 Langton Street audience of 13 May
1978 when a group that included several leading Language poets—
Ron Silliman, Tom Mandel, and Bob Perelman—made a concerted
effort to interrupt the flow of an Antin talk poem, to develop an immediate conversation.[6]
　　Antin describes Wittgenstein's mode of "lecturing":

Example was piled on example; and although the examples were often fantastic, they were sometimes merely concretizations—most often narratively situated concretizations—of some ordinary fact. And these situations were always described in precise detail in everyday language. But the students were accustomed to a particular philosophical genre in which there is a single line to an argument, no matter how ramified—a chain of consecutive connections they could hang onto. They were apparently hoping to find a pathway they could follow all the way through a performance, so that at the end they could describe where they had come from and where they ended up. (160)

Many audiences, including the Tuscaloosa audience for "black warrior," have a similar experience, particularly if they are listening for the first time to an Antin talk poem. Initially, the series of anecdotes, stories, and speculations seem to have at best a tenuous or tangential relationship to one another. After reading and listening to Antin's talk poems for fifteen years, my own impression is, oddly, the opposite. I find the various stories and questions in an Antin talk poem to be highly interconnected. In fact, talk poems such as "black warrior" exhibit an intensity of connectedness and a unity that become apparent only after the listener/reader has reflected more thoroughly upon the presentation. Thus Antin's "black warrior," by means of an underlying meditation on defamiliarization and on the value of open spaces, connects thoughts about the nature of a university (as a site to test out what is reasonable and as a place to provide open spaces for exploratory thinking), to a critique of "false" eloquence (the Lowell-Thomas Syndrome), to a detailed consideration of the baffling meaning of the place name "tuscaloosa," to the Carol-story of a familiar life that keeps taking unpredictable new directions. Antin's talk poem embodies his claim that

> there is a kind of airiness in thinking
> thinking   there should be spaces in thinking
> when you are thinking   there are places that are
> open   like holes

Antin adds that "life is filled with holes," and he values a position that

> lets things be unexplained   it's very important
> to not understand certain things

But such a failure to understand—as Antin takes us to a series of word-sites and narratives that defy clarity and conclusion—resembles Derrida's own critique of reason in "The University in the

Eyes of Its Pupils," an essay which, in its specificity of address oddly resembles an Antin talk poem, particularly as Derrida, speaking at Cornell, makes the gorge and the suspension bridge at the center of the campus the central metaphor for his talk. As Antin claims in "black warrior,"

> suddenly things that are familiar   should become
> unfamiliar   and you think   do you really know
>   them   do i really know things   i think i know
>   things   and i don't   one of the things you think
>   you know is   you think you know people   and i
>   know that when i think i know people i'm in danger
>   that is   the more you think you know people
> the more you are likely to walk off a bridge

The impression that I end up carrying away from an Antin talk poem, especially after sustained consideration of it, is that almost everything in the talk is connected to something else in the talk, and that the stories bear important off-rhymed relationships to one another.

In David's talk poems, as in "black warrior," we are placed in a defamiliarization of the immediate. Antin defamiliarizes what we know—from the identity and consistency of behavior of the people closest and most present to us (in "black warrior," Carol's essentially changing and unknowable nature is the prime example, but so too are the neighbors, a key concluding example) to the names of things such as the cities and rivers and legendary historical figures that we live among.

But Antin's process of defamiliarization is unlike that in much American lyrical poetry of the 1960s to the present, which often constitutes a process that ends in a rhetorical and/or lyrical apotheosis of dumb wonder—i.e., "wow, isn't the world so beautifully and mystically strange; how little we can truly know." Antin, on the other hand, is interested *very precisely* in taking our knowing/thinking (and his talk poems) into areas that short-circuit certainty and comfort and that lead to irresolvable questions. In fact, his talk poems provide the openings—most often realized narratively, through accreted homeomorphic stories—to reside in such a space of negative capability. Or, as Antin describes Wittgenstein's work: "Wittgenstein's is a poetic practice based on the interrogation of the meaning of words in the context of life practices. That was what he meant by grammar, and it is a practice very close to that of the Socrates represented in Plato's quasi dialogues—the improvising sophist in performance, exploring meaning by thinking while talking" (161).

In "black warrior," Antin's investigation of the limits of knowing—his vernacular version of Derrida's *aporia?*—pivots about a
central meditation on the meaning of the name "black warrior,"
which is a translation of the "Indian" name Tuskaloosa, the name
for a famous chief, whose name is the name of the city where the
University of Alabama is located, and the name, in translation, for
the river that runs through Tuscaloosa. Though the issue never
arose directly nor in our subsequent conversations, I always had
the sense that this central story was also Antin's indirect way of
touching on the endlessly complex and tempting topic of race relations in Alabama. For it would have been unwarranted and ineffec-
tual chutzpah, though a chutzpah all too frequently visited upon us,
for David to have engaged in a frontal critique of race relations and
racial history in Tuscaloosa and in Alabama. So David works up
very obliquely to issues of race by means of an interrogation of the
name of the place where he is speaking. Chief Tuskaloosa, as the
common telling of local history has it, was a heroic warrior-chief
who had dark skin—hence, as the standard litany goes, the term
means "black warrior."[7] David doesn't even pause to force us to reflect on this odd over-layering: of the city name where Governor
George Wallace attempted to block integration of the state's pre-
mier public university using the name (from an Indian language)
for a dark-skinned warrior. Antin does ask us to think about the
meaning of *black* in such a context and to consider what sorts of
other color terms might go with *warrior* and whether it would have
been plausible for there to have been women who were "black warriors":

```
              i'll give you an example      today we went to
     a restaurant on the tuscaloosa river      they call it
         the black warrior river      it occurred to me
           immediately that this was something i really
         didn't understand      what do they mean black
           warrior      what to an indian      did the word black
         warrior mean      is it alternatively replaceable with
     white warrior      blue warrior      what does it
             mean to call a warrior black      for an indian to
         call another indian black      what did the word black
     mean      did it mean earthy      powerful
           energetic      warrior      is black a sacred color
             did the word black warrior mean something different
             before and after emancipation      i have no idea
     think of it      blue warrior      is there a blue
         warrior      were they creeks or choctaw      imagine
```

> they are creeks   what other names do these people
> have   this guy is a black warrior   but do they
> have a man called black hatchet   could he be
> called black laughter   blue embarrassment
> suddenly the word is absolutely   astonishing
> to have somebody called black warrior   black is
> not an immediate adjective that you would normally
> attribute to a warrior   so you wonder what could
> this black mean under these circumstances   black in
> what way   why did we translate it black

It is always easy to mis-hear David, as when, near the end of his meditation on the term *black warrior,* he says

> were the women given color names   a warrior
> is obviously not going to be a woman

I am increasingly aware that David's talk poems are built around a number of provocative booby traps—remarks that are deliberately annoying (and that often carry a design specific to the locale of the talk poem), quips that constitute that foot stuck out in the corridor of customary traffic.[8] This remark—about women and warrior-hood—obviously is not a casual sexist remark but a linguist's empirical observation. As with the seeming dismissal of Derrida, in a talk that has its own Derridean elements to it, David's remark about women and warriorhood is part of a story, about Carol, in which a woman turns out to be an extraordinary kind of warrior who supplants in strength and accomplishment a series of initially "heroic" males.

In some sense any and every David Antin talk poem is representative. This one, "black warrior," touches on many recurring Antin-issues: the value of not knowing; the value of open spaces—in art, in thinking, in education; narrative as connected to knowing, and certain kinds of narratives as instructive in the limitations of knowing and the unexpected nature of human being; the value and limitation of reasonableness; the unfamiliar nature of the familiar (particularly in language); the contingent nature of art and art-making; the value of process over product, particularly in art.

Antin in "black warrior" is quite critical of the Lowell-Thomas Syndrome and its descendants. In a remark that hit a raw nerve for many in his Tuscaloosa audience, Antin judges Randall Jarrell's work to be trivial. Jarrell is assessed as

the sort of poet who was almost good . . .
he could have been better   but he had
too many   ideas about what made it eloquent

Jarrell, lumped together with minor modes of mere loquaciousness in the writing of Robert Lowell and Dylan Thomas, is merely *eloquent*, and this term, *eloquence*, is at the heart of "black warrior" and, more generally, of Antin's concept of the talk poem. Lowell, for example, is pronounced to be merely "eloquent about being depressed," and his writing spawned "a sort of rhetorical eloquence." His many followers are described as

psychologically oriented successors
who look into their souls   and then make well-
framed expressive utterances based on their sadness

What dawned on me in re-viewing the videotape of "black warrior"—which I don't think I'd ever watched all the way through in the nearly ten years since the original presentation—is that Antin's critique of Lowell gets a bit sticky for the hosts of his reception, George and Kathy Starbuck. At the time of Antin's presentation, George Starbuck was a visiting endowed chairholder in creative writing at the University of Alabama. George, who many years earlier had won the Yale Younger Poets Award and had chaired the Iowa Writers Workshop (during an unusual period of experimentation), was quite a Boston Brahmin, a key figure in a group that included Robert Lowell, Sylvia Plath, and Anne Sexton.

I remember that after "black warrior," I had heard that George had made a number of very snide, witty remarks about the talk poem (and its lack of form), and that, seemingly, he had reenforced the creative writing students and faculty in their disdain for David's work. After a while, though, George and I had a very productive exchange about David's work and about other matters. In retrospect I understand that David had hit a nerve with his caustic remarks about Lowell & Co., but that what was even more serious was a dispute over the value, meaning, and importance of *eloquence*—a quality tremendously important in Starbuck's witty, vernacular poetry. Also, quite obviously, George and David diverged on the issue of what constituted form, particularly what constituted admirable form. What is most odd is that in spite of this awkward beginning, George and I became good friends, and George ended up—over and against the Alabama creative writing faculty—championing my poetry and introducing me when, after a fifteen year silence, I was asked to give a reading on the Alabama campus.

Perhaps it is easy to mis-hear, as George did, David's critique of eloquence. Obviously, Antin does not have a problem with loquaciousness—nor with being an active interlocutor. Perhaps for Antin, eloquence is a defect or a hazard within talking—what happens when one's thinking-by-talking becomes merely decorous, polished, and overly eager to please. I would like to think that in spite of their different assessments of Lowell, that George and David might have enjoyed one another's conversation.

When David visited me in 1990, I was about to turn forty, and after nearly twenty years of writing poetry, except for a small chapbook in 1976, I had not published a book. I showed David my proposed collection of poems, *Doublespace*, a nearly two-hundred-page manuscript which opened in two directions that meet in a blank interior space. One evening, late, I gave David a folder with about fifteen of my essays that I was shaping into a book. The next morning, at around 6:30, over coffee, David began talking to me, rapidly and intelligently, about *all* of it, analyzing for me the central preoccupations of my critical writing and urging me forward with the publication of *Doublespace*. He talked about the early publications—the interlocking networks of friendships, magazines, and small presses—for him and for Jerry Rothenberg and others in the early stages of their writing lives. He urged me *not* to introject or accept the mistaken prestige and authentification hierarchies that academic institutions cherish as part of an institutional assessment of the value of one's publications. In many ways I credit David's visit and talk with providing the energy of activation for my first book of poetry. *Doublespace: Poems 1971-1989* appeared in 1992, published by James Sherry's Segue Books—in the exact format I had employed in the mock-up which I had shown to David. Antin wrote that *Doublespace*

>   appears to present two ways of
> thinking and working that contend for the same
>   doubled space: a modernist way   the way of
>   collage that fragments and   assembles   registers
>   and styles in a junkyard of mediated texts
>   and an older   narrative way that tracks its
>   meaning through life experience under the fitful
>   lights of memory and desire   moving from
>   right to left like hebrew or left to   right like english
>   the two ways refuse to blend   each exhibiting its
>   own excellences and insufficiencies

A few months before *Doublespace* appeared, I published *INTER(IR)RUPTIONS* (Generator Press, 1992), a series of ten collage poems. That first book bears this dedication:

for David Antin—

why?

restless integrity
generous skepticism
inspiring juxtapositions

I watch and listen to David's "black warrior," and I continue a line of thinking that I have had for some years now as I consider the enduring value of his talk poems. I wonder, what is the value or context of such talking *now?* Certainly in the early 1970s the talk poem constituted a radical disturbance of the protocol of the emerging popularity of the poetry reading. But today, is the form of the talk poem an opening? And if so, an opening in or from what? As Antin himself has remarked, "the effect of an obstacle depends on its placement and the direction of traffic."[9] Clearly, the direction of traffic has changed over the past twenty-five years, and thus the efficacy of the talk poems as (productive) obstacle has changed too. Poetry readings have, if anything, become more predictable and formulaic (in spite of the proliferation of poetry slams and other vernacular poetry events). The Language poetry movement, with its emphasis on poetics and on a theory-based conversation, has had a small effect in making philosophical discussion a part of the overall conversation about contemporary poetry. Thus the philosophical and linguistics contexts for Antin's talk poems, when introduced to an audience that is familiar with Language writing, no longer register as tremendously surprising or challenging. However, when presented to audiences tutored in the expectations of most creative writing programs, Antin's mode of poetry-making is still highly disruptive, since his work remains at odds with the discretely framed lyric and with the prohibition against "abstract thinking."

By doing this form of thinking aloud for the past twenty-five years, to what extent has David's talk poem become a form of its own and thus perhaps a form subject to its own conscious and unconscious repetitions? Certainly David's mode of talking, thinking, and narrativizing does constitute an opening and a critique when placed beside the sentimentalized, breathy homespun stories of Garrison Keillor or the anguished familial psychologizing of

Spalding Gray. But in a more decidedly "literary" culture, what is the value and importance of David's talk poems? And why have they, for the most part, not been given a place in the many allegedly new anthologies of American literature?

As a longtime friend, I also wonder quite specifically what one takes (forward) from Antin's practice. I agree with the views he expresses in "what it means to be avant-garde," that, against the one-at-a-time wrestling-match line of heroic succession posited by Harold Bloom, artists share work with one another and provide one another with usable methods and materials. Antin, in contrast to Bloom, views a predecessor (or a contemporary) as someone who makes a work that is a potentially useful tool,

> and youll lean on it and feel grateful when its good
> to you   for somebody elses work   and youll
> think of him as a friend who would borrow as freely
>   from you if he thought of it or needed to   because
> there is a community of artists[10]

What then does Antin's work ask us to consider and to borrow from it? Or, put another way, what about it is usable now? Personally, my entire work in poetry—though manifestly different from Antin's—also revolves around the question of how vernacular language (though, as with Antin's work too, not exclusively vernacular language) might be an essential element in the work of philosophical/poetic thinking. Antin's work challenges us to make thinking manifest—to find ways of embodying thinking that do not become merely decorous, habitually rhetorical, severed from narrative, nor obsessed with a professionally driven need for craft-display. And the manifestation of thinking shall value process and contingency and improvisation; and it shall be decidedly of its time.

In pursuing various Antin-Wittgenstein parallels, I must acknowledge a fundamental difference: though the two of them are considering similar questions and preoccupations, the contexts for their activities remain quite different. Antin's work, though existing at the boundaries of several disciplines and genres—indeed as an activity that puts into question the stability and necessity of such demarcations—takes place nonetheless in the context of a world of language arts, particularly the point where the realms of poetry, visual arts, literary arts, lecture, and performance intersect. That is a very different context for performance and conversation from Wittgenstein's position within the ongoing conversation of philosophy.

Antin's talk poems constitute a productive impediment in two important ways. First, the intellectual adventurousness of his talk poems stands as a valiant corrective to the intuitive know-nothingism of most institutional versions of creative writing. Second, and perhaps at the other extreme, Antin's talk poems stand as a rebuke of certain consequences of a theory-based literary study—its fear of the vernacular and its growing distance from an active engagement with poetry itself (as the object of discussion increasingly has become theoretical pronouncements themselves). Antin's own intellectually energetic and philosophically informed exploration of the vernacular and of narrativity often serve to demonstrate in fact how strikingly unoriginal and uncomplicated are many of the most current theoretical fascinations.

Throughout this essay, when I suggest that Antin's talk poem exhibits many key features that are classically Derridean, I do not at all mean to suggest that David is consciously molding his talk in such a way as to mock or illuminate or imitate certain key concepts of Derrida's thinking. Quite the opposite. I think that Antin's talk illustrates how commonplace many of Derrida's "new" ideas are—indeed how inevitably they are a feature of any serious investigation of language, thinking, and meaning-making. I think that for Antin, Derrida's thinking is minor at best, and the attention given to Derrida's thinking becomes another piece of evidence for the faddish, reductive, ill-informed behavior of academic intellectual communities, particularly when literary critics attempt to fasten their thinking to something "philosophical." I think that Antin's talk poems constitute a cogent vernacular argument for the location of such "good thinking" *within* contemporary artistic practice (rather than as a thinking that must be found principally in a professionalized critical or philosophical practice).

Who, other than David, is doing such talking today? Particularly in the context of poetry and the poetry reading, what does Antin's singularity mean? Should there be others who pick up the form of the talk poem? Would that be a fit mark of influence or importance? When we look today at the many poetries marked by the influence and stylistic mannerisms of Ashbery or Creeley, is imitation necessarily an important mark of currency? What is it about David's talking that will be carried on by others? And what is it about Antin's talking that makes imitation perilous? Perhaps his example is principally one of a passionate engagement with how one might be present to others in the making of one's art, and how one might make manifest a thinking of some significance.

Antin's nearly thirty years of talk poems can be read (and heard) as a literalizing of the epigraph/question for *Talking*, the first of

Antin's books to include a talk poem ("Talking at Pomona"):

> if someone came up and started talking
> a poem at you how would you know it
> was a poem?[11]

Within the arena of the poetry reading, Antin's question still *does* constitute a radical disturbance, going to the heart (and root) of contemporary poets' ambivalent relationship to "natural" speech. Should the poem and the poetry reading not be based *fully* on the resources, possibilities, and contingencies of speech, and the particular rhythms, hesitations, and irregular music of "true" speech? Or shouldn't the poem and the poetry reading reflect an intensified, special, crafted dimension of the language arts, perhaps partially based on speech, but also resident in musical or lyrical precincts that link the poem to the more self-consciously made forms of song, chant, and prayer? Antin's talk poems provide an extreme advocacy and a powerful position for raising and examining these questions.

In a key site of difference, Antin describes Wittgenstein's relationship to intensification and concentration:

But there is a special character to Wittgenstein's poetic performances that is illuminated by another meaning of the German verb *dichten*, or more precisely by the meaning of a homophonic verb *dichten*, which has come to be associated with the poetic verb by a folk etymology meaning "to concentrate," "make dense," or "to pack." The notion of poetry as a mental concentrate has considerable significance for Wittgenstein's practice. He was apparently operating within an esthetic of "concentration" from the beginning. This esthetic commitment was the main point of the quote from Kürnberger that serves as the motto of the *Tractatus*: ". . . and everything we know that we haven't just heard buzzing and blowing around can be stated in three words." It is this combination of an esthetic of improvisation, concentration, and compression, within an exploration of the vernacular, that suggests a connection with a poet like Creeley. ("Wittgenstein" 162)

In fact, it is quite interesting to juxtapose the writings of Antin and Creeley (and especially their talking!). Creeley, whose work Antin describes as a "psychically, intense minimalist practice" ("Wittgenstein" 162), may stand in some ways as Antin's *written* opposite. In person both are great (and similarly wide-ranging) talkers. Around Creeley, one immediately senses the "naturalness" of his odd line breaks as exactly suited to his patterns of speech, where his endlessly ruminative talk takes sudden turns and is punctuated by odd pauses.

Unlike Creeley's *written* work, Antin's "intense maximalist practice" does not rely on a lyrical notion of concentration. The intensities in an Antin talk poem are slow to develop, and they are very much the accumulated reverberation of homologous narratives that serve to intensify—but very gradually and as an *aftereffect* of the talk poem—the critical (unanswerable but compelling) questions that emerge as central to the particular occasion of talking-thinking. In practical terms this anticoncentrated quality of David's talk poems explains, in part, why his work is excluded from all of the "major" anthologies of American literature and from nearly all of the "major" anthologies of contemporary American poetry. His unit of composition really is the forty-five-to-sixty-minute audiotape; his talk poems do not lend themselves to easy extraction. In fact, quite deliberately, they manifest a mode of talking-thinking that defies concentration. Perhaps for similar reasons, the entire Chautauqua movement, as a *literary* phenomenon, remains similarly underrepresented, and the talk/lectures of writers such as Thoreau and Emerson are still too often, in a significantly deracinated way, misunderstsood as exclusively *written* artifacts, severed from their occasional context as a public *spoken* performance.

And yet, as Antin reminds us, when we talk about improvisation—in writing, in jazz, and in thinking-talking—we are *not* talking about spontaneity that starts from ground zero: "There is no such thing as ground zero for any human being who hasn't suffered severe brain damage. For any performer there is always some complex of past, future, and present relevancy-conditions that makes the notion of complete spontaneity an absurdity. And in any temporal genre each successive take is experienced as a revision of the one before it" ("Wittgenstein" 162). The last sentence in this passage seems to me to be especially important to an understanding of Antin's three decades of talk poems. Antin's own early talk poems—and especially the framing material in *talking at the boundaries*—give considerable emphasis to the oppositional or disruptive nature of his activity. As audiences over the years have learned about the new mode of "literary" performance devised by Antin, the disruptive aspect—as a key heuristic and literary-cultural intervention—becomes less and less important. Some of my own moderate critique of his talk poems—that they have achieved a kind of stasis and a quality of repetition and comfort—is, then, somewhat unreasonable, particularly in light of Antin's remark about "any temporal genre." His remark also allows me to feel at ease in my claim of representativeness for "black warrior" and in my sense of each talk poem as an incremental and inevitably overlapping element in a long-range process of thinking. Like any other thinker, David Antin has a set of key questions and concerns. As Antin points out (via Charles Hartman's *Jazz Text*) about Charlie Parker—"Parker was probably the most prolific and inventive improviser in jazz. Yet Parker's improvisations are built out of a store of about a hundred 'motives' " ("Wittgenstein" 162). For "motives" substitute "narratives" and "questions" and some dedicated compiler could then, perhaps, enumerate a similarly extensive but finite storehouse for Antin's talk poems.

Marjorie Perloff's *Wittgenstein's Ladder* grants sustained attention to a range of Language poets as writers whose work extends from and values Wittgenstein's thinking. Antin's own assessment of Language writing is not nearly as generous:

On the other hand, Wittgenstein is a poet of nearly pure cognition. He is not a poet of the German language or the English language; he is a poet of thinking through language. And the Language poets Perloff cites are poets of English. They are not so much exploring as exploiting, often elegantly, the distinctive properties of the English language. If we can imagine Wittgenstein and the Language poets engaged in a similar seeming act, like sharpening pencils, the products might look the same, but the Language poets are fashioning slender cylindrical objects that come to a finely shaped point, while Wittgenstein is preparing a writing instrument. (163)

In some ways, Antin's critique of Language poets and their "exploiting, often elegantly, the distinctive properties of the English language" bears a slight resemblance to his critiques (in "black warrior") of Jarrell (for a kind of minor eloquence) and of Lowell (for a too narrow scope of psychologized lamentation). Though Antin is hardly hostile to Language poetry, ultimately, it is not for him a writing that has achieved more than a minor significance.[12] It is a poetry that may bring to attention the materiality of signification (and a few other somewhat important fundamental premises), but I do not think that for Antin such writing has in any way made an important or fundamental contribution, nor has it really done anything *fundamentally different* from what had already been done by a range of earlier modernist artists.

I would suggest that Language writing (as a movement) is rife with "foundational" poets whose work, as championed by various Language writers, gets presented in a highly problematic partial way. Antin, as someone who foregrounds the contextual nature of genre and meaning and whose talk poems stand as a philosophically informed rebuke of the minor plainspoken lyrics of mainstream poetry, certainly can be seen as reenforcing Language poets' critique of "official verse culture." But Antin's reliance on narrative and his comfort with speech (in contrast, say, to Robert Grenier's "I HATE SPEECH") make him an unlikely forebear for Language poets. So too are other "foundational" Language poets, upon more detailed examination, being claimed in obviously partial and uneasy ways. I think, for example, of Robert Duncan's mysticism, spirituality, and high romanticism or of the shamanism and surrealism of Jerome Rothenberg's work as two key instances of poets whose work may have been formative for Language writing but whose work, upon sustained examination, is seen to be perhaps equally at odds with premises of the writing that it is claimed to support.

But then the entire discussion of Language poetry, particularly now (when such discussions are an odd mixture of retrospective narration blurred with generationally conflicted assertions about the present), has often depended upon oversimplifications in order to advance a particular viewpoint or theory. That is, actual Language writing (vs. critical descriptions of it) does not equal the externally imposed critical caricatures and freeze-frame definitions of what it is or was. The present practice of writers as diverse as Susan Howe and Charles Bernstein is often at odds with fundamental axioms used to describe the movement. Howe's work, from the very beginning, has been, among other things, intensely autobiographical and familial (as one aspect of her rewriting of early American literature). Bernstein's work, certainly for the past ten years, has a strong basis in stand-up comedy and in spoken performance.

The dominant, extended story for "black warrior" is the Carol-story, which Antin begins just after he remarks that "the more you think you know people   the more you are likely to walk off a bridge." At the end of the Carol-story, David concludes,

> i thought i understood carol   at any given
> moment i kind of thought i understood carol   but what
>   carol constantly taught me is   something else is
>   going to happen you're not going   to understand
>   me   . . . she's somebody i know
>   very well   and i don't know what she's likely to do
>   at   any given moment
>   now it seems to me   that the basis for
>   my approach to poetry has always been to be unsure about
>   what i know   to be true   but one of the ways i
>   have to reassure myself about this   is to look to
>   my experience in life and say   my life has

    prepared me to be a poet   who doesn't
      know how to do it

Near the very end of this talk poem, Antin reflects briefly on the way his neighbors radically redirected their lives, from being, seemingly, a conventional suburban couple, to a family splitting apart when the wife "became a lesbian all of a sudden." Antin ends by saying of the neighbors, and of all the figures of the talk poem,

      i thought i knew them too   and i guess i did
          but no more than i know   what black is in
    black warrior

NOTES

[1]See my two chapters, "Thinking Made in the Mouth: The Cultural Poetics of David Antin and Jerome Rothenberg," *Opposing Poetries: Volume One: Issues and Institutions* (Northwestern Univ. Press, 1996), 91-125, and "Thinking about It: David Antin's *Selected Poems, 1963-1973*," *Opposing Poetries: Volume 2: Readings* (Northwestern Univ. Press, 1996), 95-109.

[2]I have done the transcribing for all passages quoted from "black warrior."

[3]*Modernism / Modernity* 5.1 (1998): 149-70; hereafter cited parenthetically.

[4]*talking at the boundaries* (New York: New Directions, 1976), 1.

[5]In an E-mail sent to me on 15 February 2000, Antin indicates: "My argument, and I think it holds, is that W[ittgenstein], in almost all the works about whose composition we have documentation of from the *Blue Book* on, seems to have proceeded from thinking-while-talking to thinking-while-writing. This procedure is not so unusual in philosophy. It's just that W's commitment to improvisation in the talking is so absolute. There is also another aspect of his work that exhibits his poetic (creative) sensibility that I mentioned but didn't make as much of. His almost inescapable and involuntary imaging of his own ideas. That is, when he came up against some kind of wall in his analytic thinking he would almost invariably crystallize the problem in an image out [of] which he would attempt to extract a solution. The solution frequently involved narrativization of the image." If there is a difference worth noting here, I would suggest that where Wittgenstein resorts to a narrativization of the image in an attempt to *solve* a problem, Antin relies on narrativization to manifest and to reenforce the problematics of the key questions or issues that arise in his talk poems. Antin's narrativization thus is not a hoped for means of solving a problem; it is a means of making the problem more immediate in its complexity and in its probable irresolvability.

[6]For a fascinating account of this talk poem and the dynamics of the interaction between Antin and the 80 Langton Street audience, see *The Po-*

etry Reading: A Contemporary Compendium on Language & Performance,
ed. Stephen Vincent and Ellen Zweig (San Francisco: Momo's Press, 1981),
particularly Ellen Zweig, "Where Is the Piece?: An Account of a Talk by
David Antin," 174-86, and David Antin's reply, "A Response to Ellen Zweig,"
187-91.

[7]In the foreword to issues of the University of Alabama's literary magazine, the *Black Warrior Review,* it is noted that "the city, the river, and the
magazine all derive their name from that of a sixteenth-century Indian
chief, Tuscaloosa (also spelled Tuskaloosa or Tushkalusa), which comes
from two words of Creek or Choctaw origin—*tasca,* meaning "warriors," and
lusa, meaning "black." In 1540 Chief Tuscaloosa battled the Spanish ex-
plorer de Soto at Mauvilla, a fortified Indian settlement about a hundred
miles north of present-day Mobile. He supposedly perished in that battle, in
which more people were killed than in any other single battle in the United
States." In Virginia Foscue's *Place Names in Alabama* (Tuscaloosa: Univ. of
Alabama Press, 1989), we learn that "Tascaluca, among other spellings,
first appeared in the journals of de Soto's secretaries in 1540, referring to a
province and a chief. . . . By 1818 the name Tuscaloosa was preferred. . . .
This name, which spread from a Choctaw tribe to a province, to the chief or
class of chieftains, to the river or the falls, and finally to the settlement, is
derived from Choctaw *tashka* 'warrior' and *lusa* 'black' " (139-40). Obviously, both of these accounts do not answer the questions (of relational
meanings of color terms and of the meaning within the tribe of *black*) that
Antin poses. In fact, these two "explanations" become classic examples of a
(Derridean) irrecoverable and infinitely regressive origin.

[8]In his framing remarks for "talking at the boundaries" in *talking at the
boundaries,* Antin explains (52),

i had tried out the idea of the artist as
obstacle   how perhaps instead of giving a more precise
or glamorous form to the platitudes of the culture
the artist might propose himself as a sort of impediment   like sticking out a foot in a corridor and changing the direction of the traffic

[9]*talking at the boundaries,* 52.
[10]*what it means to be avant-garde* (New York: New Directions, 1993), 47.
[11]*Talking* (New York: Kulchur Foundation, 1972), 8.
[12]Note that the term *minor* is my own, and not a term that Antin himself
uses. As Antin clarifies (in an E-mail to me, 15 February 2000), "As for my
comments on the Language poets, as you indicate I have nothing against
their poems, but I think their relation to W[ittgenstein] is not very significant. On the other hand I've never really thought of any poetry as 'minor.'
It's not a term I have any relation to. It's too official. I might think of much
of it as pleasurable but 'light' or 'slight'. But so were Campion and Herrick.
Is that comparison too funny? In any case, you're right in pointing out that
my commitment to the vernacular and to narratives separate me from
them quite radically." My own remark on the "minor significance" of Language poetry refers principally to its impact on Antin's own work.

A David Antin Checklist

Stephen Cope

The following is a selected bibliography of David Antin's publications. Where possible and appropriate, I have indicated inclusive page numbers (this is not always possible for out-of-print works). For a concise but complete biographical sketch of Antin—including a book by book summary of his work—see Kenneth Sherwood's entry on Antin in the Gale Research Series' *Dictionary of Literary Biography* (Detroit: Gale Research Press, 1996, 3-12).

Books

definitions. New York: Caterpillar, 1967.
autobiography. New York: Something Else, 1967.
Code of Flag Behavior. Los Angeles: Black Sparrow, 1968.
Meditations. Los Angeles: Black Sparrow, 1971.
Talking. New York: Kulchur Foundation, 1972; rpt. Normal, IL: Dalkey Archive Press, 2001.
After the War (A Long Novel with Few Words). Los Angeles: Black Sparrow, 1973.
talking at the boundaries. New York: New Directions, 1976.
Dialogue. Santa Barbara, Ca.: Santa Barbara Museum of Art, 1979.
who's listening out there. College Park: Sun & Moon Press, 1980.
Poemes Parles. Cahiers des Brisants, 1984 (selected poems in French translation).
tuning. New York: New Directions, 1984.
Selected Poems 1963-1973. Los Angeles: Sun & Moon, 1991.
what it means to be avant-garde. New York: New Directions, 1993.

Cassette/Audio

The Principle of Fit. Washington: The Watershed Foundation, 1980.
the archaeology of home. Los Angeles: Astro Artz, 1987.

Film

The Sandwich Man, a feature length screenplay written in collaboration with Eleanor Antin, to be directed by Eleanor Antin and produced by David Antin, August 1993.

Music Lessons, 46 min. 16mm color, sound. Produced by David Antin and co-written by David Antin and Eleanor Antin. Directed by Eleanor Antin. Completed November 1997. Screenings: New York Film Market, November 1997; San Diego Museum of Contemporary Art, January 1998; SUNY Stony Brook, May 1998; North Carolina School of Film, May 1998; Los Angeles County Museum of Art, June 1998; KTOP, Oakland, Ca. 1999.

Forthcoming Works

Selected Essays. Chicago: U. of Chicago P.
John Cage Uncaged. Los Angeles: Green Integer.

Selected Critical Writings

"Grey Paint: Robert Morris." *Art News* 65.2 (April 1966): 22-26, 56-58.
"Arabian Chess." *Kulchur* 5.20 (Winter 1965-1966): 75-80.
"The Silver Tenement: Andy Warhol." *Art News* 65.4 (Summer 1966): 47-48, 58-59.
"D'Arcangelo and the New Landscape." *Art and Literature* (Summer 1966): 102-13.
"Blake, Fuseli and Palmer." *Art News Annual* 22 (Fall 1966): 108-24.
"Eccentric Abstraction." *Artforum* 5.3 (November 1966): 56-57.
"Notes toward an Ultimate Prosody." *Stony Brook* 1 (December 1968): 173-78.
"Jean Tingueley's New Machine." *Art News* 67.8 (December 1968): 20-23.
"Mazes: A Show of Transient Architecture." *Arts Magazine* 43.7 (March 1969): 18-20.
"Lead Kindly Blight." *Art News* 69.7 (November 1970): 36-39, 87-90.
"The Elements." Catalog essay for the Museum of Fine Arts, Boston, 1970.
"The Role of a University Art Gallery." *San Diego Union* 28 March 1971.
"It Reaches a Desert in which Nothing Can Be Perceived but Feeling." *Art News* 70.1 (March 1971): 38-40, 66-70.
"Alex Katz and the Tactics of Representation." *Art News* 70.2 (April 1971): 44-47, 75-77.
"Déjà vu." *Art News* 70.4 (Summer 1971): 50-53, 63-65.
"Art and the Corporations." *Art News* 70.5 (September 1971): 22-26, 52-56.
"Modernism and Postmodernism: Approaching the Present in Modern American Poetry." *boundary 2* 1.1 (1972): 98-133.
"Duchamp: The Meal and the Remainder." *Art News* 71.6 (October

1972): 68-71.

"Duchamp and Language." *Marcel Duchamp*. New York: New York Graphic Society, 1973.

"Some Questions about Modernism." *Occident* 8 (Spring 1974): 6-38 (a response to questions posed by the editors).

"Television, the Distinctive Features of the Medium." *Video Art*, catalog of exhibition by the I.C.A., Philadelphia, June 1975; published in a revised version as "Television, Video's Frightful Parent," in *Artforum* 14.4 (December 1975): 36-45; republished under original title in *Video Art* (New York: Harcourt Brace Jovanovich, 1976) ed. Schneider and Corot; and in its full form in *Television: the Critical View,* 2nd ed.(Oxford, 1979).

"The King and the Queen." *Crawl out Your Window*. 1977.

"Is There a Postmodernism?" *Bucknell Review* 25.2 (1980).

"Exclusionary Tactics." Review article on Michael Fried's *Absorption and Theatricality*. *Art in America* 70.4 (April 1982): 35-42.

"Review of *Solution Passage: Poems 1971-1981*," by Clark Coolidge. *Los Angeles Times Book Review* 17 August 1986.

"Biography." *Representations* 1 (Fall 1986): 42-49.

"Thinking of Richard Allen Morris: Some Sentences." Catalog essay for Richard Allen Morris exhibition, La Jolla Museum and Mandeville Gallery, UCSD, La Jolla, 1987.

"The Stranger at the Door." *Genre* 20.3-4 (Fall-Winter 1987): 464-81.

"Thinking about Novels." *Review of Contemporary Fiction* 11.2 (Summer 1991): 210-16.

"FINE FURS." *Critical Inquiry* 19 (1992): 151-63.

"Have Mind, Will Travel." In Robert Morris catalog. New York: Guggenheim Museum, February 1994.

"The Beggar and the King." *Pacific Philological Journal* (1995).

"Wittgenstein among the Poets." Review essay of *Wittgenstein's Ladder: Poetic Language and the Strangeness of the Ordinary*, by Marjorie Perloff. *Modernism and Modernity* 5.1 (January 1998): 149-66.

Fiction

"The Balanced Aquarium." *Kenyon Review* 21.4 (Autumn 1959) 577-85.

Uncollected Talk Pieces

"talking to discover." *Alcheringa* 2.2 (Summer 1976): 112-19. Special issue on Ethnopoetics. (Talk followed by discussion).

"radical coherency." *OARS* 1 (Winter 1981): 177-91.

"the value of the real thing." *Art in America* 69.5 (May 1981): 108-

13, 150-53.

"the man with the hoe." *Bachy* 18-19 (Spring 1981): 78-84.

"the death of the hired man." Catalog essay for *Siah Armajani*, Baxter Art Gallery, Cal. Inst. of Technology. Pasadena: 1982.

"the messenger." *Journal: A Contemporary Art Magazine* (Summer 1986).

"endangered nouns." *Remembrance of Things Past*. Catalog. Long Beach Museum of Art, Fall 1986.

"writing and exile." *Tikkun* 5.5 (September-October 1990): 47-52.

"determination suspension diversion digression destruction." *Conjunctions* 19 (Fall 1992): 51-78.

"theory and practice of postmodernism—a manifesto." *Conjunctions* 21 (Fall 1993): 335-43.

"i never knew what time it was." *108 / 107* Atlanta: December 1999. (Pamphlet).

Book Reviews

Reinaldo Arenas. *The Color of Summer; Or the Garden of Earthly Delights.* Trans. Andrew Hurley. Viking, 2000. 417 pp. $28.95.

The Color of Summer is the fourth novel in Arenas's "Pentagony," his own term for a series of novels that treat Cuba, homosexuality, the process of literary creation, and the struggle for individual expression. The novel revolves around a fiftieth anniversary celebration of Fifo's (Castro's) control of a Caribbean island. (It has actually been forty years but the dictator prefers round numbers.) In order to make the celebration perfect, the dictator has ordered the resuscitation of all of his dead enemies, including a large cohort of literary figures, so that they can properly pay homage to him before he puts them to death. This Rabelaisian tale includes an extraordinary array of characters involved in biting farce and hyperbolic sex. Characters have multiple names and identities, including references to the author himself, who is alternately Reinaldo, Gabriel, or Skunk in a Funk, depending on whether he is a writer, a son, or a queer. There are references to figures like Gabriel García Márquez as La Marquesa de Macondo or Miguel Barnet, the well-known testimonial writer, as Miguel Barniz. The references to historical and literary figures abound and may be missed by some readers less familiar with Cuban history and Latin American letters, but the extraordinary strength of the prose translation and the mesmerizing originality of the narrative are certain to captivate readers new to literature from the region. One of the most compelling features of this novel is the emotional intensity of the tale: fantastic humor is combined artfully with a profound sense of sadness, loss, and suffering. The agony of the "Pentagony" is extremely sharp, especially in the sections of the narrative that are letters from the author in Cuba to his alter ego in exile. These letters, speaking of the anguish of dictatorship and of AIDS, of personal sacrifice and loss, highlight the political postmodernism of Arenas's work and mark the text as an extraordinary combination of pleasure and pain. [Sophia McLennan]

Eric Chevillard. *On the Ceiling.* Trans. Jordan Stump. Univ. of Nebraska Press, 2000. 136 pp. Paper: $15.00.

"[I]t is by fully trusting in appearances that one begins to reshape the world," declares one of the characters in Eric Chevillard's *On the Ceiling*. Chevillard's eccentric writing style puts a lot of weight in appearances, postulating reality as a potentially flexible space in which the laws of gravity, etiquette, even the form of the body, are all subject to change. The narrator of *On the Ceiling* wears a chair upside down on his head, imaginatively reinventing both "chairness" and his relationship to the world at large. Initially *On the Ceiling* reads like a philosophical parody, but Chevillard renders the odd ideas of his characters with enough respect that their situation swells and blossoms into their own world. Thus, in execution, the novel goes well beyond any notion of parody. Intriguingly, after speaking of his chair for almost eighty pages, the narrator abruptly abandons the chair to live on the ceiling of his girlfriend's apartment, using one way of life as a stepping-stone into another.

To read Chevillard is to engage with the texture of his prose, to lose oneself in long sentences and paragraphs, to move from confusion to lucidity and back again, to leap from one idea to another. Chevillard is one of the few contemporary French writers to pick up language where *Molloy, Malone Dies,* and *The Unnamable* left off, one of the few writers to offer a convincing post-Beckettian periodic prose line. Jordan Stump's admirable translation preserves Chevillard's complex sentence structures and syntax, preserving the odd feeling Chevillard's original French. Part philosophical *esquisse,* part satire, *On the Ceiling* is an intriguing book, well worth reading, and unique. [Brian Evenson]

Edmund White. *The Married Man.* Knopf, 2000. 310 pp. $25.00.

The plot of Edmund White's latest novel, *The Married Man,* is simple enough: Austin Smith, a lonely, middle-aged, American art historian living in Paris, meets a young, supposedly aristocratic, and essentially heterosexual Frenchman named Julien, who is in the process of divorcing his wife. They fall in love. Austin is seropositive, and, after much fear of losing Julien, finally discloses his HIV status. When Julien proves to be seropositive as well, Austin blames himself for infecting Julien, even though the doctor tells Austin that there is only the smallest chance that he could have done so. Julien becomes ill and dies. Only after Julien's death does Austin learn of Julien's lower-class background and extensive gay experience. Moralists might say that *The Married Man* is about deception, or about self-deception, but White is concerned about the way couples live out the myths they have created about their relationship and whether or not it corresponds to the facts of their life. *The Married Man* challenges one of the most powerful myths associated with AIDS: its power to strip away the polite, artificial surface of reality and force people to confront how they really are. White shows how, in the face of a terminal disease, people cling even more tenaciously to the narratives they have constructed about themselves and each other. Indeed, because modern medical practice strips patients so mercilessly of any sense of privacy, mystery, or dignity, patients and their families may need to hold on more than ever to the protective coloring of their personal myths. White's sexual explicitness masks a deeper discretion about the complexities and irrationalities of love. Elegantly written and grippingly narrated, *The Married Man* is White's most readable novel. [David Bergman]

António Lobo Antunes. *The Natural Order of Things*. Trans. Richard Zenith. Grove Press, 2000. 298 pp. $25.00.

António Lobo Antunes's previous books have earned him comparisons to almost every literary master of the twentieth century—writers as diverse as Dos Passos, Céline, García Márquez, and Cormac McCarthy. This newly translated novel will likely have the same results, with Faulkner's *The Sound and the Fury* the most apt comparison. Lobo Antunes has a deft touch in creating a tapestry of voices out of the jumbled interior monologues of his characters. In a piecemeal fashion, jumping from character to character across a span of over forty years, *The Natural Order of Things* recounts the disintegration of two families. As the novel progresses, Lobo Antunes foregrounds the theme of isolation in the plot, providing a touchstone for the reader to understand each character's separate history. A young man is separated from his family when he is arrested on charges of political conspiracy; his illegitimate half-sister is shunned by the family and locked in an attic with her record player; a former miner relives his past life and loves, convinced that he can fly underground; and the son of the "madwoman in the attic" connects the two families when he falls in love with the miner's daughter and spends his nights whispering the secrets of his youth to her silent back. Although the idea that entropy is the natural order of things is invoked through the sordid events and desolate images that dominate this book, the hopeful optimism of Lobo Antunes's writing is affirmed through splashes of comedy and magical coincidences. [Chad W. Post]

László Krasznahorkai. *The Melancholy of Resistance*. Trans. George Szirtes. New Directions, 2000. 320 pp. $25.95.

The more one knows, the harder it is to stop shuddering. Whom may one trust? Who can say what more or greater horrors await as all hell threatens to break loose, denying individual will, devastating the commonweal? If force must prevail, which force, and at what cost? Such concerns haunt the characters in this first of László Krasznahorkai's novels to be translated into English, dissecting their lives as residents of an ordinary Hungarian town under siege by powers alien in their hostile inscrutability. Valuska's mother, Mrs. Plauf, returning home by train, is accosted by a young man who apparently believes she means to seduce him. What can this presage? Valuska then witnesses the arrival of a traveling carnival featuring a huge whale carcass, a retinue of shady, desperate men seething in its wake. The peculiar fascination exerted by this exhibit, along with its lingering menace, increasingly baits public attention, while Valuska's peculiar gifts and pathetic innocence mark him as a victim-in-waiting. As the irruption of the threat posed by the show's hangers-on enfolds Valuska in its spread, a larger flood of savagery is unleashed on the town until order finally is restored. Mrs. Plauf falls before the wholesale rapine, but her friend Mrs. Eszter, cannily taking the measure of the situation, seizes the initiative to rout the intruders and assume effective control of local affairs. Flushed with triumph, she enshrines Mrs. Plauf as a martyr, but her ruthless efficiency augurs no good.

For narrative sophistication and acute discernment of contemporary social unrest, Krasznahorkai's artistry merits serious notice. Unraveling his long, rhapsodic sentences, which suggest a language of bad dreams, proves captivating entertainment. May further translations grant him the wider notice he deserves among English-speaking readers. [Michael Pinker]

Don DeLillo. *The Body Artist*. Scribner, 2001. 125pp. $22.00.

This taut drama makes a startling contrast with the historical spread of *Underworld*. The action centers on a couple and then a widow living in a large frame house in an unnamed village on the American coast. The first section describes the negotiations between a film director and his wife over holding a meaningful dialogue, which turn into a meditation by the wife on experiential authenticity. In the second chapter we are given news reports of the director's suicide and descriptions of his technique which bear implicitly on the novel itself: "His subject is people in landscapes of estrangement." That is exactly what happens in *The Body Artist,* where the widow Lauren returns to the house to try to reconstruct her life after the death. As she explores the upper floors she finds a man who has been sleeping there for some time and engages him in conversation in order to understand where he comes from. His replies are so cryptic, however ("I know how much this house. Alone by the sea"), that each encounter becomes a struggle to impose meaning on his words. As these attempts gradually fail, DeLillo places more emphasis on Lauren's nonverbal skills. She is the body artist of the title and uses her dancing as a way of consciously existing in time. While this gives her a structure, Lauren's identity remains elusive and shifting. One reviewer sums up her performances by stating: "She is acting, always in the process of becoming another or exploring some root identity." To the very end of the novel this process remains enigmatic and inconclusive, but DeLillo keeps our interest through the unpredictable twists and turns of Lauren's thoughts. [David Seed]

Rick Moody. *Demonology*. Little, Brown, 2001. 320 pp. $24.95.

Although most of the stories in this collection have previously appeared in various periodicals, a number of interesting effects occur when they are assembled in *Demonology*. First, Moody's range of talent is revealed right away; the difference in storytelling between the heart-wrenching, intimate title story and the cold observation of pieces like "Hawaiian Night" and "Boys" proves once again that Moody has earned his reputation as one of the best contemporary American writers. Second, Moody is nothing if not a chronicler; his characters in "The Double Zero," "Hawaiian Night," and "The

Carnival Tradition" reflect a huge range of social/economic/American expe-riences, yet each is presented in an incredibly accurate manner. What makes Moody's reflections more innovative, though, is his representation without excessive "comment." He simply lets the voices of the characters hang in the air. Last, the collection shows Moody's amazing ability to present a seemingly conventional story in a different and effective way. Al-though *Demonology* has its pieces that are experimental in form ("Wilkie Ridgeway Fahnstock, The Boxed Set," for example, which consists of liner notes to the soundtrack, on casette, of one man's life), these seem less inter-esting and more showy. Moody shines when he lets his talent for storytelling take over. Both "The Mansion on the Hill" and the title story il-lustrate this point extremely well; serving as end pieces in the collection, they will keep Moody's fans happy and surely enlist quite a few more. [Amy Havel]

Sylvie Germain. *The Book of Tobias*. Trans. Christine Donough. Dedalus, 2000. 196 pp. Paper: $12.99.

Sylvie Germain, like many writers and artists, is a metaphysician. She believes in the transcendental nature of simple objects: a peasant song, a loaf of bread, the family dog. With these objects, she composes a mystical, allegorical world, a world of legend and myth, a world of magic. Objects, characters, and gestures are charged with a spirit, an aura of generosity, affection, and forgiveness. Accordingly, *The Book of Tobias* is a retelling of the biblical story of Tobit, which details the journey of a young man (Tobit), accompanied by the angel Raphael, who undertakes a journey for his father (Tobiel). They encounter Sara, who has survived seven young suitors, and both biblical story and novel quickly proceed to happy conclusions. *The Book of Tobias* translates the story into twentieth-century France. The bib-lical narrative is merely a structure from which Germain can weave out her fabulous characters and situations. There's the story of Deborah, Tobias's grand aunt, who survives two wars, immigration to and deportation from America, and the deaths of most of her family, including Tobias's mother Anna, whose accidental beheading begins the novel. There is also the story of Theodore, Tobias's father, who searches in vain for his wife's missing head; Arthur, Tobias's jealous uncle, who has hidden the head in his chim-ney; and Valentine, Arthur's wife and Anna's sister, who turns mad with grief. It is in this fecundity of storytelling where Germain is at her best. The novel remains problematic, however. While the world she creates is well imagined and self-contained, Germain takes her angels seriously, and so the novel sometimes borders on the mawkish and sentimental. I recom-mend *The Book of Tobias* only to those who don't mind a touch of the celes-tial in their fiction. [Jeffrey DeShell]

Carlos Fuentes. *The Years with Laura Díaz*. Trans. Alfred MacAdam. Farrar, Straus & Giroux, 2000. 516 pp. $26.00.

Carlos Fuentes seldom sets out to create psychologically rounded characters in naturalistic scenes. Instead, his fiction is driven by the ideas his characters represent, especially in his interpretation of Mexican history. So it might seem natural for Fuentes to model his latest novel, *The Years with Laura Díaz,* as if it were one of those great Mexican murals, say the one by Diego Rivera that graces its jacket: a stylized panorama of factory workers and revolutionaries rendered with the boldness and flatness of a cartoon that is as crowded as the time line of the novel itself, and in which the title character makes a cameo appearance. Moving Laura Díaz from the periphery of Rivera's mural to the center of his novel, Fuentes takes readers on a decade-by-decade tour as she bears witness to Mexico's modern transformation, from her family's prerevolutionary legends, through the stasis that marks Mexico by the end of the novel's main action in 1972. An acknowledgment page details the numerous friends and relatives Fuentes drew on for the stories that make up his panorama. It doesn't list the breadth of learning he also brought to the novel. Unfortunately, the fusion of the two in this stylized depiction often reads like a straight-forward family saga, peppered with talking-heads discoursing on politics. Its affinities with a TV miniseries format is surprising, coming as it does from an author known for narrative complexity. Indeed, richness, density, and line-by-line virtuosity arguably make his magnum opus, *Terra Nostra,* one of the most profound novels of the century, nostalgically recapitulated in *Laura Díaz*. If that earlier book was philosophy, a groundbreaking novel that, through its understanding of history, showed what a literature of the Americas might look like, then *The Years with Laura Díaz* is the sociology of the familiar, both in theme and aesthetics. [Steve Tomasula]

Javier Marías. *A Heart So White*. Trans. Margaret Jull Costa. New Directions, 2000. 288 pp. $24.95.

This celebrated European best-seller opens with an unexplained suicide in Madrid forty years before the narrator is born, when the aunt he'll never meet leaves the lunch table and shoots herself in the chest. The next chapter jumps to his honeymoon, as he overhears lovers plotting murder, perhaps, in the next room of a Havana hotel. His father is a curator who regularly defrauds major museums. This seems like material for a thriller, but *A Heart So White* is a reflective book. It is narrated by Juan, a United Nations interpreter, acutely aware of gesture and the ambiguity of language. So while he uncovers the facts behind some of these intrigues, the understanding he longs for remains elusive. On assignment in New York, he spends time with an old flame. She is searching for romance by sending out anonymous videos of herself. Her strange hunt for affection is an amplification of the isolation of all the characters in this book. Dark secrets remain dark even when they are shared, because they are an internal experience, part of the loneliness of individuality. Translating for two heads of state, Juan misinterprets what they say, just to see what happens. There are no consequences. Marías's novel mixes philosophy and kinkiness, suspense and contemplation. As in the works of Martin Amis and Paul Auster, the elements of mystery writing are used as a catalyst for existential observation. Everyday events coalesce into tragedy. Connections are made, symmetry forms, but discovering truth has a way of making life more complicated. Even when people speak plainly, it seems, it is hard to know whether they have learned anything about their true selves. [Ben Donnelly]

Günter Grass. *Too Far Afield*. Trans. Krishna Winston. Harcourt, 2000. 658 pp. $30.00.

Grass's wonderful novel is to be read by anyone interested in the role of literature at the end/beginning of the century. Like the sofa stuffed with secrets in the Ministries' basement, *Too Far Afield* bulges with German cultural history, opening with a chronology (1598-1990) and emphasizing the political and literary from Luther forward. Creating a partnership reminiscent of *Faust* between two contemporary East Germans—Theo Wuttke (a minor lecturer and clerk in the Stasi archives with a "time-defying understanding of politics and literature") and his shadow, the Havana-smoking, suddenly appearing Ludwig Hoftaller—the novel unravels their intersections and that of their historical doubles, Theodor Fontane (for whom Wuttke is called "Fonty" because he seems to know, write, speak Fontane's every word) and *his* spy/shadow, Tallhover. The nineteenth and twentieth centuries echo with similar occurrences—German unification in the Franco-Prussian War (celebrated by Fontane) and at the fall of the Wall (doubted by Wuttke); also, Grass's characters' lives repeat Fontane's plots; Turks have replaced the Jews as the alien group. An archivist (the Fontane Archive is in Potsdam) provides the narrative perspective while his group embodies the spying techniques that are such a part of German history; the archivists observe, speculate, fictionalize, and include various perspectives on an incident to fill in gaps in knowledge. The five-section structure—as well as references to *Macbeth,* the tragedy of over-reaching—suggests drama. While the novel ends without resolution, the necessity that doubt replace Luther's absolute reliance on faith comes along with the fear that the future once again will repeat the past. [Richard J. Murphy]

José Saramago. *All the Names*. Trans. Margaret Jull Costa. Harcourt, 2000. 238 pp. $24.00.

All the Names is the story of Senhor José, a largely solitary and blandly consistent clerk employed on the lowest rung of the city's Central Registry of Births, Marriages, and Deaths. Having no life, no connections outside of his job, José entertains himself by collecting newspaper clippings, keeping track of the most notorious and most photographed celebrities. One day, by accident, he stumbles upon the birth certificate of an unknown woman. He becomes obsessed with discovering all he can about her, though it puts his job and his life at risk. The Central Registry, a massive and labyrinthine building in which researchers must hold to a thread or become lost, seems a setting lifted from Kafka. Indeed many of the elements that appear in *The Trial* are to be found here: a seemingly anonymous clerkish bureaucracy, an arcane hierarchy with rigid etiquette, a stifling mass of records, a sense of the irrepressible weight of all that remains unavailable to the central character. Yet, finally, *All the Name*s moves toward a (sometimes tenuous) sense of human connection that Kafka would eschew. As José follows the thread of the unknown woman's life, making connections he has always shied away from, he gradually discovers how little can be known about anyone, including oneself. But rather than leading him to despair, such discoveries open his life up in ways he cannot imagine.

Stylistically, *All the Names* employs the devices of Saramago's earlier work: multiclaused and sinuous sentences in long paragraphs, with little done to set off the difference between narration and quoted speech. The novel has many of the strengths of Saramago's most compelling novel, *Blindness,* yet while *Blindness* has a velocity and brilliance in its first half never quite equalled in the second, *All the Names* manages to sustain its force to the end. Symbolically permeating the line between life and death, *All the Names* is Saramago at his most compassionate and least sentimental, at his very best. [Brian Evenson]

David Mitchell. *Ghostwritten*. Random House, 2000. 448 pp. $24.95.

Nine narratives told from a corresponding number of far-flung locales compose this ingenious first novel by David Mitchell. The wildly alternating voices and settings of *Ghostwritten*'s chapters (a Japanese cult member, an Irish physicist, a New York disc jockey) are so compelling and authentic that one may initially mistake this novel for a book of stories. Each first-person chapter introduces a new character, and the connections that the reader draws among all these voices ultimately form the novel's core. The overlap among the novel's sections varies from direct contact between characters to implied metaphors, but the end result is a finely woven tapestry that is nearly seamless. It is to Mitchell's great credit that the novel's odd links never seem forced or contrived. *Ghostwritten*'s great achievement is that it incorporates fairly heady scientific ideas into its structure while remaining readable, intellectual, and humanist. While the novel is sufficiently confounding to upset any easy conclusions, ultimately that's part of its allure. Heisenberg's uncertainty principle roughly means that the more you try to conduct an accurate measurement, the more you interfere with what's being measured. In a sense *Ghostwritten* cleverly mirrors this theory, for a reader who can draw on a working knowledge of quantum mechanics may have more unanswered questions than those who cannot. Despite the number of narratives and disparate places, *Ghostwritten* remains thematically cohesive. The deep sense of connection among these narratives suggests a global interdependence that manifests itself in the most unimaginable ways possible. This novel reads like a brilliant daydream that attempts to explain plausibly how a seemingly insignificant event in one person's life can irrevocably alter the life of a complete stranger halfway around the globe. It's probable that Mitchell wrote the novel to show just this. [Jason Picone]

Padgett Powell. *Mrs. Hollingsworth's Men*. Houghton Mifflin, 2000. 144 pp. $20.00.

Padgett Powell's splendid new novel begins: "Mrs. Hollingsworth likes to traipse." And traipse the novel does, through wonderfully imaginative fog, surreal and real. The novel starts by situating Mrs. Hollingsworth at her kitchen table, ostensibly to consider a shopping list. What she manages, however, is the construction of a narrative surrounding her desire to identify the ideal of Southern masculinity. To come to terms with the new Southern male, Mrs. Hollingsworth looks back to the Civil War, specifically to Nathan Bedford Forrest, a notorious Confederate general. Mrs. Hollingsworth's shopping-list narrative, however, does not restrict Forrest to the past. In fact, he pays her a visit near the end of the novel, and earlier in the narrative he meanders around as a fifty-foot hologram. The surreal environment of the shopping list narrative is anchored by the reality of Mrs. Hollingsworth's life: the real fog. She is a realtor, a mother of two, and a wife. While her family questions her sanity, Mrs. Hollingsworth relishes her moments alone with her shopping list: "Mrs. Hollingsworth retook her kitchen, headquarters for her recent lovely campaign." Given the mundanity of her daily life, Mrs. Hollingsworth relishes her imaginative exploits. Padgett Powell's text, however, is more than just an investigation into what it means to be a housewife in the new South. Powell's text is also about language. By way of beautiful prose, Powell has produced an imaginative novel of remarkable fluidity. There is no moment in the book that isn't delightfully crafted. Given the strength of the language alone, *Mrs. Hollingsworth's Men* would be worth reading. Since there is also a compelling narrative drive, *Mrs. Hollingsworth's Men* should be placed at the top of every list. [Alan Tinkler]

Raymond Queneau. *Stories and Remarks*. Trans. and intro. Marc Lowenthal. Univ. of Nebraska Press, 2000. 155 pp. Paper. $15.00.

Few writers can claim as various and influential a body of work as Raymond Queneau, and nearly every aspect of his distinctive art is on offer in this slender volume. The twenty-one short pieces included here range in date of authorship from the twenties, when Queneau was a young man deeply involved in the surrealist project, to the early seventies, well after he'd made his reputation as the founder of the Oulipo group. As well as chronological diversity, the book demonstrates considerable formal diversity; it contains fablelike stories, fragments of uncompleted novels, pseudoacademic treatises, "texticles," and even a playlet. Not surprising then, that there's a hodgepodge quality to the collection. *Stories and Remarks* is saved from being a mere desk-clearing effort, though, by at least two things. First, the translator, Marc Lowenthal, has extensively annotated each story and almost every remark, providing a publishing history and establishing a context for them all. More important, there's a consistent tone of humor throughout. Some have termed Queneau's brand of comedy black, since he considered any subject, scatological or eschatological, as pun worthy, but his attitude wasn't bitter enough to warrant that assessment. Here as elsewhere in his oeuvre, whimsy abounds and the darkest mood is one of rueful amusement at the banality of life. Lowenthal notes that Queneau's first published work was an account of a dream, and the final piece in this miscellany, written near the end of his life, purports to recount several more. The events of each narrative are mundane—a woman shells peas, another walks a cat on a leash—but their atmosphere is the recognizable strangeness of our own nocturnal imaginings. It turns out that the bland tales are true and the only oneiric quality about them is the intentionally stilted way in which they're told. Queneau may have begun by turning a dream into prose, but by the end of his fifty-odd-year career, he could make the most prosaic detail dreamy. [James Crossley]

———————

Roger Martin du Gard. *Lieutenant-Colonel de Maumort.* Trans. Luc Bebion and Timothy Crouse. Knopf, 2000. 778 pp. $35.00.

The pace of this old-fashioned bildungsroman is geologically slow, the events of the Lieutenant-Colonel's boyhood stretched to breaking between lavish descriptions of the various settings. At times, du Gard's evocations of place seem merely digressive, as if he could not curb his (very nineteenth-century) descriptive impulse. However, when the plot, or a subplot, breaks though the expository overcast, it shines that much more brightly. The interpolated tale of an affair between a school teacher and a baker's assistant is a tragic, affecting romance, while Maumort's sexual awakening with a mature Martiniquan woman is an almost perfect rendition of what is often, in lesser writers' hands, a trite watershed of bildungs-heroic youth. (Du Gard's style, objective but muscular, is ideally suited to matters erotic.) Old-fashioned, then, but also artfully fashioned, at least in part. "In part" because the trouble with *Lieutenant-Colonel de Maumort* lies not in du Gard's art, but in the simple fact that the book is unfinished. The translators, with the irrationality of true fans, claim that this is one of the century's greatest novels. It is not. It is a work-in-progress, abbreviated here, rough-hewn there, and sans denouement. (Though the translators claim otherwise, *Lieutenant-Colonel de Maumort*, unlike Robert Musil's *Man without Qualities*, does not philosophically support its own incomplete state.) That said, this hefty seminovel will chiefly please two groups: du Gard's admirers, and other novelists. The former will happily sift through the fragments and composition notes that comprise the last three hundred pages of this book, in search of glimpses into du Gard's (decidedly blue) perspective; the latter, after carefully reading the rest, *should* sift through the aforementioned miscellany for insights into the craft and magnitude of proper novel-making. Readers, however, ought to start with *Jean Barois* or *The Thibaults* to sample this neglected master's work. [Harold Davis]

———————

John Taylor. *Some Sort of Joy*. Cedar Hill Publications, 2000. 149 pp. Paper: $15.00.

John Taylor's latest is a "daybook." He recounts his various walks in a small French village, describing passages through various streets as he shops or takes his son to school. His descriptions are, on the surface, routine and commonplace. But he finds that even ordinary walks are surprising. Indeed, he discovers that existence is mysterious, and thus he becomes a fascinating observer and participant. Almost every page offers inquiry but few solutions. In the very first description, Taylor, bringing a cartload of produce to market suddenly spots a cathedral, "its two spires blended—in profile—into one knife blade thrusting high in the heavens. This knife blade is the only familiar sight I recognize, however. To my left extends an enormous discount shoe store and to my right I read 'Marché d'Intérêt National.' " The passage is representative. Taylor recognizes the unfamiliar in the familiar and vice versa; there is a sudden change of perspective and the subsequent risk of acceptance. It is appropriate that he juxtaposes cathedral and discount store, or rather, that he sees the juxtaposition. How can he find "some sort of joy" in an odd mixed world. He tells us: "It is difficult to obtain a correct perspective on the world, on what one should do with one's life, in such a place." Taylor's plain prose is appropriate; although he thinks about the most difficult philosophical questions, he brings them down to earth. And as we read Taylor's apparently simple prose we see that its surface hides deep secrets, uncommon perplexities. This brilliant book is a kind of pilgrim's process, offering no final answer. [Irving Malin]

———————

Michel Houellebecq. *The Elementary Particles*. Trans. Frank Wynne. Knopf, 2000. 272 pp. $25.00.

The French, in literature at least, love their bad boys, their Célines and Rimbauds, and Houellebecq, author of this best-selling, award-winning novel variously compared to work by Balzac, Camus, and Beckett, is the latest of these. Many reviews have stressed the book's schematic—halfbrothers, children of the sixties, raised apart and undone by heritage, inner failings, and the many failings of their era; others the novel's frank sexuality. Often, in fact, reviewers have seemed at a loss for what to say, and little wonder: this novel speaks the language of profundity, but speaks it poorly, tenses incorrect, articles awry, phrases misplaced. The mark of our time— that great dislocation identified by Virginia Woolf—is that our lives have become discontinuous. Houellebecq's novel well attests to this, self-generating from the tension between the continuous filament and discontinuous currents of the brothers' lives as they careen through the sixties in the wake of their own disabilities, sexual liberation, social confusion. The author sometimes seems to have had as little clue as reviewers as to where the book was going, what was intended, his many grafts of philosophical cant and op-ed discursions a manifest of this, as he casts about for handholds. That being said, it must also be remarked that the novel is compulsively readable—readable almost in spite of itself—not for its profundity but for all the small verisimilitudinous touches against which structure and author seem pitched in Jacob-like struggle. Houellebecq wants to stand apart, to be witness to his times. But his characters, like drowning men, grasp him and pull him down with them: he cannot help caring, he cannot help loving them, cannot help drawing with them that final, fatal breath. [James Sallis]

James Chapman. *Daughter! I Forbid Your Recurring Dream!* Fugue State Press, 2000. 217 pp. Paper: $8.00.

Readers of James Chapman's four previous novels—particularly his 1995 *Glass (Pray the Electrons Back to Sand)*, an astonishing critique and simultaneous indulgence of the tele-voyeurism of the Persian Gulf War—will again find themselves in the presence of a truly remarkable literary alchemist. If the adage holds true that an author's books are in many ways her/ his children, Chapman's *Daughter!* is perhaps the brightest and most beautiful test-tube baby in his family of experimental novels. In detailing the otherwise ordinary life of our narrator Frieda from her preconception to her postmortem, Chapman blends elements of creation mythology, semiotics, religion, the artifice of music, and the banality of family life into a grand poetic prose that is as hauntingly disembodied as the best texts of Kathy Acker and as strikingly visual as any Paul Thomas Anderson film. In opening *Daughter!*, Frieda reminds us that "Believing what you cannot see, that is believing." And while faith hangs in the balance as we trip through Frieda's life and her forays into art, love, politics, self-actualization, and self-destruction, thematic justice seems to be among the least of Chapman's concerns. It is Chapman's ongoing experiment in his fiction—his exploration of the serious limitations on our ability to communicate in a largely inarticulate culture that has become dangerously obsessed with violence, veneer, and volume—that weighs most heavily. For as Frieda believes that she can "rescue us all out of the performance" of our parents' lives by setting her own agendas and interpreting the "instructions my own way," Chapman may too believe that his *Daughter!* can deliver Barnes & Noble-ized fiction from its current infantile regression by creating entirely new rules and setting different expectations. I believe with his newest enfant terrible that he may just be right. [Trevor Dodge]

Gerhard Köpf. *Piranesi's Dream: A Novel*. Trans. Leslie Willson. George Braziller, 2000. 240 pp. $22.50.

Winds of disaster blow through this fictional autobiography of the eighteenth-century Italian artist Giovanni Battista Piranesi. Calling to mind Browning's crazed creative narrators, Piranesi, in a hermetically sealed voice, as though speaking from the crypt, rails against the Catholic church, against critics, against his wife Angelica who cuckolded him, and against his nemesis, the German aesthetic Johannes Winckelman, whose effete brand of Hellenism he denounces as a sham—a preposterous veil thinly concealing Winckelman's pederasty. Piranesi's unrelenting passion is to build. He characterizes architecture as "a sublime symbol for the tension between what you want to do in your mind and what you are able to do in reality." Too fantastic, monumental, and unwieldy to be built, Piranesi's architectural schemes find their sole form in drawings and engravings. Ironically, what Köpf's Piranesi laments as a grand failure is transfigured into a marvelous triumph. The narrator does seem to realize (in a way reminiscent of Nietzsche's description of the posthumous man) that while his work is scorned by his contemporaries, it will be understood by subsequent generations. Piranesi's drawings and engravings, as he himself admits here, are reflections of a tormented soul. Certainly this can be seen in his towers, torture chambers, byzantine corridors, and shadowed archways. This narrative itself is claustrophobic. There seems to be no way out. Even when he wants to die, he finds that route of escape blocked. He is condemned to eternal life. Indeed, the story is told with an omniscience unconfined by history. Haunted by the compulsion of eternal return, Piranesi is left adrift in the Australian desert, still dreaming of reconstructing the ancient city of Rome. [Allen Hibbard]

Donatien-Alphouse-François de Sade. *The Mystified Magistrate and Other Tales*. Trans. and intro. Richard Seaver. Arcade, 2000. 211 pp. $23.95.

The Marquis de Sade is not known for restraint, either in the length or subject matter of his fiction. So it's surprising to see how successful and charming some of his shorter works are. This volume, which contains a novella and eleven shorter pieces, is a fascinating addition the Sade canon (if we can speak of such a thing) in English. The novella "The Mystified Magistrate" is a splendid introduction to Sade's work. It contains most of the elements that make him great: humor (a pompous judge wallowing in pig sty), cruelty (buttocks glued to a toilet seat and then burned from below), sexual experimentation (flogging, cuckolding, drugging, and interracial coupling), as well as his sometimes tedious philosophical digressions. It's all here, although in greatly abbreviated form. What's obviously missing is the sheer scale and repetition of Sade's imaginative obsessions, obsessions which readers can only grasp in the longer works. Two stories, "Emilie de Tourville or Fraternal Cruelty" and "Augustine de Villebanche or Love's Strategy," even hint at Sade's possible feminism. "Emile" decries the cruelty and hypocrisy of punishing young women for their supposed loss of honor. "Augustine" begins with a spirited defense of lesbianism and details a story where a young bisexual male cross-dresses to seduce a young bisexual female, who herself is in drag. Roles are reversed, then reversed again; pronouns are confused, and the Douglas Sirk ending doesn't dissipate the story's radical questioning of traditional gender roles. This is not to say that all of the stories are equally interesting. Some of the briefer pieces don't even rise to the level of short shorts and remain simple jokes or anecdotes. Still, much of the volume makes rewarding, important, and fascinating reading. [Jeffrey DeShell]

Carmen Martín Gaite. *The Back Room*. Trans. Helen Lane. City Lights, 2000. 215 pp. Paper: $11.95.

In the second chapter of Carmen Martín Gaite's hypnotic novel, the narrator remarks: "There is always a dreamed text, vague and fleeting, that precedes the one that is actually recited and is swept away by it." This is the essence of *The Back Room*. The plot itself seems unspooled from a dream. A writer relates her coming-of-age tale to an apparition which has awakened her in the middle of the night. Gaite uses this scenario to explore the dichotomy between dream and reality. The back room of the title exists in a dream, where the simplest movements yield the greatest pleasures. The action therein depicts quite wonderfully how a dream can be more real than the conscious, while still maintaining the thread connecting the ethereal and the happenstance and making both not only believable but desirable. Gaite is careful not to take the simple for granted and derives beauty and intrigue from all aspects of her narrator's tale. When objects—the paper on which she writes, the books strewn across the floor, photographs—become "fingered for such a long time, they become emptied of all their content," they become memory, dream. Gaite sidesteps the notion that dream is inherently psychological and instead makes it tangible, filtering the objects in the room and the bodies of her characters through the dream state until all that exists between the narrator and the stranger, as well as between narrator and author, is the dreams. *The Back Room* is an exquisite creation, elegant, smart, and sad—a remarkable story of the nature of a consciousness. [Brian Budzynski]

Ludmilla Petrushevskaya. *The Time: Night*. Trans. Sally Laird. Northwestern Univ. Press, 2000. 155 pp. Paper: $14.95.

Anna Andrianovna's night thoughts begin almost comically, providing an intimate glimpse of her life and thought as the Soviet hegemony wanes. Her mordant remarks, punctuating a journey with her grandson Tima in search of food for the hungry child, reveal Anna's near-desperate plight in hues of gray and black. She is a poet who gives readings, when she can get them, to children. Of late, Anna lives from hand to mouth with little Tima, while her estranged daughter, Alyona, the boy's mother, moves in and out of her flat, taking lovers, bearing children, and finally fleeing when she no longer can stand Anna's constant criticism. Anna's son, Andrei, equally feckless, remains the apple of his mother's eye. A youthful felon released from prison under an amnesty, later crippled tumbling out of a second-story window, Andrei is no longer a young hood, but a drunkard who periodically hits up Anna for cash while keeping well beyond her urgent embrace. Anna's expectations for her children receive little respect and much scorn. Her ceaseless harping, intended to make them feel guilty, only drives them away. To top it off, Anna's schizophrenic mother lives in a mental institution to which her daughter consigned her some years ago. With its closing imminent, mother must be moved, but where? To Anna's home? To another institution, farther away? Though scraping together a living for herself and her sometime dependents, even while she tries to cope with the tangled affairs they create, takes its toll, still Anna would be, is, lost without them. This reprint of Petrushevskaya's 1992 novel purports to present Anna's literary remains, dubbed "Notes from the edge of the table." In their harassed, frequently sarcastic reflections, life appears reduced to a series of strains taken and accommodations made, her troubled story mirroring that of the society collapsing about her. [Michael Pinker]

———————

David Means. *Assorted Fire Events*. Context Press, 2000. 181 pp. $22.00.

In this new collection of stories, David Means is interested in "how people go about their daily lives . . . how they bide their time and what they fill up that time with. Not the big motions but the little ones. . . ." Using these "little motions" and moments of life Means expertly crafts thirteen intensely incisive explorations into the depths of the American mind. One of the best in the collection, "The Gesture Hunter," is concerned with the mission of a man to find the perfect gesture. It is made explicit in this story that Means, like his narrator, is looking for truth among all the false gestures we practice and experience every day and examining the very real pain behind the gestures we perform to get through the day. In "The Reaction" a doctor reflects on the gestures he performs on his patients—the routine touch of the shoulder, a hug, the occasional kiss on the cheek or forehead. He remembers using these routine gestures in his last meeting with his estranged daughter and comes to the realization that "the evil thing about pain is that it makes us sensitive to the smallest nuances of movement." This idea is central to these subtle and deeply moving stories. The language is stark and the settings often brutal, as Means, like his gesture hunter, seizes moments, probes into the everyday remembrances, regrets, longings, and losses buried deep in the hearts of his Americans. These wonderfully penetrating stories are lamentations for the dead, the un-known, and the unloved. In his search for the perfect gesture Means creates just that, beautifully articulating the human capacity for pain and for rev-elation. [Christy Post]

———————

Emily Barton. *The Testament of Yves Gundron*. Farrar, Straus & Giroux, 2000. 305 pp. $25.00.

Emily Barton explores notions of society and societal changes in her first novel, *The Testament of Yves Gundron, Yeoman Farmer of Mandragora Vil-lage, Being a Treatise on the Nature of Change and on the Coming of the New World*. Ruth Blum, an anthropology Ph.D. candidate from Boston, who is researching the isolated village of Madragora, edits Yves's testament, providing editorial insights into the rudimentary village where the inven-tion of a horse's harness is cause for celebration. Even though Ruth at-tempts to remain an objective, noninterfering observer, she brings about enormous change, albeit accidentally. Ruth inadvertently helps Yves, the village's inventor, make the harness more productive; specifically, she sug-gests the concept of a wagon with breaks. With such advances, it is only a matter of time before the village becomes productive enough to support lei-sure activities, particularly the fashionable Sunday afternoon drive. Given the new transportation trend, the village's perimeter expands, making in-evitable contact with the surrounding twentieth century. Yves's *Testament,* accordingly, becomes a narrative concerned with the nature of change. Ironically, Yves becomes Mandragora's historian, hurriedly attempting to record the history of the uncorrupted, prewagon society. While the preindustrial world maintains a privileged position, the narrative acknowl-edges the import of technological advances. The narrative, though, is not a didactic call for the return to nature, but rather an interesting exploration of the tensions that result during times of transformation. Emily Barton is a clever writer. She takes advantage of narrative techniques, specifically narrative layering, to explore her subject more fully. In a less competent writer the structural multiplicity could suggest narrative trickery, but that is simply not the case. Emily Barton is to be commended; *The Testament of Yves Gundron* is a fine first novel. [Alan Tinkler]

———————

Denis Johnson. *The Name of the World*. Harper Collins, 2000. 129 pp. $21.00.

Denis Johnson is haunted by the ghostly remains of the Catholicism he once accepted. He writes about lost souls who cannot accept heaven or earth, and he recounts their desperate wanderings and longings in a vision-ary style. The narrator of this stunning novella is a middle-aged widower. He cannot stop thinking of the accident that killed his wife and children. He lives (or tries to) in the academic world, but he cannot accept its abstract, secular, meaningless rituals and conventions. So instead, he tries to find solace in strip clubs, in imaginary conversations with the guard of a museum, and in a music student, Flower Cannon, who both strips and plays cello. He returns obsessively to a painting. He looks at the youthful skaters and yearns for their perfect movements. In the last two pages we learn that the events the narrator has described so vividly occurred in the past. He is now a journalist covering the insanity of the Gulf War. He has found a kind of perverse salvation in the vast wastes of the desert. The last sentence describes his ascent in helicopters above blazing tank battles—the vantage offers him a view of "the world pocked by burning oil wells like flickering signals of distress, of helplessness." The ending is, of course, ambiguous. Has the narrator finally found significance in his overview of the wasteland? Is he capable of naming the world? Or is he merely a victim of the fiendish, nameless delusions which have finally abused him? The novella, like *Wise Blood* or *The Moviegoer,* marries religion and madness. It offers inexplicable solutions, and confirms Johnson's angelic/demonic talent. [Irving Malin]

———————

John Lanchester. *Mr Phillips*. Putnam, 2000. 292 pp. $24.95.

John Lanchester's cookbook/novel *The Debt to Pleasure,* a formal experiment in the tradition of Nabokov's *Pale Fire*, poked fun at English elitism and Francophilia and gave us the soul of a snob to taste. In his second book, by deliberate contrast, Lanchester serves up a member of the middle class, Mr. David Phillips, philistine, mediocrity, and ogler of girls. *Mr Phillips* has a certain affinity with Nick Hornby's fiction of male infantilism, and the influence of Nicholson Baker may be discerned in Lanchester's connoisseurship of the mundane. In writing a novel about a day in the life of a middle-aged London accountant, Lanchester affords his audience tingly pleasures of recognition, but the effect is far from complacent. The restrained precision of the third-person narration blends the appalling with the wonderful, as the habitual privacy of a lifelong commuter is punctured, in turn, by an accosting pornographer, a Jehova's witness, and a nutcase in the Tate Gallery, to mention some of the eccentrics who buttonhole Lanchester's *flâneur.* The tired male in Cool Britannia has little to shout about: "[T]he city is inhabited by people 99.999 per cent of whom will never have a monument built to them, and who know it, and who repay the compliment by ignoring all the monuments and memorials to toffs and nobs and heroes and famous victories." The knife is out for postimperialist complacency. Lanchester's generous humor draws on the wholesome, cleansing traditions of urban fiction in English: echoes here of Mrs. Dalloway, Mr. Pickwick, and Leopold Bloom. [Philip Landon]

———————

Brain Evenson. *Contagion and Other Stories*. Wordcraft of Oregon, 2000. 152 pp. Paper: $11.00.

With this new collection of short stories Brian Evenson further stakes out his own disturbing, sometimes hilarious, and always bizarre narrative terrain. The stories here often take place in an abstract western landscape that grafts John Ford's sweeping vistas to Samuel Beckett's stark stage sets. In the barbwire-inspired title story, two fence checkers follow a ceaseless fence line across a vast plain, cataloging the victims of a mysterious and deadly contagion as they advance. In "A Hanging" sophist horsemen force a stranger into killing another and then himself. In "Prairie" a Corronado-like party of explorers takes a gory trek across a waterless plain in which "at times one discovers the living hidden among the dead." The characters in *Contagion* effuse a severe Old Testament sensibility and enunciation that has a strong Mormon bent. Polygamists, patriarchs, and self-proclaimed prophets abound here. In "Two Brothers" the patricidal Theron rebels against the *Holy Word of God as revealed to Daddy Norton,* while his placid brother Aurel watches. In "By Halves" two half-brothers enter a suicide pact to resist the strong-arm father who "preached them awake" each morning. In one of the most powerful stories, "The Polygamy of Language," a renegade linguist (of sorts) attempts to solve "the problem of all possible language," beginning with killing his two polygamist neighbors. Throughout *Contagion*, various written texts and acts of writing appear regularly, as if language itself were an inescapable contamination, an ontological quandary that each character must unravel, as the narrator of "The Polygamy of Language" says, "not from a distance, but from within." *Contagion and Other Stories* challenges readers in daring and unexpected ways. [Peter Donahue]

––––––––––

Antonio Tabucchi. *Dream of Dreams*. Trans. Nancy J. Peters. City Lights, 2000. 136 pp. Paper: $10.95.

"I have often been seized by the desire to know the dreams of artists I have loved," Antonio Tabucchi writes in a brief note preceding this little book. Propelled by this desire, Tabucci fabricates short dreams of Dedalus, Ovid, Apuleius, Angiolieri, Villon, Rabelais, Caravaggio, Goya, Coleridge, Leopardi, Collodi, Stevenson, Rimbaud, Chekhov, Debussy, Toulouse-Lautrec, Pessoa, Mayakovsky, Lorca, and Freud. (The list itself says a good deal about Tabucci's tastes and interests.) As intriguing as the conceit is, these dreams hold little surprise; they are all too predictable. Rabelais meets the fantastic glutton Sir Patagruel in his dream. Coleridge's dream holds a vision of a captain, a ship, and an albatross. In his dream Caravaggio receives the vision for *The Calling of St. Matthew.* The night before his death Sigmund Freud dreams he is Dora, and as Dora he seems to enjoy the advances of a young man. And so on. "The Last Three Days of Fernado Pessoa: A Delirium," which follows these ficticious dreams, blurs the line between reality and fantasy, or illusion, in more satisfying ways. As in Broch's *Death of Virgil* (though far more compressed), Tabucchi conveys the marvelous sense of a whole life as the modern Portuguese poet conjures imaginary conversations with a handful of old friends: Alvaro de Campos, Ricardo Reis, Alberto Caeiro, Bernardo Soares, and Antonio Mora. Clearly Tabucci (qua Pessoa!) creates these characters, or "heteronyms," as they are termed: "voices that spoke in him and had autonomous lives and biographies." All of this imagining is exhausting business. "But now I've had enough, dear Antonio Mora, living my life has been like living a thousand lives," Tabucchi's Pessoa sighs wearily before expiring [Allen Hibbard]

Julio Cortázar. *62: A Model Kit*. Trans. Gregory Rabassa. New Directions, 2000. 281 pp. Paper: $14.00.

The love triangle at the heart of Cortázar's *Hopscotch* gave rise to prose in which desire was poured out in long, breath-taking passages of unrestrained lyricism. *62: A Model Kit*, which takes its cue from chapter 62 of *Hopscotch*, is shorter and more subdued than its predecessor. The atmosphere is less orgasmic, more postcoital, shrouded in gray and grounded in what the novel calls depressence—"A depression is like something that makes you go lower and lower. . . . On the other hand, a depressence keeps raising up everything around you. You fight against it but it's useless, and finally you are left on the ground like a leaf." Rather than *Hopscotch*'s triangle, *62: A Model Kit* is structured around overlapping pairs and parallels. As with most of Cortázar's work there is a loose, dreamy quality to the prose, which is played up by a point of view which can drop from third into first person midsentence. The prose is still gorgeous, but gains its power not through overflowing exuberance, but through saturation and condensation. The novel opens with the main character, Juan, overhearing an innocent enough phrase spoken by a customer in a restaurant. But for Juan, who is an interpreter by trade, it immediately becomes anything but innocent. The phrase takes on a double meaning which continues doubling and expanding in Juan's mind. What is important in the novel that ensues is not plot in the traditional sense, but the unpacking of the resonances and associations embedded in that simple moment of eavesdropping. While much of the attention given *62: A Model Kit* stems from its connection to *Hopscotch*, the novel is important in its own right. New Directions' reissue repairs what was a regrettable gap in the available works of Cortázar. [T. J. Gerlach]

Tom Paine. *Scar Vegas and Other Stories*. Harcourt, 2000. 215 pp. $22.00.

The stories in Tom Paine's first collection of short stories are filled with the ugliest Americans, although Paine's characters do more than simply sport fanny packs and garish Bermuda shorts. In "The Hotel on Monkey Forest Road," an arrogant real estate developer in Bali tramples on the spiritual offerings of the Balinese people that stand in the path of his mega-hotel development. He then turns his exploitative ways into a barroom tale. In "A Predictable Nightmare on the Eve of the Stock Market First Breaking 6,000," Melanie Applebee, a down-and-out management consultant, broke and stranded in Mexico, gleefully recalls the restructuring maneuvers that made her a corporate star: "The plan closed down marginal stores, bought a chain of cut-rate drug stores, slashed the pension program, reduced employee stock options, severely limited the health plan, and cut wages." Paine serves these characters up as models of the booming global economy. But in these geopolitical parables the international robber barons get their comeuppance and watching them get their just deserts is wicked fun. American economic arrogance is met with swift violence and deadpan humor. But *Scar Vegas* isn't all revenge fantasy. Paine's world is more balanced and true; the virtuous and downtrodden suffer, too, often at the hands of the more economically privileged. The deftly drawn characters keep the tales from sinking into the type of morality tales in which characters are stand-ins for Truth or Capitalism or Evil. In this respect, Paine succeeds where many political fiction writers fail; his characters remain individuals and that allows him to make the political personal. Furthermore he offers no windy historical exposition or clunky, self-righteous, didactic summation. In these compressed, savage stories there isn't a wasted word or action. [Nicole Lamy]

Tobias Wolff, ed. *Best New American Voices 2000*. Harvest/Harcourt, 2000. 434 pp. Paper: $14.00.

Readers of excellent but somewhat predictable and homogenous fiction anthologies like the *Best American Short Stories* series will be excited that there is a new kid on the block. This inaugural volume of a yearly series collects short stories by new writers rather than by established masters of the form. Contributors come from workshops and creative writing programs across the country, not from the pages of the *New Yorker*. Volume editor Tobias Wolff has selected twenty fine stories that vary greatly in terms of tone, subject matter, even length (with one selection, "The Hatbox," by Jennifer Vanderbes, pushing the boundaries toward the length of a novella). These stories are by no means uniform and don't fit together neatly like Lego blocks. The question most readers will ask is whether the collection also varies in terms of quality. Of course it does—what anthology doesn't?—but the distance between the best and the worst of these stories is slight, and the overall impression the collection conveys is not that these emerging writers have a long way to go, but rather that there are some very exciting and promising new voices coming up over the horizon. In terms of energy, passion, artistry, and intellect, this collection is a winner, and it should appeal to readers generally interested in the short-story form, and particularly to aspiring writers of short fiction who want to find out what's really current. Where else could one find stories about a rivalry between a punk rock drummer and a heartless record promoter, about a soon-to-be married playboy cyclist who follows an adolescent girl into her parents'

bakery and nearly falls in love with her, and about inmates facing imminent death in the AIDS ward of a prison? What is noteworthy is that these
writers explore this fresh material with such accomplishment. It is a daring
collection that is well worth our attention. [D. Quentin Miller]

Theodore Pelton. *Endorsed by Jack Chapeau*. Starcherone Books, 2000. 80
pp. Paper: $7.95.

Theodore Pelton's first collection of short stories explores an America
plagued by media misinformation, conspiracy theories, academic socio-
paths, and pubic-hair fetishes, where televisions have replaced fireplaces
as the warming-yet-disaffected glow in our collective homes and hearts.
Pelton's seven short fictions problematize the reality of postwar America by
asking us to think beyond what we've come to know as numb spectators of
the electric box and bored participants in the theater of our own absurd
lives. In "Friendly Fire" Pelton examines the rhetoric of the Persian Gulf
War as a spaghetti Western starring Dr. Seuss, George Bush, and Tonto,
separated from his Lone Ranger. "Pawns" depicts Bobby Fischer as the sad,
deflated character he has become in the post-Cold War era: a corporate
shell hawking chess timers to a world that no longer has any use for him.
"From Comboria" posits the possibility that the Tomb of the Unknown Soldier actually contains a surveillance camera which records the serious expressions and morose contemplations of the Tomb's passersby. And while
yellow-ribbon conspiracy ("Where did the yellow ribbons come from?") and
technophobic paranoia ("twenty-eight people were killed yesterday by a
glitch") are certainly on Pelton's mind throughout the collection, he's realistic in his assessment that "most people think of conspiracies as hazy
dreams which probably occurred but no longer fit their current lifestyles."
In our United States of Apathy we may acknowledge that the buffalo will
not come back and J. Edgar Hoover probably *did* have something to do with
JFK's death, but ultimately these realities are more annoying entries on a
to-do list than inspirational calls to action and reform. [Trevor Dodge]

Mark Axelrod. *Capital Castles*. Pacific Writers Press, 2000. 192 pages. Paper: No price given.

Mark Axelrod concludes his *Castles Trilogy* with another freewheeling
quest novel that takes his artist hero, Duncan Katz, on a trip to Holland
and France, and then on a strange expedition through the United States.
Resolution is in the air from the very beginning of the book. Duncan's travels are in fact occasioned by his marriage to Hadara Halevi. Their ensuing
honeymoon in Europe and move from New York to California provide the
motivation for the whole itinerary. The structural importance of Duncan's
marriage goes to show that even cynics such as he buy into the system they
allegedly despise. However, to take his occasional jibes at face value would

be to miss the point of the novel. Axelrod produces mild satire, whose purpose is to entertain rather than incite, and his book should therefore be judged on the basis of the fun it is able to provide. While the many metafictional moments in *Capital Castles* may seem generally outmoded, they are quite often amusing, such as when his narrator gives the reader an exam about the book and provides a neat quizstrip for good measure. The book's real attractions, however, derive from Axelrod's hilarious extension of its locales. Highpoints include an explanation of why the Dutch leave their shades undrawn in the evening; a meeting with Samuel Beckett in Paris; and an episode in Philadelphia during which Katz sees elaborate proof of the assistance Jefferson received from his concubine's brother in drafting the Declaration of Independence. [Luc Herman]

Hilary Mantel. *Fludd.* Owl Books, 2000. 181 pp. Paper: $13.00; Hilary Mantel. *Every Day Is Mother's Day.* Owl Books, 2000. 225 pp. Paper: $13.00.

The disturbing world of British novelist Hilary Mantel has until now been little known by the American reading public. Henry Holt has remedied that omission by publishing for the first time in the United States six of her novels, most recently the quirky *Fludd*, and the darker *Every Day Is Mother's Day*. Both novels take place in twentieth-century Britain, a land that is so haunted by its historical and spiritual past it almost seems poisoned.

Fludd is the stronger of the two novels; it interrogates the nature of faith in a way that would amaze Trollope. Father Angwin, the priest of the dismal village of Fetherhoughton, pretends to have faith even though he lost it thirty years ago. Something supernatural happens to cause him to investigate his faith, although it's not clear whether Fludd is an otherworldy visitor, a new curate, an angel, a devil, or a seventeenth-century alchemist. Fludd helps him defy his bishop, who has ordered that the statues of saints be taken away from the church, and aids in his struggles against a group of strong-minded nuns who spend their time alternating between cruelly educating children and working on a tapestry of the plagues of Egypt. There is black humor as well in *Every Day Is Mother's Day*, but little hope. Set in modern London, the novel details the miserable life of a widow with a mentally disturbed daughter, Muriel, and the complications arising from Muriel's pregnancy. There are possibly supernatural beings in this novel too, although they may also be the evil vibrations of a house where memories of child abuse and murder exist.

Mantel's prose is striking and witty, especially when the out of the ordinary happens. Her vision of the world is bleakly humorous and allows for the possibility, however remote, of a kind of grace. [Sally E. Parry]

Edward Sanders. *The Poetry and Life of Allen Ginsberg: A Narrative Poem.*

Overlook Press, 2000. 252 pp. $27.95; Edward Sanders. *America: A History in Verse, Volume I, 1900-1939*. Black Sparrow, 2000. 385 pp. Paper: $16.00.

Poetry, Ed Sanders wrote in his 1976 manifesto *Investigative Poetry*, must "again assume responsibility for the description of history." The urge to produce such poems has been with Sanders at least as far back as "The Entrapment of John Sinclair," but it was with his book-length verse biography *Chekhov* and *1968: A History in Verse* that Sanders began to answer his own call for a politically engaged, data-intensive poetry of epic proportions. This self-imposed project continues with *The Poetry and Life of Allen Ginsberg* and the first installment of his three-volume work-in-progress, *America: A History in Verse*.

For many who grew up in the fifties and after, the author of *Howl* has been our Archilochus, Blake, and holy madman, and *The Poetry and Life of Allen Ginsberg* walks us carefully through what Sanders terms "the Forest Ginsberg." It is an affectionate, personalized biography that presents the poet as "a great and positive beacon," whose poetic genius, inexhaustible energy, and commitment to social justice placed him at the center of much that happened culturally and artistically in this country and elsewhere during the past half-century. Sanders covers familiar ground ably (the Gallery Six reading, Ginsberg as sixties guru) but is perhaps best when proffering the sort of insider information to which he was privy—Ginsberg making Ezra Pound listen to the Beatles and Dylan, for instance—and when recounting Ginsberg's final decades, productive years still largely overshadowed by the legendary events of the fifties and sixties. Sanders accomplishes for his long-time friend and mentor what partisan criticism at its best must always do: to advocate for and thereby to send readers back to the poetry for a more informed, more sympathetic look.

What Sanders does for Ginsberg, he likewise accomplishes for the U.S. in volume 1 of *America*, which locates the first forty years of the American century in the context of world history—its politics, culture, scientific/technological advances—with particular attention to the working class and the American Left as both negotiated internal conflicts, capitalism's hostility, the threat of fascism, and disappointments with Soviet communism. Like the Ginsberg biography, *America* occasionally threatens to sag beneath its accumulation of facts, sometimes frustrating a desire for elaboration and speculation or escaping the author's control. But rewriting Howard Zinn's *A People's History* is not exactly where Sanders is at in *America* any more than competing with Barry Miles (*Ginsberg*) and Michael Schumacher (*Dharma Lion*) is his purpose in writing a narrative of Ginsberg's life. Which leads to the question of what has been gained by producing biographies and histories in verse. Both books are prosodically of a piece with *Chekhov* and *1968*, offering free-verse "data clusters" interrupted by small illustrations and headings that draw attention to certain events. The result is verbal collage (although strung along linear "time-tracks") in which conventionally poetic lines are few. However, cumulatively the data clusters generate considerable power and a forward momentum that carries the reader feelingly through a world or a life.

Avoiding the prosaic requirements of textbook history or conventional biography, Sanders offers instead elegy and eulogy while avoiding the temptation to impose upon his subjects an undue interpretive/explanatory tidiness. If *The Poetry and Life of Allen Ginsberg* is "a temporary path" through sacred terrain, a homage to one of the best minds of Sanders's generation, *America* is a chant of praise and condemnation meant to inspire and outrage, a song of gratitude for the too-often unsung women and men who struggled to help secure a bit more of our birthright of freedom. Ginsberg was one bard in this struggle; Sanders is another. [Brooke Horvath]

Jorge Luis Borges. *This Craft of Verse*. Ed. Calin-Andrei Mihailescu. Harvard Univ. Press, 2000. 160 pp. $22.95.

This series of six lectures was delivered extempore at Harvard in 1967-68, and Professor Mihailescu has transcribed, edited, and thoroughly annotated them from tapes that were abandoned in a library vault for three decades. Each lecture focuses on a different aspect of poetry, but only loosely so. Whether Borges's topic is metaphor, epic narrative, or the nature of poetry, his basic aim is to reproduce the experience of wonder that poetry inspires. Accordingly, he shies away from poetic theories and instead allows his examples and personal impressions to speak for themselves. Sometimes he delves into philological matters; at other times, he offers characteristically postmodern insights on literary history: "I no longer believe in expression: I believe only in allusion. After all, what are words? Words are symbols for shared memories."But on the whole, these lectures warn against the pitfalls of literary-historical awareness, especially when it leads us to approach books not as "occasions for beauty" but as collections of outmoded views and etymological curiosities. Although Borges's readings betray his own notorious encyclopedic knowledge, he suggests that an over-developed historical awareness threatens our openness to the experience of wonder. Today, thirty years after he delivered these lectures, historical awareness (some call it "knowingness") pervades literary scholarship, and many historicist critics would scoff at Borges's suggestion that "there is an eternity in beauty." But to those who want to approach poetry as enthusiasts rather than curators, the value of these lectures lies in their frequent success at conveying the passions and joys in the experience of artfully arranged words. [Thomas Hove]

Suzanne Jill Levine. *Manuel Puig and the Spider Women: His Life and Fictions*. Farrar, Straus & Giroux, 2000. 448 pp. $27.50.

Suzanne Jill Levine's biography of Manuel Puig is a model of tact and gossip: she has included essential information that anyone enamored of Puig's novels needs to know, and she has passed on important data about Puig's love life which, at least for this reader, would be difficult to gather anywhere else. Particularly impressive are the details of family life and the oppressive atmosphere of General Villegas, the village where Puig grew up. Levine is quite perceptive about both sides of Puig's influences; here are Hollywood's presentation of the real world and a romanticized paradise, and both his literary background (Puig's acquisition of foreign languages and his broad reading during the Boom) and Freudian background (his cousin Bébé, who would become a psychologist, instructed him early in theories of homosexuality). Levine is very thorough, moreover, to keep us abreast of which people in Puig's life became incarnated as characters and which events he fictionalized. At times the biographical and the critical impulses clash, such as when Levine, narrating the tortuous process by which the Spanish edition of *Betrayed by Rita Hayworth* gets published, neglects to tell us how it ended up at Jorge Alvarez. Although she has an excellent sense of which traits of the author appear acted out in the novels, her contention that Molina and Valentín (of *Kiss of the Spider Woman*) represent two sides of Puig seems unconvincing to me. *Manuel Puig and the Spider Woman* deserves high praise for its insights about the literary process that go beyond Puig's own work. It should remain an essential reference on Puig, a writer who, in Goytisolo's words, "knew no other commitment than the one he had contracted with writing and with himself." [Keith Cohen]

Alexis Lykiard. *Jean Rhys Revisited*. Stride Publications, 2000. 281 pp. £11.95.

Impressionistic, roving, idiosyncratic, Alexis Lykiard's *Jean Rhys Revisited* is not a scholarly book, yet scholars and readers alike will find much of interest in its observations of Rhys, whom Lykiard befriended during the last years of her life, and in its perceptive reading of her work. A Greek-British novelist, poet, and translator, Lykiard is a writer's writer, well and widely read, and his insights into Rhys's work are peppered with allusions to Rilke, Gissing, Duras, and others, as well as to various critical studies of Rhys. The book is best read as an appreciation, as one writer's homage to another, informed by Lykiard's clear affection for Rhys and his careful, comprehensive knowledge of her work. The chapters, often as brief as a page or two, have titles like "Dreams and extremes" and "Her and not her, " and the volume closes with an original poem inspired by what Lykiard describes as the visit of Rhys's ghost. This unusual, elegantly written treatment offers vivid descriptions of Rhys in her late years (and a handful of previously unpublished photographs), and insightful, sensitive readings of her fiction. Given Lykiard's own good but minor reputation, however, it is surprising that *Jean Rhys Revisited* often dwells less on Rhys than on the various trials of the author himself, particularly as a writer in rural isolation and as a true Rhys initiate forced to contend with feminist critics and "hackademic" know-nothings who inevitably misconstrue her work. Lykiard's hubris occasionally amuses, as when he notes that "bafflingly enough" Rhys chose to have one of her stories reprinted without incorporating his suggested changes. In sum, Lykiard's warm tribute offers a great deal that illuminates Rhys and her work, and much that does not. [Joy Castro]

———————————

Arthur Saltzman. *This Mad "Instead": Governing Metaphors in Contemporary American Fiction.* Univ. of South Carolina Press, 2000. 232 pp. $39.95.

Metaphor is the holy grail of literary art—an intriguing amalgam calling attention to itself not only as a carefully crafted linguistic prize but also as a mysterious and elusive truth. Arthur Saltzman's *This Mad "Instead": Governing Metaphors in Contemporary American Fiction* examines the successes and failures contemporary novelists meet when using metaphor in the construction of their fictional worlds. Saltzman begins with the notion that "language is an especially suspicious artistic medium and must be frisked for the meanings it smuggles," and while figurative language resides more comfortably in the world of poetry and poetics, because it is both expected and anticipated, fiction employs metaphor no less strategically or effectively. Although the approach to metaphor may be slightly different in the contemporary text due to philosophical changes in how we view the stability of language, nevertheless "metaphor aspires beyond the role of ornamentation to become a means of knowledge." Saltzman's selection of authors focuses on the past fifteen years of contemporary American fiction and represents a diverse cross-section of the landscape—Paul West, Don DeLillo, Steven Millhauser, Paul Auster, William Gass, Kathy Acker, and John Updike. In each of these authors, Saltzman envisions the employment of metaphor as a point of departure rather than an end in itself, an opportunity for the examination of language's seeming ambiguity. Contrary to indictments against contemporary fiction's lack of moral reliability, Saltzman very convincingly argues that these authors move beyond linguistic ornamentation and/or mere literary playfulness to provide an underlying structure or method of inquiry governed by a dynamic and extraordinarily active search for meaning. For anyone who believes that contemporary fiction has somehow failed to live up to its literary predecessors, Saltzman's book shines a remarkable light, not only on individual texts but on the very language of their construction. [Anne Foltz]

———————————

Douglas Glover. *Notes Home from a Prodigal Son.* Oberon Press [Canada], 1999. 171 pp. Paper: $17.95.

In this new book Douglas Glover includes essays on Christa Wolf, Margaret Atwood, Leonard Cohen, and Hubert Aquin; three interviews and a memoir; and three considerations of the nature of fiction and one on comedy. In them, he establishes paternity, explanations and justification for the non-narrative novel, what Glover refers to in one essay title as the novel as poem. Again and again he cites John Hawkes's much-quoted remark that the enemies of the novel are "plot, character, setting, and theme." And he rounds up the usual suspects in marshalling his arguments: Nabokov, Paul Valéry, Samuel Beckett, Victor Shklovsky. This kind of writer, Glover argues, chooses less than he is chosen. Writing becomes an act of survival, if it is even, ever, that: "Christa Wolf is hiding in California, living the life of one of her own characters, hounded out of Germany for being politically incorrect. Leonard Cohen stopped writing novels after *Beautiful Losers*. And Hubert Aquin killed himself. Exile, silence and death, which are optional modes in a piece of fiction, seem, in the lives of certain writers, to take on a kind of necessity—there is only this and writing, or, perhaps, this or writing. For this kind of writer, there are no safe havens, no fire exits, and the patient never recovers." It is a particular strength of this collection that Glover not only demonstrates how much Canadian fiction is part of the avant-garde non-narrative novel but also that the circumstances of Canada invite just such writing: "These are writers and artists . . . who see marginality (Canadianness) as a metaphor for the self in the modern age—that self which everywhere feels somehow exterior and irrelevant to its own destiny." To understand it this way is to see Canadian writing in a new way. [Robert Buckeye]

Mark Osteen. *American Magic and Dread: Don DeLillo's Dialogue with Culture.* Univ. of Pennsylvania Press, 2000. 299 pp. $42.00.

Although there have been books (by Tom LeClair and Douglas Keesey) and collections of criticism (by Frank Lentricchia), Mark Osteen's book on DeLillo is surely the most comprehensive and daring yet. His title is taken from *White Noise*—Murray Siskind, an expert on tabloid culture and shopping, wants to "immerse himself in American magic and dread." The phrase points toward DeLillo's beginnings as a Catholic. His religious background—his desire to find a kind of transcendence in our underworld—is one of the secret sources of all DeLillo's fictions. Osteen's previous book on Joyce, his awareness of Catholic rituals and language, his belief in the supernatural, all provide the central part of his criticism. I need merely note some of his chapter titles—"The Theology of Secrets," or "The Nature of Diminishing Existence"—to demonstrate the religious subtexts. If I turn to any page by Osteen I find a brilliant explanation of details I have missed in my previous readings. On page 79, for example, he refers to the Nobel Laureate Shazar Lazarus Ratner (who gives his name to *Ratner's Star*) and suggests that his middle name "implies his potential for regeneration. A believer in kabbalistic number-mysticism, Ratner (an avatar of Pythagoras) appears in Chapter 10 as if to verify that 10 embodies perfection." On page 140 Osteen uses Tap's interest in glossalalia to discuss the relation of language and theology in *The Names*. Likewise, Nick's fascination with "The Cloud of Unkowing" in *Underworld*, is elaborated brilliantly. I find it interesting that *Underworld*, like *The Recognitions, Mason and Dixon*, and *Women and Men*, assumes or denies a spectral dimension. Such a brief clue provides an antidote to the usual criticism of these works as merely paranoid. It broadens the awareness that texts do not merely engage in contemporary concerns. [Irving Malin]

Books Received

Alex, Kirk. *Working the Hard Side of the Street.* Tucumcari Press, 2000. Paper: $14.95. (F,P)

Anderson, Robert. *Ice Age.* Univ. of Georgia Press, 2000. $24.95. (F)

Ashbery, John. *Other Traditions.* Harvard Univ. Press, 2000. $22.95. (NF)

——. *Your Name Here: Poems.* Farrar, Straus & Giroux. $23.00. (P)

Aylett, Steve. *Atom.* Four Walls Eight Windows, 2000. Paper: $14.95. (F)

Banks, Ian. *The Business.* Simon & Schuster, 2000. $25.00. (F)

Banville, John. *Eclipse.* Knopf, 2001. $23.00. (F)

Barnes, Julian. *Love, Etc.* Knopf, 2001. $24.00. (F)

Baxter, Charles. *The Feast of Love.* Pantheon, 2000. $24.00. (F)

Beattie, Ann. *Perfect Recall.* Scribner, 2000. $24.00. (F)

Belpoliti, Marco, and Robert Gordon, eds. *The Voices of Memory: Primo Levi.* Trans. and preface by Robert Gordon. Intro. Marco Belpoliti. New Press, 2000. $24.95. (NF)

Benali, Abdelkader. *Wedding by the Sea.* Arcade, 2000. $23.95. (F)

Bennet, Barbara. *Understanding Jill McCorkle.* Univ. of South Carolina Press, 2000. $29.95. (NF)

Birk, John F. *Tracing the Round: The Astrological Framework of Moby-Dick.* Minerva, 2000. Paper: $29.95. (NF).

Black, Baxter. *A Cowful of Cowboy Poetry.* Coyote Cowboy Company, 2000. $24.95. (P)

Boutilier, Nancy. *On the Eighth Day Adam Slept Alone: New Poems.* Black Sparrow, 2000. Paper: $16.00. (P)

Broderick, Damien. *Transrealist Fiction: Writing in the Slipstream of Science.* Greenwood, 2000. $65.00. (NF)

Byatt, A. S. *The Biographer's Tale.* Knopf, 2000. $24.00. (F)

Carter, Emily. *Glory Goes and Gets Some.* Cofee House, 2000. $20.95. (F)

Chadwick, Cydney. *Benched.* Avec Books, 2000. Paper: $7.50. (F)

Chester, Laura. *Kingdom Come.* Creative Arts Book Company, 2000. Paper: $14.95. (F)

Clark, Tom. *The Spell: A Romance.* Black Sparrow, 2000. Paper: $16.00. (F, P)

Cole, C. Bard. *Briefly Told Lives.* St. Martin's, 2000. $22.95. (F)

Cormier, Ken. *Balance Act.* Insomniac Press, 2000. Paper: $9.99. (F, P)

Creeley, Robert. *Life & Death.* New Directions, 2000. Paper: $9.95. (P)

Cronin, Anthony. *Dead as Doornails.* Lilliput Press/Dufour Editions, 2000. Paper: $17.95. (NF)

Cuéller, José Tomás de. *The Magic Lantern.* Trans. Margaret

Carson. Ed. with an introduction by Margo Glantz. Oxford Univ. Press, 2000. $30.00. (F)

Cullin, Mitch. *Tideland.* Dufour, 2000. $22.00. (F)

Cuoco, Lauren, and William H. Gass, eds. *Literary St. Louis: A Guide.* Missouri Historical Society Press, 2000. Paper: $19.95. (NF)

Davidson, Toni. *Scar Culture.* Norton, 2000. Paper: $14.00. (F)

Dembowski, Nancy. *Only the Ghost Has Lasted.* Insomniac Press, 2000. Paper: $9.99. (P)

Denino, Kae. *Glow.* Livingston, 2000. Paper: $12.00. (F)

Dinh, Linh. *Fake House: Stories.* Seven Stories, 2000. $23.95. (F)

Dirda, Michael. *Readings: Essays and Literary Entertainments.* Indiana Univ. Press, 2000. $24.95. (NF)

Dissanayakee, Ellen. *Art and Intimacy: How the Arts Began.* Univ. of Washington Press, 2000. $29.95. (NF)

Ditsky, John. *John Steinbeck and the Critics.* Camden House, 2000. $59.00. (NF)

Drury, Tom. *Hunts in Dreams.* Houghton Mifflin, 2000. $22.00. (F)

Duranti, Francesca. *Left-Handed Dreams.* Delphinium Books, 2000. $20.00. (F)

———. *The House on Moon Lake.* Trans. Stephen Sartarelli. Dephinium Books, 2000. Paper: $13.95. (F)

Enright, Anne. *What Are You Like?* Jonathon Cape, 2000. Paper: £10. (F)

Eve, Nomi. *The Family Orchard.* Knopf, 2000. $25.00. (F)

Fanning, Charles, ed. *New Perspectives on the Irish Diaspora.* Southern Illinois Univ. Press, 2000. Paper: $19.95. (NF)

Farrell, Joseph, and Antonio Scuderi, eds. *Dario Fo: Stage, Text, and Tradition.* Southern Illinois Univ. Press, 2000. $49.95. (NF)

Feltman, Becky Anne. *The Eclipse for the Final Son.* Vantage, 2000. Paper: $6.95. (P)

Fiddian, Robin W. *The Novels of Fernando del Paso.* Univ. of Florida Press, 2000. $49.95. (NF)

Finucan, Stephen. *Happy Pilgrims.* Insomniac Press, 2000. Paper: $15.99. (F)

Fitzgerald, Penelope. *The Knox Brothers.* Counterpoint, 2000. $26.00. (NF)

Flanagan, Richard. *Death of a River Guide.* Grove, 2000. $24.00. (F)

Fowles, John, and A. L. Kennedy, eds. *New Writing 9.* Intro. A. L. Kennedy. Vintage, 2000. Paper: £7.99. (F)

Frazer, Vernon. *Relic's Reunion.* Beneath the Underground, 2000. Paper: $16.00. (P)

Friedman, Bruce Jay. *A Mother's Kisses.* Univ. of Chicago Press. 2000. Paper: $14.00. (F)

Fuentes, Carlos, and Julio Ortega, eds. *The Vintage Book of Latin*

American Stories. Vintage, 2000. Paper: $14.00. (F)

Glave, Thomas. *Whose Song? And Other Stories.* City Lights, 2000. Paper: $12.95. (F)

Glickfield, Carole L. *Swimming toward the Ocean.* Knopf, 2001. $25.00. (F)

Grangé, Jean-Christpohe. *Blood-Red Rivers.* Harvill, 2000. Paper: £5.99. (F)

Grealy, Lucy. *As Seen on TV: Provocations.* Bloomsbury USA, 2000. $23.95. (NF)

Grombrowicz, Witold. *Ferdyduke.* Trans. Danuta Borchardt. Forward by Susan Sontag. Yale Univ. Press, 2000. Paper: $14.95. (F)

Haigh, Joshua. *Letters from Hanusse.* Ed. with a preface by Douglas Messerli. Green Integer, 2000. Paper: $12.95. (F)

Hajdu, Lazlo. *Viennese Story.* 1st Books, 2000. Paper: No Price Given. (F)

Hammond, Paul, ed. *The Shadow and Its Shadow: Surrealist Writings on the Cinema.* 3rd edition, revised and expanded. Trans. and intro. by the editor. City Lights, 2000. Paper:$17.95. (NF)

Handke, Peter. *On a Dark Night I Left My Silent House.* Trans. Krishna Winston. Farrar, Straus & Giroux, 2000. $23.00. (F)

Harte, Liam, and Michael Parker, eds. *Contemporary Irish Fiction: Themes, Tropes, Theories.* St. Martin's, 2000. $49.95. (NF)

Hawes, James. *Dead Long Enough.* Jonathon Cape, 2000. Paper: £10. (F)

Hearon, Shelby. *Ella in Bloom.* Knopf, 2000. $23.00. (F)

Hitchcott, Nicki. *Women Writers in Francophone Africa.* Berg, 2000. $65.00. (NF)

Hô, Xuân Huong. *Spring Essence: The Poetry of Hô Xuân Huong.* Ed. and trans. by John Balaban. Copper Canyon, 2000. Paper: $15.00. (P)

Hollander, Gad. *Benching with Virgil.* Avec Books, 2000. Paper: $7.50. (F)

Hume, Kathryn. *American Dream, American Nightmare: Fiction since 1960.* Univ. of Illinois Press, 2000. $39.95. (NF)

Ireland, Perrin. *Ana Imagined.* Graywolf, 2000. $22.95. (F)

Jabra, Jabra Ibrahim. *In Search of Walid Masoud.* Trans. Roger Allen and Adnan Haydar. Syracuse Univ. Press, 2000. $26.95.(F)

Jones, Stephen Graham. *The Fast Red Road.* FC2, 2000. Paper: $13.95. (F)

Jones, Suzanne W. *Crossing the Color Line: Readings in Black and White.* Univ. of South Carolina Press, 2000. Paper: $16.95. (F)

Kanafasi, Ghassan. *Palestine's Children: Returning to Haifa and Other Stories.* Trans. and intro. Barbara Harlow and Karen E. Riley. Lynne Rienner, 2000. Paper: $13.95. (F)

Khorrami, Mohammad Medhi, and Shouleh Vatanabadi, eds. and trans. *A Feast in the Mirror: Stories by Contemporary Iranian*

Women. Lynne Rienner, 2000. Paper: $17.95. (F)

Kimmel, Keith. *Jeremy's Prophecy Dot Com.* Veneer Publishing, 2000. Paper: $12.95. (F)

Kirchheimer, Gloria DeVidas. *Goodbye, Evil Eye.* Holmes & Meier, 2000. 21.95. (F)

Kittredge, William. *The Nature of Generosity.* Knopf, 2000. $25.00. (F)

Königsdorf, Helen. *Fission.* Trans. Susan H. Gillespie. Northwestern Univ. Press, 2000. Paper: $18.95. (F)

Kopperud, Gunnar. *The Time of Light.* Trans. Tiina Nunnally. Bloomsbury, 2000. £15.99. (F)

Kumin, Maxine. *Always Beginning: Essays on a Life in Poetry.* Copper Canyon, 2000. Paper: $17.00. (NF, P)

——. *Quit Monks or Die!* Story Line, 2000. Paper: $13.95. (F)

Kuusisto, Stephen. *Only Bread, Only Light: Poems.* Copper Canyon, 2000. Paper: $15.00. (P)

Julavits, Heidi. *The Mineral Palace.* Putnam, 2000. $23.95. (F)

Largo, Miachael. *Welcome to Miami.* Tropical Press, 2000. Paper: $14.95. (F)

Leavitt, David. *Martin Bauman; or, A Sure Thing.* Houghton Mifflin, 2000. $ 26.00.

Leefeldt, Ed. *Lighter than Air.* Lighter Than Air, L.P., 2000. Paper: $9.95. (F)

Leong, Russell Charles. *Phoenix Eyes and Other Stories.* Univ. of Washington Press, 2000. Paper: $16.95. (F)

Levertov, Denise. *The Great Unkowing: Last Poems.* New Directions, 2000. Paper: $9.95. (P)

Liberi, Antoni. *Madame.* Farrar, Straus & Giroux, 2000. $26.00. (F)

Linnet, Deena. *Rare Earths.* Foreword by Molly Peacock. BOA Editions, Ltd., 2000. Paper: $12.50. (F,P)

Liu, Alvin. *The Hell Screens.* Four Walls Eight Windows, 2000. $22.00. (F)

Machado de Assis, Joaquim Maria. *Esau and Jacob.* Trans. Elizabeth Lowe. Ed. with a foreword by Dan Borges. Afterword by Carlos Felipe Moisés. Oxford Univ. Press, 2000. $35.00. (F)

Manguel, Alberto. *Into the Looking-Glass Wood.* Harcourt, 2000. Paper: $13.00. (NF)

Marías, Javier. *All Souls.* Trans. Margaret Jull Costa. New Directions, 2000. Paper: $13.95. (F)

Marsh, Nicholas. *D. H. Lawrence: The Novels.* St. Martin's, 2000. $59.95. (NF)

Mayer, Patricia. *Terminal Bend.* Livingston Press, 2000. Paper: $14.00. (F)

McGrath, Patrick. *Martha Peake: A Novel of the Revolution.* Random House, 2000. $24.95. (F)

McNally, John. *Troublemakers.* Univ. of Iowa Press, 2000. Paper: $15.95. (F)

McNamara, Katherine. *Narrow Road to the Deep North.* Mercury House, 2000. Paper: $15.95. (F)

Mitchell, Lauren Porosoff. *Look at Me.* Leapfrog Press, 2000. Paper: $14.95. (F)

Murakami, Haruki. *Norwegian Wood.* Trans. Jay Rubin.Vintage Books, 2000. Paper: $13.00. (F)

Murdoch, Iris. *Something Special: A Story.* Illustrations by Michael McCurdy. Norton, 2000. $15.95. (F)

Næss, Atle. *Doubting Thomas: A Novel about Caravaggio.* Peter Owen Ltd./Dufour Editions, 2000. $29.95. (F)

Nakhjavani, Bahiyyih. *The Saddlebag: A Fable for Doubters and Seekers.* Beacon, 2000. $22.00. (F)

Nelson, Antonya. *Living to Tell.* Scribner, 2000. $24.00. (F)

Oliver, Mary. *The Leaf and the Cloud.* Da Capo, 2000. $22.00. (P)

Olson, Toby. *Write Letter to Billy.* Coffee House, 2000. Paper: $15.95. (F)

Oness, Elizabeth. *Articles of Faith.* Univ. of Iowa Press, 2000. Paper: $14.95. (F)

Osborne, Ralph. *Just for Comfort.* Insomniac Press, 2000. Paper: $15.99. (F)

Ozick, Cynthia. *Quarrel & Quandry: Essays.* Knopf, 2000. $25.00. (NF)

Peabody, Richard. *Sugar Mountain.* Argonne Hotel, 2000. Paper: No Price Given. (F)

Peach, Linden. *Toni Morrison.* 2nd edition. St. Martin's, 2000. $35.00. (NF)

Ponte, Antonio José. *In the Cold of the Malecón.* City Lights, 2000. Paper: $10.95. (F)

Porter, Joe Ashby, *Resident Aliens.* Ivan R. Dee, 2000. $19.95. (F)

Price, Reynolds. *Learning a Trade.* Duke Univ. Press, 2000. Paper: $21.95. (NF)

Rhodes, Dan. *Anthropology.* Villard, 2000. $18.95. (F)

Rice, Ben. *Pobby and Dingan.* Knopf, 2000. $16.00. (F)

Rifkin, Libbie. *Career Moves: Olson, Creeley, Zukofsky, Berrigan and the American Avant-Garde.* Univ. of Wisconsin Press, 2000. Paper: $16.95. (NF)

Ríos, Julián. *Monstruary.* Trans. Edith Grossman. Knopf, 2001. $25.00. (F)

Rorem, Ned. *Lies: A Diary, 1986-1999.* Intro. Edmund White. Counterpoint, 2000. $30.00. (NF)

Rothenberg, Michael. *Punk Rockwell.* Tropical Press, 2000. Paper: $14.95. (F)

Ruebsamen, Helga. *The Song and the Truth.* Trans. Paul Vincent. Knopf, 2000. $26.00. (F)

Russell, John. *Reciprocities in the Nonfiction Novel.* Univ. of Georgia Press, 2000. $35.00. (NF)

Sallis, James. *Bluebottle.* Walker & Company, 2000. Paper: $8.95. (F)

Santos-Febres, Mayra. *Sirena Selena.* Trans. Stephen Lytle. Picador, 2000. $21.00 (F)

Scannell, Vernon. *Feminine Endings.* Enitharmon/Dufour, 2000. Paper: $19.95. (F)

Schmidt, Richard. *The Aerialist.* Overlook, 2000. $26.95. (F)

Schneider, Peter. *Eduard's Homecoming.* Trans. John Brownjohn. Farrar, Straus & Giroux, 2000. $25.00. (F)

Self, Will. *How the Dead Live.* Grove, 2000. $24.00. (F)

Sgulia, Eduardo. *Fordlandia.* St. Martin's, 2000. $22.95. (F)

Simpson, Philip L. *Psycho Paths: Tracking the Serial Killer through Contemporary American Film and Fiction,* Southern Illinois Univ. Press, 2000. Paper: $18.95. (NF)

Singh, Amritjit, and Peter Schmidt, eds. *Postcolonial Theory and the United States: Race, Ethnicity, and Literature.* Univ. of Mississippi Press, 2000. Paper: $26.00. (NF)

Slethaug, Gordon E. *Beautiful Chaos: Chaos Theory and Metachaotics in Recent American Fiction.* SUNY Press, 2000. Paper: $19.95. (NF)

Smith, Roch C. *Understanding Alain Robbe-Grillet.* Univ. of South Carolina Press, 2000. $29.95. (NF)

Stuefloten, D. N. *The Wilderness.* FC2, 2000. Paper: $10.95. (F)

Tanner, Tony. *The American Mystery.* Cambridge Univ. Press, 2000. $59.95. (NF)

Tarbox, Gwen Athene. *The Clubwomen's Daughters: Collectivist Impulses in Progressive-Era Girls' Fiction.* Garland, 2000. $50.00. (NF)

Taylor, Patrick. *Pray for Us Sinners.* Insomniac Press, 2000. Paper: $15.99. (F)

Toynton, Evelyn. *Modern Art:* Delphinium Books, 2000. $22.00. (F)

Treat, Jessica. *Not a Chance.* FC2, 2000. Paper: $12.95. (F)

Ultan, Loyd, and Barbara Unger. *Bronx Accent: A Literary and Pictorial History of the Borough.* Rutgers Univ. Press, 2000. $32.00. (NF)

Upward, Edward. *The Coming Day and Other Stories.* Enitharmon Press/Dufour Editions, 2000. Paper: $18.95. (F)

Valtinos, Thanassis. *Data from the Decade of the Sixties.* Trans. Jane Assimakopoulos and Stavros Deligiorgis. Northwestern Univ. Press, 2000. Paper: $19.95. (F)

Vázquez Díaz, René. *The Island of Cundeamor.* Trans. David E. Davis. Latin American Literary Review Press, 2000. Paper: $16.95. (F)

Vega, Janine Pommy. *Mad Dogs of Trieste: New and Selected Poems.* Black Sparrow, 2000. Paper: $16.00. (P)

Vera, Yvonne. *Butterfly Burning.* Farrar, Straus & Giroux, 2000. Paper: $12.00. (F)

Vizenor, Gerald. *Chancers.* Univ. of Oklahoma, 2000. $19.95. (F)

Wallace, Mark. *The Big Lie.* Avec Books, 2000. Paper: $7.50. (F)

Wanatabe, Jun'ichi. *A Lost Paradise.* Trans. Juliet Winters Carpenter. Kodansha, 2000. $24.00. (F)

Wattar, Tahir. *The Earthquake.* Trans. William Granara. Saqi Books, 2000. $29.50. (F)

Williams, Jonathon. *Blackbird Dust: Essays, Poems, and Photographs.* Turtle Point Press, 2000. Paper: $16.95. (NF, P)

Winkler, Martin. *The Case of Dr. Sachs.* Seven Stories, 2000. $27.95. (F)

Winterson, Jeanette. *The Powerbook.* Knopf, 2000. $24.00. (F)

Wolfe, Tom. *Hooking Up.* Farrar, Straus & Giroux, 2000. $25.00. (NF, F)

Wuori, G. K. *An American Outrage: A Novel of Quillifarkeag, Maine.* Algonquin Books of Chapel Hill, 2000. $22.95. (F)

Yuknavitch, Lidia. *Liberty's Excess.* FC2, 2000. Paper: $12.95. (F)

Zivkovic, Zoran. *Time Gifts.* Trans. Alice Copple-Tosic. Northwestern Univ. Press, 2000. Paper:$14.95. (F)

Contributors

A former student at the École Normale Supérieure, HÉLÈNE AJI (born in Paris in 1969) holds a Ph.D. in twentieth-century American poetry and has written on David Antin, Ezra Pound, Jerome Rothenberg, and William Carlos Williams. She is currently Assistant Professor of American literature at the Sorbonne in Paris, France. Her research and reflection are focused on poetry as a performative art.

CHARLES BERNSTEIN's most recent books include *Republics of Reality: 1975-1995*, poems from Sun & Moon Press and *My Way: Speeches and Poems*, from the University of Chicago Press, and, as editor, *Close Listening: Poetry and the Performed Word* (Oxford Univ. Press). Bernstein is Director of the Poetics Program at SUNY-Buffalo (epc.buffalo.edu/authors/bernstein).

STEPHEN COPE's poems and/or reviews have appeared in *XCP: Cross-Cultural Poetics*, *The Germ*, *Jacket*, *Mirage / A Period(ical)* and elsewhere. Cope is currently editing the American poet George Oppen's uncollected writings, selections of which have appeared or are forthcoming in *Facture*, *The Germ*, and *Sagetrieb*. He teaches literature and writing at University of California—San Diego.

HANK LAZER's publications include *3 of 10* (poetry, Chax Press, 1996) and *Opposing Poetries* (criticism, two volumes, Northwestern Univ. Press, 1996). With Charles Bernstein, Lazer edits the Modern and Contemporary Poetics Series of the University of Alabama Press. Lazer is an Assistant Vice President and Professor at the University of Alabama.

GEORGE J. LEONARD wrote *Into the Light of Things: The Art of the Commonplace from Wordsworth to John Cage* (Univ. of Chicago Press, 1994), selected by the American Library Association as "One of the Outstanding Academic Books of the Year." His novels include *The Ice Cathedral* and *Beyond Control*. He edited, and wrote half of, the 700-page essay collection, *The Asian Pacific American Heritage: A Companion to Literature and Arts* (New York: Garland, 1999.)

CHRISTIAN MORARU is an Assistant Professor of English at University of North Carolina—Greensboro, where he teaches primarily modern and postmodern American literature and critical theory. He also is an Associate Editor of *symplokē,* a journal of theory and comparative studies. A chapter of his 1990 book on mimetic ideologies in twentieth-century theory, *The Archeology of Mimesis*, has recently been reprinted in the SUNY Press anthology *The Play of the Self*. Such journals as *Names, Critique, Nabokov Studies*, the *Comparatist, Canadian Review of Comparative Literature, Studies in the Novel, Modern Fiction Studies*, and the *Journal of Narrative Technique* have published his essays. His new book, *Rewriting. Postmodern Narrative and Cultural Critique in the Age of Cloning*, is forthcoming from SUNY Press.

MARJORIE PERLOFF's most recent books are *Poetry on & off the Page* (Northwestern, 1998) and *Wittgenstein's Ladder* (Chicago, 1996). Perloff is Sadie D. Patek Professor Emerita of Humanities at Stanford University. Her *Poetics of Indeterminacy*, which has a chapter on David Antin, has recently been reissued by Northwestern University Press (1999).

LOU ROWAN just completed the autobiography of an American superhero, *My Last Days*. He writes fiction, poetry, essays. He lives in Seattle and earns his living as an institutional money manager. A native of California, he first heard David Antin "read" (by playing a tape of himself and his wife) at St. Mark's-Church-in-the Bowery in the sixties.

HENRY SAYRE is Distinguished Professor of Art History at Oregon State University. He is author of *The Object of Performance* (Chicago, 1989) and the widely used textbooks, *A World of Art* (Prentice Hall, 4th ed., 2000) and *Writing about Art* (Prentice Hall, 3rd ed., 1999). He also produced the television series *Works in Progress* for public television.

other voices

Studies in Twentieth Century Literature

Volume 25, No. 1 (Winter, 2001)

*The Literature and Popular Culture
of the U.S.-Mexican Border*

Guest Editor: Charles Tatum

Contributors include:

J. Douglas Canfield
Roberto Cantú
Debra A. Castillo
Javier Durán
David William Foster
Claire Fox
George Hartley
Amy Kaminsky
Gary D. Keller
Francisco Manzo-Robledo
Alberto López Pulido
Ellen McCracken
Maarten van Delden

In Preparation:

Perspectives in French Studies at the Turn of the Millennium
Guest Editors: Martine Antle and Dominique Fisher

Silvia Sauter, Editor
Kansas State University
Eisenhower 104
Manhattan, KS 66506-1003
Submissions in: Spanish and Russian

Jordan Stump, Editor
University of Nebraska
PO Box 880318
Lincoln, NE 68588-0318
Submissions in: French and German